Towards Effective Place Brand Management

Towards Effective Place Brand Management

Branding European Cities and Regions

Edited by

Gregory Ashworth

Professor of Heritage Planning and Urban Tourism, University of Groningen, the Netherlands

Mihalis Kavaratzis

Associate Professor of Marketing and Tourism, International Business School – Budapest, Hungary

Edward Elgar
Cheltenham, UK • Northampton, MA, USA

Published by
Edward Elgar Publishing Limited
The Lypiatts
15 Lansdown Road
Cheltenham
Glos GL50 2JA
UK

Edward Elgar Publishing, Inc.
William Pratt House
9 Dewey Court
Northampton
Massachusetts 01060
USA

A catalogue record for this book
is available from the British Library

Library of Congress Control Number: 2009941148

Mixed Sources
Product group from well-managed
forests and other controlled sources
www.fsc.org Cert no. SA-COC-1565
© 1996 Forest Stewardship Council

ISBN 978 1 84844 242 9

Printed and bound by MPG Books Group, UK

Contents

Figures

Tables

Contributors

THE EDITORS

Gregory Ashworth was educated at the Universities of Cambridge, Reading and London (PhD 1974). He has taught at the Universities of Wales, Portsmouth and (since 1979) Groningen. Since 1994 he has been Professor of heritage management and urban tourism in the Department of Planning, Faculty of Spatial Sciences, University of Groningen (NL). His main research interests include tourism, heritage and place marketing, largely in an urban context.

Mihalis Kavaratzis was born in Athens, Greece. He has studied Business Administration in Greece (Pireas) and Marketing in Scotland (Stirling). He soon discovered that he wanted to devote the working part of his life on something other than helping rich companies get richer and he went to the Netherlands where he obtained his PhD on city marketing from the University of Groningen. His research interests include place marketing and place branding, tourism planning and development, and the application of marketing in non-business situations. He lives in Hungary (Budapest) where he teaches marketing and tourism related courses.

THE CONTRIBUTORS

Mirza Mohammed Ali Baig BMedSci, MBA is a Research Assistant at Bradford University School of Management. He has researched into hard-to-reach communities and businesses within a predominantly South Asian area of the city of Bradford. More recently he has undertaken focus groups in order to understand how a city's brand and identity can influence business performance and what impact businesses themselves can have on the identity of a city. He has taught Strategic Management and Product Innovation and is currently preparing doctoral research on how Marketing Communications can be adapted for non-mainstream audiences.

Nicola Bellini is Director of the Institute of Economic Planning of the Tuscany Region (IRPET) in Florence, and of the Management and

Innovation–MAIN Lab at the Scuola Superiore Sant'Anna, Pisa (Italy). He is author of several books and articles on local and regional development, innovation policies, the management and marketing of business support services and place marketing.

Claire Colomb is Lecturer in Urban Sociology and European Spatial Planning at the Bartlett School of Planning, University College London. She is a sociologist and a planner with a first degree from the Institut d'Etudes Politiques de Paris and a PhD in Planning from University College London. Her research interests include urban governance, planning and urban policies in European cities; place marketing, culture and urban regeneration; urban sociology; European spatial planning and transnational territorial cooperation.

Nelarine Cornelius is Professor of Human Resource Management and Organizational Studies at Bradford University School of Management. She is Director of the Centre for Research into Emotion Work (CREW) and Head of the Organizational Behaviour and Employment Relations Research group at Brunel Business School. Her research interests include identity management, fairness and ethics at work, emotion and reason, and organizational change and learning. She is Visiting Professor at McGill University, Canada, and the University of Valenciennes, and co-leader (with Professor Eric Pezet, École des Mines, Paris) of a joint Anglo-French project on mentoring supported by the Centre de Gestion Scientifique at the École Nationale Supérieure des Mines. Other research projects include an ESRC-funded research with Miguel Martinez Lucio (University of Manchester) and city regeneration and identity (with Myfanwy Trueman).

Alex Deffner, Dipl. Arch. NTUA (Athens), MSc Urban & Regional Planning (London School of Economics and Political Science: LSE), PhD Planning Studies (LSE). Since 2008 he has been Associate Professor of Urban and Leisure Planning, and since 2003 he has been Director of the Laboratory of Tourism Planning, Research and Policy, Department of Planning and Regional Development, University of Thessaly, Volos, Greece. He has been scientific coordinator of the various programmes relating to cultural heritage. His publications in English focus on urban cultural and time planning, and city marketing.

Magdalena Florek is a Doctor of Science in Marketing, Adjunct at the Poznan University of Economics, Poland. In 2006–07 she was senior lecturer in the Marketing Department, University of Otago, New Zealand. She is a scholarship participant of the Fulbright Foundation at Northwestern University and Kellogg School of Management, USA. She has gained experience in place branding and marketing as a member of research and project teams in the USA, Italy, Poland and New Zealand. Her recent research focuses on place brand equity, place brand loyalty, place satisfaction and special events. She is also a founder of the Place+ consulting company in place marketing.

Henrik Halkier is Professor of regional and tourism studies at Aalborg University, Denmark. His main area of research is public policy, including place branding, tourism policy, and knowledge processes in regional economic development.

Graham Hankinson began his career as a market researcher before joining the Survey Research Centre at the London School of Economics. He has since held professorial positions at Thames Valley University and the University of Lincoln. He has also been Dean of the Business School at the University of Lincoln and was Head of the School of Marketing and Corporate Strategy at Kingston University. He now teaches and researches at London Metropolitan University Business School. His writing and research has been in the area of brands and their management, and more recently focused on the creation and maintenance of places as brands.

Assumpció Huertas Roig is a Senior Lecturer of Public Relations at Rovira i Virgili University, Tarragona (Spain). She is also a lecturer in Advertising at UOC (Universitat Oberta de Catalunya). She has a background in sociology, advertising and public relations. Her research spans tourism marketing, destination branding, new technologies applied to tourism, e-commerce, e-marketing and tourism communication. She is working in a project about new technologies and tourism at Pompeu Fabra University and she is also doing research on identity and destination branding. She is in the executive committee of Public Relations Researchers Association (AIRP).

Andrea Insch is a Lecturer and Researcher at the University of Otago, New Zealand. She has a PhD in International Business and Asian Studies from Griffith University. Her research is focused on place-based marketing and the ways that place identity can create stakeholder value. Currently Andrea is working on defining and measuring place brand equity in New Zealand's cities and hopes to extend this research to other countries.

Ole B. Jensen is Professor of Urban Theory at the Department of Architecture and Design, Aalborg University, Denmark. He is coordinator of the Urban Design Research Group at Aalborg University, and a board member and co-founder of the Centre for Mobility and Urban Studies (C-MUS). His main research interests are city branding/culture planning with particular emphasis on the relationship between representations and physical spaces, and mobility studies with particular emphasis on the relationship between physical movement and social identity/culture.

Ares Kalandides is a Berlin-based urban planner and consultant in place branding. As the managing director of Inpolis he consults cities, neighbourhoods and regions. He has a degree in Urban Planning from the National Technical University of Athens, where he still researches in urban geography. He is a member of the Georg Simmel Centre for Metropolitan Studies at the Humboldt University in Berlin, the Association of Place Branding & Public Diplomacy and a board member of the designer association Create Berlin.

Joyce Liddle is a Professor of Public Management and Head of the International Centre for Public Services Management at Nottingham Business School, NTU. She was Associate Professor and Director of the MPA at the University of Nottingham, Director of MA in Management at Durham Business School and Director of the MBA at Sunderland Business School.

Anna Loffredo graduated in geography at the University of Pisa. She is a Research Fellow at the Management and Innovation–MAIN Lab of the Scuola Superiore Sant'Anna, Pisa (Italy). Her research interests include local development policies and place marketing.

María Cristina Mateo currently works for the International Strategy and Action Bureau of Madrid City Council, in charge of the design and implementation of the strategy for the internationalization of the city of Madrid. Previously she worked as marketing manager and acting manager for Spain and Portugal in VisitBritain, Madrid. Before moving back to Spain she lived in London, where she lectured at several universities on the topics of the media in Spain, and Spanish contemporary culture. Cristina has a consultancy background in advertising, media, retail, tourism, utilities and the public sector, with a focus on new media and online marketing. (Marchfirst – AT Kearney). Cristina holds a PhD in Sociology (Goldsmiths College, University of London) and an executive MBA. A trained journalist, she writes regularly on consumer trends. She is also an Associate Researcher of the Instituto de Empresa, Madrid, specializing in place branding.

Dominic Medway is a Senior Lecturer and Head of the Marketing Group at Manchester Business School. His research interests bring together his academic roots in marketing and geography, with a particular focus on place marketing and management.

Theodore Metaxas is an Economist with a PhD in Planning and Regional Development. Since 2009 he has been Lecturer at the Department of Economics, University of Thessaly, Volos, Greece. Since 2002, he has been a researcher of the Regional Analysis and Forecasting Laboratory, Department of Planning and Regional Development, University of Thessaly, Volos, Greece. His research interests include: urban development and competitiveness, place marketing, tourism and strategic planning.

Nigel Morgan is an academic who combines publication and consultancy with a background in research, policy development and marketing acquired at national agency and local government levels. He is currently Professor of Tourism Studies at the Welsh Centre for Tourism Research in the University of Wales Institute, Cardiff. Whilst much of his research focuses on issues of identity and citizenship in tourism, he has an interest in destination marketing.

Cecilia Pasquinelli holds degrees in local development from the University of Pisa (Italy) and University of Newcastle (UK). Currently she is a PhD student at the Scuola Superiore Sant'Anna, Pisa (Italy), with a research program focusing on place branding.

Annette Pritchard is Professor of Critical Tourism Studies and Director of the Welsh Centre for Tourism Research in the University of Wales' Cardiff School of Management. She has worked in sports and tourism research and strategy at national agencies and has degrees in sociology and international politics, media studies and tourism studies. She publishes on tourism's visual culture and destination marketing. She has undertaken consultancy and advisory roles for public, private and third sector organizations, including UNESCO and national tourist boards and international tourism organizations.

Gildo Seisdedos is Professor of Marketing at IE Business School. He combines teaching, research and consulting activities in the fields of urban planning, local policies and city marketing and on the way cities deal with the new competitive environment, advocating city development strategy approach, which relates traditional planning with strategic urban planning, city branding and city marketing. He has prepared studies on urban planning and design at the London School of Economics and Political Science, the University of California in Los Angeles (UCLA), and Universidad de San Andrés (Buenos Aires). He holds a PhD in Urban Economy from Madrid's Autonoma University, a Bachelor in Business Administration (E3) from ICADE, Madrid, a MBA Degree in Sales and Marketing Management from IE Business School and he is a member of the Madrid Bar Association and a qualified estate agent. He has served as director of IE Business School's marketing programmes for eight years.

Anette Therkelsen is Associate Professor of tourism studies and market communication at Aalborg University, Denmark. She is head of the Tourism Research Unit at Aalborg University and co-editor of Scandinavian Journal of Hospitality and Tourism. Her main areas of research are tourists' consumer behaviour and market communication with a special focus on decision making, image formation, identity construction and destination branding.

Myfanwy Trueman BA, MSc, PhD is Lecturer in Marketing at Bradford University School of Management. Her research interest is in how perceptions of identity and place can influence city brands and regeneration. She has examined urban corridors, hard-to-reach communities in multicultural societies, and how brand 'ownership' can generate social capital for change.

Gary Warnaby is a Senior Lecturer in marketing at the University of Liverpool Management School. His research interests include the marketing of places (in particular the marketing of towns and cities as retail destinations), town centre management and retailing more generally.

1. Place branding: where do we stand?

Mihalis Kavaratzis and Gregory Ashworth

The overall aim of this book is to examine and clarify several aspects of the recently popularized concept of place branding. Many of the constituents of the application of branding to places, such as identities, image, promotion or sense of place, have been around for a long time. However, the need to analyse their nature in the context of branding and to examine their relationships in detail has grown rapidly in the last decade or so, as places all over the world have put branding activities higher than ever in their agenda. Many controversies, confusions and discords will be discussed in the chapters that follow. This introductory chapter examines contemporary place branding understanding in the literature and describes how the issues discussed in the chapters of this book relate to the general topic and to each other. To start with, it is worth taking a brief look at the wider setting of place marketing.

BEFORE PLACE BRANDING

The application of marketing techniques and the adoption of a marketing philosophy in order to meet operational and strategic goals of places have been well established both in practice and in theory. The rapid rise in popularity of place marketing over the past decade, to the extent that it has become an acceptable and commonplace activity of place management, may give the impression that this is a recent phenomenon. It is not. Places have long felt a need to differentiate themselves from each other in order to assert their individuality and distinctive characteristics in pursuit of various economic, political or socio-psychological objectives. The conscious attempt of governments to shape a specifically designed place identity and promote it to identified markets, whether external or internal, is almost as old as government itself. The phenomenon of places transferring marketing knowledge to their own operational needs is not as novel as one might think. As Ashworth and Voogd (1994:39) describe: 'since Leif Ericson sought new settlers in the 8th century for his newly discovered "green" land, the idea of the deliberate projection of favourable place images to potential customers, investors or residents has been actively pursued'. Thus, any consideration of the fundamental geographical idea of sense of place must include the deliberate creation of such senses through place marketing. However, the way it has been used, the instruments available, the active agencies, and the goals pursued have all evolved as a result of sets of changes in both the marketing and planning disciplines as described below. The transfer of marketing knowledge to the operational environment of cities has caused difficulties and misalignments, which could be attributed to several reasons, all of which are related to the peculiar nature of places as marketable assets. Several ways in which marketing has been related to places have been identified (Kavaratzis and Ashworth, 2008). Despite the accumulated experience, significant issues surrounding the application of place marketing remain in need of further practical clarification as well as clearer theoretical development. Indeed, as Skinner's (2008) comprehensive review of the literature has concluded, place marketing is suffering from a 'confused identity', which stems, along with other factors, from the different subject areas and professional interests of the various commentators (Skinner, 2008).

It is accepted here that place marketing can be treated as an instrument of place management undertaken in pursuit of objectives that relate to the management of the place (Ashworth and Voogd, 1990a). At its simplest level, it is merely the recognition that places exist within competitive markets, even if these are difficult to delimit. Places compete with each other and always have done because there are always alternative places that could be selected for any particular use. Place marketing not only recognizes the existence of competition: it also responds by discovering or creating uniqueness in order to improve the competitive position of the place marketed. However, it is important not to equate the stimulation of identity, and thus identification, with place marketing. The former is certainly a part, and usually an important initial condition, of the latter; it does not however encompass it. The identification of people with places is more than place marketing, and place marketing is more than the creation and promotion of place images as part of place management.

The concordance of a number of commentators (including Barke, 1999; Kavaratzis, 2007; Braun, 2008) suggests that the practice of place marketing has developed through discrete phases over time; phases that differ in the general approach towards marketing as well as their level of refinement. These can be grouped into three broadly delimited stages which have not followed a strict timeline, nor have involved geographical distinctiveness. The progress from one stage to the next was more a result of growing understanding and experience of the application of marketing.

Also, each stage was not superseded by the next but rather coexisted so that at any one time a number of these stages can be found, often even in the same place (for a detailed description see Kavaratzis and Ashworth, 2008). The first stage has been the stage of place promotion or place boosterism as described in the many historical cases in Gold and Ward (1994). Then came the stage of place marketing as a planning instrument. Place marketing came of age due to changes in both marketing and planning independently that led to a convergence. Place marketing in planning was made possible, by a series of conceptual and practical developments within marketing over the past 40 years. In particular, three necessary precursors to place marketing were the emergence of 'social marketing', 'non-profit marketing' and 'strategic image marketing'. It was changes in the priorities of planning that made place marketing desirable. These changes related to new competitive arenas in which places now operate and to the way society organizes itself (particularly the relationship between government and the governed). Furthermore, these changes concerned the way places are viewed and experienced, and thus the expectations that people hold of places and their managers. The third stage is that of place branding as a distinct focus within place marketing again resulting from a merge between interests of planning and developments in marketing. Particularly, the advent of the concept of corporate branding, which appears to mesh well with the general idea of 'communicative planning', which involves will-shaping, identity forming, and consensus creation.

In practice what was first adopted was the implementation of purely promotional activities, undertaken by several independent actors with an interest in promoting the place (selling what we have). The adoption of marketing alongside other techniques within place management planning in the collective interest was as much a reaction to a crisis of confidence within planning, and perhaps within public service provision in general, that shifted the attention on to finding out what potential consumers or citizens wished to buy or experience (Kavaratzis and Ashworth, 2008). Finally, we arrive at a hopefully more refined and clearly targeted place marketing and branding of the future in which the creation of new forms of representation of places and major concerns over the image of the place emphasize distinctiveness transcending mere advertising. It is the latter that is examined in this book, accepting that it is possible to use branding tools and to adopt a branding philosophy for managing places and, at the same time, it is necessary to adapt concepts methods and tools to the specific conditions and characteristics of places. In other words, the contention of this book is that place branding will be legitimate only if it is developed as a distinct form of branding within a framework that applies specifically to places. There have been such attempts in the past, albeit fragmented, and the chapters in this book signify a new attempt.

PLACE BRANDING IN THE LITERATURE

In general terms, branding is a process which attempts to influence how consumers interpret and develop their own sense of what a brand means and '. . . a brand is a product or service made distinctive by its positioning relative to the competition and by its personality, which comprises a unique combination of functional attributes and symbolic values' (Hankinson and Cowking, 1993:10). A brand embodies a whole set of physical and socio-psychological attributes and beliefs which are associated with the product (Simoes and Dibb, 2001). Branding is a deliberate process of selecting and associating these attributes because they are assumed to add value to the basic product or service (Knox and Bickerton, 2003). Place branding attempts to transfer those meanings to the operational environment of place management and it centres around the conceptualization of a specific place as a brand. That means that for the purposes of branding the place, whether a country, a region, a city or a neighbourhood, is understood and treated as a brand or a multidimensional construct, consisting of functional, emotional, relational and strategic elements that collectively generate a unique set of associations with the place in the public mind (Kavaratzis and Ashworth, 2005).

In the literature, however, distinct trends of discussion have emerged and not all adopt this view (Kavaratzis, 2005). The subject of place branding is indeed a complex subject and those trends represent the various aspects that bring about this complexity.

a) Place of Origin Branding (e.g. Kotler and Gertner, 2002; Papadopoulos and Heslop, 2002). This trend has developed within the marketing discipline and has grown to a large body of publications. It concerns the usage of the place of origin in branding a product. Using the qualities, images and, in most cases, stereotypes of the place and the people living in that place to brand a product that is produced in that place is considered an effective strategy. In essence though, it has little to do with the concept of place branding. Interesting as it may be (and useful for product marketing), this practice does not constitute a place branding strategy, in the sense that it can not be considered a place management strategy.

b) Nation Branding (e.g. van Ham, 2001; Gilmore, 2001; Anholt, 2002; 2007). This trend has also developed within the marketing discipline and especially within the circles of marketing consultants, who act as advisors to national governments, that have realized the potential advantages of branding their country but do not have the knowledge and skills necessary to design and implement branding campaigns and strategies. The interest lies usually in the positive effects of branding the nation for the benefit of tourism development and the attraction of foreign investment. The topic has grown considerably, so that some commentators propose that the whole foreign affairs policy of the country should be thought of as a branding exercise. A growing number of researchers are examining the potential and suitability of branding nations (e.g. O'Shaughnessy and O'Shaughnessy, 2000) or specific methods and cases (e.g. Endzina and Luneva, 2004; Gilmore, 2001).

c) Destination Branding (e.g. Brent-Ritchie and Ritchie, 1998; Morgan et al., 2002). Perhaps the most developed in theory and most used in practice trend within place branding has been the investigation of the role of branding in the marketing of tourism destinations. Starting, arguably, from the realization that destinations are visited because of their prior images, and they are consumed based on a first-hand comparison of those images with the reality faced in the destination itself, this trend has offered much to the theory of place branding. The largest part, at least of the theoretical development in this field comes from Hankinson (2001; 2004a; 2007). Starting from his belief that 'as yet no general theoretical framework exists to underpin the development of place brands apart from classical, product-based branding theory' (Hankinson, 2004a:110), he provides a refined framework for understanding cities as brands even if focusing on cities mainly as tourism destinations. Brent-Ritchie and Ritchie (1998) recognize that a destination brand has the potential to play a coordinating role 'for a broad range of community development efforts' (p. 19), and stress the need for other agencies to agree with branding the destination, in this way realizing that destination branding is only part of the whole branding effort of any place.

d) Culture/Entertainment Branding (e.g. Evans, 2003; Greenberg, 2003; Hannigan, 2004). Another interesting and steadily growing trend has been the examination of the effects of cultural and entertainment branding on the physical, economic and, sometimes, social environment of cities. Widely applied in cities all over the world, this cultural branding owes its development to the growing importance of the cultural, leisure and entertainment industries within the contemporary economy, as much for tourists and other visitors, as for the local population. At the same time, attempts to incorporate this trend in planning the city (e.g. Evans, 2001; Ashworth, 2004) and the increased importance of image-based industries and the people these employ (Florida, 2002) are reinforcing the processes involved in this form of place branding. Connected with this trend, one can identify a more recent discussion, especially among urban designers, on the effects of high-profile buildings on the city's image and the use of such buildings and other 'landmarks' in general in the city's promotion.

e) Integrated Place Branding A final trend in the literature can be found in a number of articles that try to discuss the possibilities of using branding as an approach to integrate, guide and focus place management. Borrowing from the techniques and ideas developed within general branding, and especially the advent of the increasingly popular concept of corporate branding, these articles discuss the appropriateness of central branding concepts for place branding (Kavaratzis and Ashworth, 2005) and attempt to either provide a general framework for developing and managing place brands (Hankinson, 2004a; 2007; Kavaratzis, 2004; 2009) or examine the suitability of specific branding tools for city branding (Trueman et al., 2004). This last trend is characterized by the attempt to implement the concept of corporate branding and specific methodologies developed in this field in place branding (Rainisto, 2003; Trueman et al., 2004; Hankinson, 2007; Kavaratzis, 2009).

The above distinctions cannot be exhaustive, especially since the literature on place branding is steadily growing together with the number of international conferences and special issues in academic journals devoted to the topic. The field has even seen the launching of three specialized journals in the last five years (*Place Branding and Public Diplomacy*, the *Journal of Place Management and Development* and the *Journal of Town and City Management*). All the above approaches and most of the articles published, despite their varying suggestions and focus, have one thing in common: they make arguments for the implementation of branding within place management. These arguments are rooted in the assumption that, in essence, people 'understand' cities in the same way as brands (Ashworth and Kavaratzis, 2009). It is in peoples' minds that the city takes form through the processing of perceptions and images about the city. This process is the same as that followed in the formation of images of other entities like products or corporations, which have long been managed as brands. Extending this assumption raises the argument that the best way to attempt to influence peoples' perceptions and images about cities must be similar to the way that businesses have been successfully attempting the same for their products, namely branding. The above assumptions are, of course, subject to scrutiny as is found in the academic literature on place and city branding (e.g. Kavaratzis and Ashworth, 2005; Freire, 2005).

Each of the trends mentioned above has made its contribution towards a general understanding of the phenomenon of place branding and has proven its usefulness for specific fields of action. This variety in approaches to place branding, coupled with several practical developments in cities around the world that interpret concepts in their own way and adopt their own approach, has lead to a certainly useful and exciting discussion but, at the same time, problematic development of place branding theory and practice. There are several fundamental questions that remain unanswered and are overlooked (deliberately or not) in the study and practice of branding nations, regions and cities. First of all there still seems to be no general agreement as to how to understand place branding and how this differs from place marketing or even simply promotion. The terms are still often used interchangeably (Skinner, 2008; Kalandides and Kavaratzis, 2009). Is place branding part of place marketing or the other way around? Is place branding (or place marketing for that matter) a strategic orientation or a tactical practice? Secondly, the non-geographical thinking of many commentators and practitioners who work in the field has lead to confusion in terms of the social and spatial implications of place branding. Questions of place-scale, place-function and place-identity should come to the foreground. Thirdly, all these questions mentioned above seem to interest researchers in particular fields, but are secondary for practitioners of city marketing. Practitioners need fast, easy answers, which theoreticians cannot offer; or when they do, these answers seem to have the quality of recipes or toolkits (Kalandides and Kavaratzis, 2009). All those might lead sceptics to an essential question: is place branding effective or even useful? To even tackle this question, there is a need to create a common body of knowledge and vocabulary among different disciplines working in the field.

This book is an attempt to contribute towards that ambition. The chapters included in the book, separately and collectively, set out to demonstrate that branding needs to be thought of as a continuous process interlinked with all marketing efforts and with the whole planning exercise. Place branding can be the means both for achieving competitive advantage in order to increase inward investment and tourism, but also the means for achieving community development, reinforcing local identity and identification of the citizens with their city and activating all social forces to avoid social exclusion and unrest. This is the underlying principle of all chapters presented here and this principle guides the theoretical suggestions, the evaluation of specific cases and the concluding section of the book.

PLACE BRANDING IN THIS BOOK

Although the topic of place branding has attracted the interest of commentators from several academic disciplines, its origins lie in marketing science. It is in essence only the application of marketing to a special sort of product, namely places. Most of the rest of this book is concerned with the ramifications and implications of that application. Thus although most chapters examine how place marketing is a distinctive form of marketing, it is salutary at the outset to examine the opposite proposition. Indeed, the underlying argument of the first chapter by Hankinson is that the lack of an overarching comprehensive theory as repeatedly noted in the literature (e.g. Kavaratzis, 2005; Skinner, 2008) and the resulting lack of precision in terminology, is largely a consequence of the over-hasty adoption of terms and techniques from marketing, in order to serve new purposes, divorced from their conceptual origins in marketing. To remedy this, the chapter provides a comprehensive and thorough review of the relevant literature derived from marketing as the 'mother' discipline. The author traces the beginning of place branding studies in the literature on place images and place promotion, in an attempt to stem the tendency of place branding to develop separately from mainstream marketing literature. The contribution of each relevant discipline is highlighted with the intention of providing a basis for generating future research. Particularly useful to the readers of this book is the description of the evolution of classical product branding and its relevance to places. The author also outlines currently developing areas within mainstream marketing that could or should contribute to our knowledge and understanding of place branding. Such areas include particularly the burgeoning field of services marketing and the notion of corporate rather than specific product branding.

This recently investigated idea of corporate-level marketing is an issue taken further in Chapter 3 by Kavaratzis, where the corporate branding literature is examined in a search for relevant concepts and tools. The main contention is that corporate level marketing has brought marketing theories closer than ever before to the peculiarities and needs of places. The chapter starts with an overview of corporations as entities that need to be marketed and branded and goes on to assess the similarities between corporate and place branding. A particularly useful contribution of the chapter is the comparison of several place branding frameworks found in the literature and the outline of their commonalities and differences in an attempt to provide the basis for an integration, which this book examines further in the last chapter.

One of the major issues surrounding the conceptualization of place branding is the question whether, and to what extent, the place's brand can be based on the place's identity, which raises the ever-present question, 'whose identity?' Similarly, is place branding simply another form of image creation and projection? The chapter (4) by Deffner and Metaxas attempts to delineate the differences between brand, identity and image and their role in place branding. The two cases examined in the chapter, namely Nea Ionia, Magnesia, Greece and Pafos, Cyprus, demonstrate the not unfamiliar struggle of places to find a balance between the 'old', well-established traditional character and the 'new', sought-after character and the ways in which the effort to find this balance determines the setting of branding goals and the processes that occur. The chapter starts from the need for competitiveness and describes the process of creating and communicating place brands based on the place's vision for the future and its distinctive characteristics. The focus of the chapter lies on culture and tourism, broadly defined in terms of their contribution to and reflection of identity, although it highlights the need for the agreement of local communities, particularly evident in the case of Pafos.

A frequently raised criticism against place marketing (and its derivative place branding) is that it tends, by its nature, to project an overly positive image of the place, disregarding (or even camouflaging) negative aspects that do not contribute or even contradict the elements being showcased. In other words it is argued that it is intrinsically in the nature of place marketing to exacerbate the gaps between projected image and experienced reality. The chapter by Mateo and Seisdedos (5) deals with this issue, albeit from an opposite angle. The core question they pose is what happens when a place (a city in this case) does not have the image that reality suggests it deserves? In their chapter the authors discuss Madrid's efforts to close the gap between perception and reality, arguing that the city indeed is deserving of a stronger international image in comparison with its competitors. The chapter describes the move from mass (and largely untargeted) marketing to targeting specific segments and the decision to establish a network of allies that would plan strategic initiatives designed to improve Madrid's international positioning. As the chapter demonstrates, Madrid has chosen several tools to achieve this improvement, which the authors call 'a new generation of city marketing tools'. These focus on building partnerships and include several interesting propositions such as place-product co-branding, the British Council's Open Cities programme and a distinct focus on Madrid's relations to Asia. The authors, although approving the goals and techniques, are rather sceptical about the seemingly ad-hoc nature of those partnerships as well as the city's apparent failure to implement more obvious and commonsense practices.

Place images are examined further in the chapter (6) by Bellini, Loffredo and Pasquinelli with their evocative and engaging analysis of the images of Tuscany. The authors remind us of the often forgotten fact that place branding is a highly political process and they demonstrate how the communication of place images is in many cases used to form and force through policy agendas, particularly in an effort to 'control representations of the past, present and future' of places. The focus of the chapter is on 'other Tuscanies' whether elsewhere (places in and outside Italy that present themselves as the new Tuscany – only better) or within the region (areas that show a divergence from the region's overall image). Of particular interest is the authors' assessment of the problems emanating from a particularly strong image developed for the needs of the tourism industry. As demonstrated in the case of Tuscany, a strong, positive tourism image may prevent the emergence of other images that would reflect the visions of other sectors and would fulfil the need for more dynamic future prospects for the region. In other words, the chapter demonstrates how images of the same region may compete against each other, thus highlighting the complexities involved in the place branding endeavour. The inertia of established stereotypes and the implicit goals of policy-making are only two of the factors that deem place branding a process of excluding as much as including; a process of legitimizing already stagnant development goals as much as supporting alternative opportunities and models of development. The place brand inevitably interacts with the place's constantly changing identities held by insiders and outsiders. Is it then desirable or even possible to develop stable and consistent place brands, serving the multiple goals of heterogeneous regions?

The interaction between brands and territorial identities is also examined in the chapter (7) by Huertas, Morgan and Pritchard but from a different perspective. The chapter centres on an in-depth analysis of two regional brands: Wales and Catalonia. The analysis discloses the ways in which identities derived from a use of history are influencing both brand-building efforts and brand perceptions in the two regions. Despite the focus on destination branding, the chapter highlights the need for the destination brand to be rooted in a more-encompassing place brand. The authors discuss one of the many unresolved issues in place brand management, namely branding at different spatial scales, analysing the relationships between the two regional brands in their context of the 'higher' national brands (UK and Spain) as well as with 'lower' capital-city brands (Cardiff and Barcelona). In this way, the subject of brand-architecture and its relevance to place branding is brought into focus. The intriguing part of the chapter emerges from the choice of the two cases analysed and the ways that selective histories and their concomitant symbols and relics are used in place branding initiatives. The paramount importance of such fundamental issues as ethnic identification, cultural distinctiveness and, in both cases, a unique language is revealed as the chapter explores the identity-building aspects of place brands in what the authors call 'place-making'. This is a matter that goes deeper than the often claimed attempt to foster community-feelings and local pride through branding campaigns.

The underlying question is, can place branding respond to this challenge? Another interesting point raised by the authors is the confusion between the place brand (in this case the destination) and the brand of the tourism promotion agency; an issue also discussed later in the chapter (8) by Therkelsen et al.

A major difficulty of the place branding endeavour is that internal and external markets and audiences are both important and place branding is often called upon to cover the needs of both. Another difficulty or point of disagreement is whether the focus of branding lies on a symbolic representation of the landscape (see Chapter 12 by Warnaby and Medway), a physical 'making' of the landscape itself or upon some combination of the two. Therkelsen, Halkier and Jensen, in their chapters successfully integrate these two issues into their theoretical framework using contributions from the disciplines of marketing, urban studies and policy studies. Place branding is certainly about selling places but the nature of this selling is radically different from the common understanding of the term. Multiple offers, simultaneous selling to multiple audiences and other issues explained more fully elsewhere (see Ashworth and Voogd, 1990a) make it a unique type of selling and, therefore, a unique type of branding. The opportunity to create a sense of belonging – to build a place-based community – is inherent in the nature of place branding as is the need to pursue this opportunity. As the chapter clearly demonstrates, this has been, so far, a missed opportunity for the Danish city of Aalborg as, unfortunately, for many other such cities. The analysis included in the chapter, however, leads to several suggestions about the significance of the community-building goals of place branding and practical proposals about how to pursue them.

One particular community-building endeavour with relevance to many contemporary cities is examined in the chapter (9) by Trueman et al. It is the task of understanding ethnic minorities and attempting to take into account their cultural differences if place branding is to be effective. The chapter examines stakeholder involvement in policy-making and landscape or place-making interventions (see also Kavaratzis, 2009), particularly focusing on the Asian business community in the post-industrial city of Bradford, in Northern England. It investigates the networks of opinion-leaders, critical in any attempt to reach otherwise hard-to-reach communities. It involves utilizing several communication channels as well as developing significant relationships through trust-building efforts in order to enhance a local quality of life. As indicated in the chapter, there is often a mismatch between the agenda of city planners and the needs and objectives of local communities. The chapter highlights differences in the ways local people understand their immediate environment (their 'neighbourhood', as spatial and social entity) and the city planners' approach to the same environment (the same neighbourhood as one zone in a larger zoning system). One of the main findings of the authors' research is that this mutual lack of understanding often may lead to an absence of trust and even resentment by local communities towards top-down interventions by outside agencies.

The double target of internal and external audiences is an issue also tackled in the chapter (10) by Colomb and Kalandides, which includes a detailed and revealing review of place marketing and branding practices of the city of Berlin after the fall of the Wall. The review shows that creating a sense of local identity and civic pride is a common and admirable goal of place branding but it is the opportunities for participation and the ways in which these goals are pursued that determine the effectiveness of such internal place branding. The chapter includes a summary of the criticisms levelled against place marketing and place branding raising as devil's advocate many fundamental issues that underlie, implicitly or explicitly many chapters throughout this book. Particularly illuminating is the authors' evaluation of the recent branding campaign, '*be* Berlin', against the main points of this criticism. The analysis demonstrates that '*be* Berlin' can be considered a step forward, however haltingly, in terms of a more broad-based participation and, perhaps, what the authors would regard as a more 'honest' place branding. At least in its first stage, the campaign was directed at Berliners themselves, who featured centrally in the advertising, a positive and, unfortunately not common, feature of such promotional campaigns.

It is widely accepted that place marketing and branding have three main target groups: visitors, investors and residents. The first two are commonly believed to be more or less predictable in their behaviour towards places to visit or invest in. However, that is not the case with the place's residents and there is little conceptual or empirical research work addressing this group. If place branding is called upon to satisfy the needs and wants of residents, there is an obvious need to develop an understanding of how residents perceive their own place and consequently behave in it. What determines their satisfaction and in what ways do they attach to places? This is an issue directly addressed in the chapter (11) by Insch and Florek, which discusses the concept of resident place satisfaction and its importance for place branding. The authors, using contributions from environmental psychology, sociology and marketing, outline the factors that contribute to the satisfaction residents feel with their place of residence and that determine their attachment to their place. A framework to measure resident satisfaction is developed and is evaluated through the findings of the authors' own research on residents of the city of Dunedin, New Zealand. Such an analysis of the existing satisfaction, or as often the absence of it, and especially its causes is clearly an essential precursor to branding campaigns directed at residents.

The search for differentiation is certainly one of the major forces that push places towards the use of branding techniques because places have long felt the need to present their distinctiveness to the outside world. The development of logos has thus far provided the main expression of this search for distinctiveness and uniqueness and it is the single branding element that has been applied with relative ease, if not always precision, within place management. The chapter (12) by Warnaby and Medway deals with place representation through logos that incorporate the natural or built environment. The authors use semiotic theories to examine logos as visual identification systems. They reveal the reasons why and the ways in which places use logos that are designed to enhance a place's unique identity, applying a novel and useful categorization of logos. The chapter explores several areas of tension. Logos may be assumed to simultaneously meet the needs of several different groups, separate agencies may use separate logos to promote their own field of activity within the same place and more broadly logos have an intrinsic capacity to develop 'associative property' between certain phenomena and the places within which these phenomena are located.

The search for distinctiveness and uniqueness has also found another expression in the efforts of places to associate themselves with certain personalities. This is the issue dealt with in the chapter (13) by Ashworth, which clarifies several matters that surround such practice and provides several well-known and less-known examples of personality association as an instrument of place branding. The logical, at first glance, assumption is that as people are unique individuals then places will acquire this character of uniqueness through this association with a nominated person. Whether real or fictional, whether actually at some point in time associated with the place or not, whether world renowned or locally significant, the life and work of specific people seems to provide an obvious tool for places to exploit in their branding efforts. The viability of this practice, however, as well as its relation with wider branding policies and the pitfalls involved are analysed and recommendations made. Issues of 'ownership' of such associations (as illustrated in the competition between several places for the ownership of Robin Hood or Santa Claus), the durability of the reputation of the personality selected and the implications of the place size on the use of personality association are all raised and exemplified in the chapter.

All the selected chapters were written by authors experienced in a particular academic approach or area of practical expertise. We hope that their synthesis of the issues raised in the book and the conclusions that can be

drawn from the cases investigated, will provide the basis for a better implementation of place branding, so that its potential as an extremely powerful
tool of management, despite the drawbacks and difficulties discussed at
length above, can at last be fully realized.

2. Place branding theory: a cross-domain literature review from a marketing perspective

Graham Hankinson

Place branding has its origins in the literature on place promotion, which is primarily associated with the literature on urban policy, a domain of study that has attracted researchers from a variety of academic areas including geographers, sociologists, anthropologists and regional economists. For several reasons this literature has largely developed separately from mainstream marketing literature; indeed, a significant section of this literature has been critical of place promotion as a process leading to the 'commodification' of places (Urry, 1990). In addition, those taking a more positive view of place promotion have regarded place branding theory as inappropriate, based as it has been on fast-moving consumer goods marketing practised by private sector organisations in contrast to place products which have largely been the responsibility of the public sector. The link with marketing has primarily been through tourism where the focus has been on places as visitor destinations, but even in this domain researchers have sought to differentiate place marketing from mainstream marketing. It is only recently that these differing perspectives are beginning to be brought together and, as a consequence, a richer and more useful theory of place branding is beginning to emerge (Hankinson, 2007).

The purpose of this chapter is therefore to review the literature within the domains with an interest in place branding, namely marketing, urban policy and tourism. It will evaluate the contributions of each area of study in order to provide an overarching framework both as an aide to practitioners and as a basis for future research. It is accepted that this analysis cannot be comprehensive, but such is the nature of literature reviews. The aim is to give the reader a 'feel' for the range and balance of the literature in these areas.

The chapter begins with a review of the evolution of classical branding and is followed by a similar discussion with regard to the urban policy and tourism literatures. The chapter then examines emerging areas within mainstream marketing theory, which can help to develop a more comprehensive understanding of place branding. Finally, the chapter presents a multi-disciplinary framework of the place branding domain.

THE EVOLUTION OF MODERN BRANDING

The term brand was originally an Old English word meaning a piece of wood that had been burning on a hearth (Oxford English Dictionary, 1936). In the early nineteenth century however, it was more positively applied and used with reference to 'trademarks, made by burning or otherwise. Applied on casks of wines or liquors, timber, metals and any description of goods . . . .' (Oxford English Dictionary, 1936:1055). The concept of a brand is therefore, neither new nor static; it has evolved as its usage has changed and will continue to evolve as the practice of branding is applied to new 'product' areas.

Although the practice of branding for commercial purposes can be traced back to the early nineteenth century, branding as a modern commercial practice began in the USA, around the end of the 1800s. Around this time, brand champions, usually owner-entrepreneurs, began developing and promoting brands, which included Coca-Cola, Gillette, Colgate and Heinz in the US and Rolls Royce and Cadbury's in the UK. All these brand names exist today because of the enthusiasm, energy and status of their owner-entrepreneurs. However, as companies grew, the task of brand management was taken over by teams of functional specialists occupying middle and upper middle management positions (Low and Fullerton, 1994). Such teams typically were comprised of an advertising specialist, a market researcher, a product technician and a sales manager. Brand management thus became more about cooperation and teamwork than vision and entrepreneurship.

From 1930 to the late 1940s, against a backdrop of economic depression and the Second World War, consumers became more cynical of the rather lavish advertising claims being made. Retailers also became more selective in the brands they stocked and there were growing concerns amongst producers about the effectiveness of the team-based approach. Such criticisms led Procter and Gamble to introduce the so-called 'brand manager system' in 1931, by which each brand became the responsibility of one person. Although Johnson and Johnson followed suit, in general, few other firms adopted the system until much later (Low and Fullerton, 1994). The 1950s however, saw a much wider acceptance of the brand manager system. Under this system, brand managers had the authority to ensure the most effective marketing of the company's brands backed by significant corporate resources. As a result, branding raised profit margins and expanded into new product areas, while brand managers were seen as the linchpins of marketing oriented organisations. At this point, branding was predominantly associated with fast-moving consumer goods reflecting the domination of manufacturing across all developed economies. As a result, branding theory until recently was largely developed around the experiences of product marketing.

Some of the early papers on branding were published at around this time (for example, Gardner and Levy, 1955; Boulding, 1956). These papers focused on image as a central component of a brand. The primary role of brand management was to create positive images in the mind of the consumer (Boulding, 1956) in order to establish differentiation and build preference and loyalty in the minds of the consumer (Knox and Bickerton, 2003). Brand images communicate a brand's meaning through a set of associations, which consumers hold in their memories (Keller, 1993; Aaker, 1991; Kapferer, 1997; de Chernatony and Dall'Olmo Riley, 1998).

Most models of brand image classify these associations into two categories: functional attributes, that is the tangible features of a product, and emotional or symbolic attributes, that is the intangible features which meet consumer needs for social approval, personal expression or self-esteem (Keller, 1993; Hankinson and Cowking, 1993; de Chernatony and McWilliam, 1989). Other authors add a third category. In particular, Keller (1993) and Park et al. (1986), add experiential attributes. These relate to what it feels like to use the product or service and satisfy internally generated needs for stimulation and variety (Park et al., 1986; Wilkie, 1986).

In more recent times brand image has become inextricably linked to the concept of brand positioning (Ries and Trout, 1981) based on the recognition that consumer choices are based on comparisons between competing brands. In these circumstances the role of brand management was to create a unique positioning for the brand in the mind of the consumer based upon an attractive set of strong associations (Keller, 1998). This approach to branding focused the management process on brand communications.

In recent years, brands have increasingly been seen as value enhancers providing value not only to organisations but also added value to consumers, activities at the core of the concept of brand equity (Hankinson, 2004a). To the accountant, brand equity is about the brand's financial value, as reflected in its future income potential. To the marketer brand equity is about indicators of financial value such as relative price, brand loyalty, distribution and awareness levels. This conceptualisation has laid the foundations for a strategic approach to brand management. The role of brand management from this perspective is to add value for consumers and for the organisation. Thus brands have come to be regarded as strategic assets able to build long-term value for the company by building long-term value-based relationships with consumers.

THE DEVELOPMENT OF PLACE BRANDING

Like mainstream branding, place branding can be traced back a long way, but the origins of modern-day practice seem to have begun primarily in the USA in the mid-1800s. Place marketing features prominently in the literature of urban policy. The objective of this activity was similarly the creation of differentiation and preference in order to assert competitive advantage over other places, a process that focused like mainstream branding largely, but not exclusively, on advertising (Ward, 1998). However, the term branding has only recently been used to describe the process; more commonly used terms have been 'place selling' and 'place promotion' (see for example Ashworth and Voogd, 1990b; Gold and Ward, 1994; Ward, 1998). In contrast to the normative approach adopted by most of the mainstream marketing literature however, the approach in the urban policy literature has been more varied. These approaches vary from the historical approach, which sees place selling and promotion as part of a broader process of social and economic change (e.g. Ward, 1998) to the critical approach (see for example, Burgess, 1990; Philo and Kearns, 1993; Lash and Urry, 1994), which takes an anti-marketing stance arguing that to treat places as marketable products is to ignore their cultural and social realities. However, the era of Thatcherism that began in the 1970s saw a lasting shift in prevailing attitudes (Ashworth and Voogd, 1994; Ward, 1998). The more positive perspective on the selling and promotion of places that emerged recognised the important contribution of such activities to the efficient social and economic functioning of an area (for example, Ashworth and Voogd, 1994; Ward and Gold, 1994). This was accompanied by the emergence of managerial forms of governance by public administrators and the use of marketing techniques from the private sector as the means by which places sought to compete in an increasingly global marketplace. Frequently, the economic *raison d'etre* for these activities has been the need to regenerate declining, former manufacturing cities and regions (Bradley et al., 2002). Studies in this body of the literature also focus on the outputs from place marketing and examine the degree of success associated with alternative urban marketing strategies (see for example, Ashworth and Voogd, 1990b). As the application of private sector-based marketing techniques became more widespread, the term brand entered the consciousness of the public sector and, shortly afterwards, place branding entered the consciousness of mainstream marketing academics (Hankinson, 2001).

A recurring theme in the urban policy literature has been the nature of the place product, its historical development and the marketing implications of its distinctive features (Ward, 1998; van den Berg and Braun, 1999; Ashworth and Voogd, 1994). Sleipen (1988) argues that the place product is dualistic, consisting of a 'nuclear' product (the place as a holistic conceptual entity) and its contributory elements (the services, activities and features that comprise the place). Van den Berg and Braun (1999) divide the place product into three levels, the individual service (e.g. a tourist attraction), clusters of related services (e.g. tourism services) and urban agglomeration, referring to the collection of all services that make up the place. Ashworth and Voogd (1990b) similarly point out that places operate at different spatial scales from regions to towns and cities to individual buildings with different spatial purposes intended to meet the needs of different consumer groups. Within these spaces, consumers assemble their own unique product from the range of services offered by the place. As a consequence a space can be sold for different purposes to different groups of people by different producers (Ashworth and Voogd, 1994). Thus, places can be both multi-functional and co-consumed. In addition, consumers are free to choose their own unique combination of services from the varied selection on offer and therefore, the place marketer has little control over the consumer experience.

Also, places are not designed to meet a market need in the way that new products and services are. They evolve organically and are defined geographically by statute without reference to commercial considerations. Thus, when the consumer selects a unique combination of experiences across two or more jurisdictional areas (Ashworth and Voogd, 1994), the product consumed may not have been promoted as this combination. The consumption of places that combine two or more separate jurisdictional areas makes place product development and place brand management more difficult.

The process of place branding is usually carried out by a partnership between the public and private sector stakeholders who are involved in the place product delivery. This process can be overlaid by political objectives requiring the Place Branding Organisation (PBO) who is coordinating the process to achieve not only marketing and economic objectives but also political and social aims as well.

All this bears little resemblance to branding in the private sector where brands are built and maintained through a system of direct managerial authority. Consequently, decisions can be made more quickly and there is greater managerial control over the branding processes.

There are, however, also differences in orientation between the urban policy perspective and the mainstream marketing perspective on branding. The role of marketing in the urban policy literature frequently seems to adopt a selling approach to place promotion rather than the consumer-focused role encapsulated in the marketing concept. The role of marketing has often focused on strategies to 'communicate and promote an image' (Burgess, 1990) rather than develop a product that meets the needs and desires of potential consumers.

THE TOURISM PERSPECTIVE

It is in the tourism literature that the concept of the place image has been most fully developed (Selby, 2004). The tourism marketing literature in particular, is dominated by the perceptual perspective of branding, which is based around the task of image development as the principle objective of place promotion. Evidence suggests that visitors' choices of destinations are based upon the degree to which they generate favourable images (Gartner, 1989; Woodside and Lyonsky, 1989). Destination images are thus the means by which a prospective tourist determines a destination's potential for satisfaction (Pearce, 1982). The more favourable the image of a destination, the greater the likelihood of choice (Goodrich, 1977). A destination's brand image is therefore crucial to its marketing success (Leisen, 2001). Thus Sirgy and Su (2000) argue that the propensity to visit a place is dependent upon a match between the visitor's destination image and what the authors refer to as the tourist's self-concept – their image of themselves. Similarly, Hall and Hubbard (1998) see the core objective of destination branding as the production of a positive, focused and consistent communication strategy.

The literature also focuses on image associations. For example, one article alone includes a systematic review of fifteen articles in this area (Echtner and Ritchie, 1993). Similarly, Hankinson (2005) in his review of the leisure tourism literature identified five categories of individual image associations utilised for tourism promotion purposes: economic, physical environment, activities and facilities and people characteristics. Examples of each category are set out in Table 2.1.

One of the earliest contributors to the tourism development literature, Gunn (1972), sub-divides destination image into three categories: (1) organic images that are embedded over a long period of time, based upon 'the totality of what a person already knows or perceives about that

Table 2.1   Brand image attributes associated with leisure tourism

Attribute category	Author(s)
Economic	
Commercialised/not commercialised	Walmsley and Jenkins (1993)
Expensive/inexpensive	Echtner and Ritchie (1993)
Physical environment	
Physical environment/economic dev't	Embacher and Buttle (1989)
Attractive/ unattractive	Walmsley and Jenkins (1993)
Busy/quiet	Walmsley and Jenkins (1993)
Relaxed/fast pace of life	Walmsley and Jenkins (1993)
Weather/climate	Embacher and Buttle (1989)
Resort atmosphere	Embacher and Buttle (1989)
Boring/interesting	Walmsley and Jenkins (1993)
Natural state	Echtner and Ritchie (1993)
Comfort/security	Echtner and Ritchie (1993)
Activities and facilities	
Food	Embacher and Buttle (1989)
Suitability for children	Embacher and Buttle (1989)
Suitability for different types of vacation	Embacher and Buttle (1989)
Tourist facilities and infrastructure	Embacher and Buttle (1989)
Accessibility	Embacher and Buttle (1989)
Interest/adventure	Echtner and Ritchie (1993)
Brand attitudes	
Overall appeal	Embacher and Buttle (1989)
People	
People	Embacher and Buttle (1989)
Culture	Embacher and Buttle (1989)
Trendy/not trendy	Walmsley and Jenkins (1993)
Lack of language barrier	Echtner and Ritchie (1993)
Cultural distance	Echtner and Ritchie (1993)

Source: Author's own.

destination. . . . From newspapers, radio and TV news, documentaries, periodicals, dramas, novels, and non-fictional books and classes on geography'; (2) induced images formed by exposure to a destination's projected image and (3), a modified induced image based upon the interaction of actual experiences of visiting the destination with existing organic and induced images.

However, while the academic literature contains a considerable body of research into the development of induced images, less attention appears to have been given to the significance of images formed through organic processes despite their recognised significance to destination marketing (Hankinson, 2004b).

These models of destination image contrast with the recent mainstream marketing literature that has focused primarily on the classification of brand associations. From this, two principal categories emerge, namely functional associations and symbolic associations. However, at least two papers can be identified that include a third category, namely experiential associations (Park et al., 1986; Keller, 1993). In the context of destination brand images, Hankinson (2005) suggests that brand associations are more likely to fall into the two categories of functional and ambience/ experiential. This study also found evidence of symbolic associations but these appeared to be less important. Similarly, Echtner and Ritchie (1993) provide a conceptual model of the components of a destination image also based upon the three categories of brand association, individual attributes versus holistic impressions, functional versus psychological characteristics and common versus unique characteristics.

Research has shown that destinations that focus purely on the brand communications however, fail to address issues associated with organisational structure, managerial control and product development. For example, Hankinson (2004a) argues for a relationship approach based around a network of partnerships, which can more adequately reflect the reality of place brand management. Selby (2004) also supports the need for a more integrated approach, focusing on both the images and the experiences of the consumer.

Pride (2002) similarly combines a relationship perspective with the communication perspective. Other articles also link these perspectives. Kotler and Gertner (2002), for example, adopt the American Marketing Association's definition of a brand but link this to a brand personality that speaks to the consumer. Morgan et al. (2002) argue for increasing product parity combined with creating unique identities in order to differentiate places from their competitors.

RECENT DEVELOPMENTS IN MAINSTREAM BRANDING THEORY

Corporate Branding

Recent theoretical developments in the area of corporate brands, it has been argued, are of relevance to place branding (Hankinson, 2007;

Karavatzis, 2004; Trueman et al., 2004; Rainisto, 2003). First, both place brands and corporate brands involve interactions with multiple stakeholders (Knox and Bickerton, 2003; Trueman et al., 2004). Secondly, both brands play a strong overarching role, adding value across a variety of business activities through a process of brand endorsement (Keller, 1998; Hankinson, 2001). Finally, both brands provide the focal point for several consumer segments simultaneously (Kotler et al., 1999).

The practice of corporate branding began to develop around the late 1980s and early 1990s, following a series of take-overs of several large organisations, whose success had been built around their strong product brands, highlighting the value of brands as strategic assets (Doyle, 1990). The value of brands and their vulnerability to acquisition by predators led practitioners and academics to consider new ways of managing them (see for example, Piercy and Cravens, 1995). A particularly significant response to the changing commercial environment was the emergence of corporate brands as umbrellas under which sheltered a range of different and sometimes only loosely related product brands. A review of the corporate brand literature by Hankinson (2005) suggests five key requirements for successful corporate branding.

First, central to the delivery of a successful corporate brand is a brand supportive culture (Hatch and Schultz, 2003). A corporate brand must not only communicate its values – what it stands for – but it must also deliver those values, i.e. keep its promise to its target market. Hatch and Schultz (2003) argue that it is this '. . .concern with values that brings corporate branding practice into direct contact with organisational culture' which they define as '. . .the internal values, beliefs and assumptions that embody the heritage of the company and communicate its meaning to its members' (p.1047). Kapferer (2000) similarly argues that to be successful, there needs to be consistency between brand values and organisational culture if the brand is to have credibility in the eyes of its stakeholders. In order for this to happen, corporate brand values must be rooted in the cultural values of the organisation.

Secondly, senior management and, in particular the Chief Executive Officer (CEO), must set a clear vision for the organisation and ensure alignment between that vision, the corporate culture and the brand image (Hatch and Schultz, 2003). The strategic vision forms the basis for the development of corporate values, which, in turn, guide the development of the brand values that form part of the brand identity to be communicated. Through a process of training and mentoring, top management must develop, communicate and embed the strategic vision and values in the culture of the entire organisation and ensure that the performance of the brand reflects the brand promise (Hankinson, 2007).

Thirdly, to deliver the brand promise, it is also necessary to have in place the procedures and processes necessary to ensure a coordinated response to customer needs. In a study of three contrasting organisations, Knox and Bickerton (2003) found that all three organisations highlighted the importance of aligning the relevant business processes with corporate brand values in order to delivery customer value. The principle of inter-departmental coordination is the central component of a brand orienta-tion organisation (Urde, 1999). In many organisations, there can be a different understanding of the brand in different parts of the organisation. Thus, implementing brand orientation requires a fundamental review of all marketing and non-marketing departments' procedures and processes and their re-orientation around the brand's core values (Tilley, 1999).

Fourthly, corporate brands deal with a wide range of external stake-holders; in addition to shareholders, suppliers, distributors and govern-ment agencies these can also include the media, education and the arts, all of which can have a profound influence on the brand image over a long period of time. In addition, many organisations have insufficient resources to respond quickly enough to the changing market environment. A swifter and more effective response may be made through cooperative partner-ships and alliances. Thus, Leitch and Richardson (2003) suggest that it will be increasingly important for new economy organisations to create and manage their brands in partnership with other organisations, including competitors, rather than fighting for exclusivity.

One brand therefore, must address these multi-dimensional and multi-disciplinary interfaces in a way that is consistent with the designated brand values. This requires strong, long-term relationships with stakeholders in order to provide the stability needed to build brands and deliver the brand values embodied in the brand images that they have created (Zineldin, 2004; Murphy et al., 2005). It is therefore important to establish an appro-priate institutional framework for the creation of a cooperative network that can take the branding process forward. Warnaby et al., (2002) suggest such frameworks should allow for both formal and informal interactions. While formal meetings facilitate decision-making, informal interaction allows dialogue to continue between meetings and helps resolve partner-ship problems.

Fifthly, corporate brands are required to build a wider appeal than product brands through the development of brand identities with meaning across a range of stakeholders. Therefore, in addition to conventional, media-based marketing communications aimed at consumers, corporate brands must seek to build and maintain strong partnerships with other stakeholders through more suitable media such as face-to-face meet-ings, events, reports, training programmes and manuals. Such inter-organisational communications need to take place at both strategic and operational levels in order to ensure common understanding of the brand and its values and the behaviours necessary to deliver them.

Services Branding

Little attention has been given in the literature to place branding from a services marketing perspective; yet, places as marketable entities are largely positioned as collections of services. This is particularly the case with respect to places positioned as tourism destinations but it is arguably equally true of places positioned as financial centres, retail centres and events and cultural centres. Even in the case of manufacturing, it could be argued that firms increasingly relocate on the basis of services benefits such as logistical convenience or the presence of suppliers and supporting businesses such as financial services. Services are provided by private sector organisations which provide most, but not all of the primary (customer-facing) services such as retailing, entertainment, hotels and restaurants. Services are also provided by the public sector, which is responsible for many of the infrastructural services such as policing, environmental health, and the maintenance of the public servicescape (Shostack, 1977) such as parks and other open spaces, public buildings and monuments (Hankinson, 2004a).

In essence, people and organisations visit or locate in a place because of the services that they provide. Therefore, it is services that form the core of the place product and provide the benefits that the place brand offers. It is logical therefore, that the services marketing and branding literatures should form part of this review.

There is now a well-established literature on services marketing reflecting the fact that, in developed economies, services now account for around 75 per cent of GDP (Lovelock and Wirtz, 2007). In contrast, only around 25 per cent of the world's top 60 brands are services brands (Clifton and Maughan, 2000) and as a consequence, the literature on services branding is only just emerging. There is however, much that can be learned about place branding from both literatures.

Much of the attention in this literature has focused on the conceptual differences between products and services. As a result, the distinctive characteristics of services are now widely accepted as being intangibility, inseparability, variability, inability to store and inability to own. Of these, intangibility, inseparability and variability are perhaps the most relevant from the point of view of branding (de Chernatony and Segal-Horn, 2001). For example, financial services are generally regarded as nearer to the 'pure' end of the product/services continuum. Most of the service benefits they offer are intangible; yet there are tangible elements to the service including bank notes and coinage, and other financial documents associated with financial assets. Towards the other end of the continuum are products with service accompaniments such as are offered by retail businesses. The greater the service component of an organisation's offering, the greater the intangibility and the consequent need for physical evidence of the service including that provided by brand communications. Staff also form part of physical evidence, as does the environment or servicescape in which the service takes place (Shostack, 1977). In most services, the service encounter (Shostack, 1984) between the consumer and service personnel constitutes the core service product. The consumer is actively involved with the service production and as a result the two are regarded as inseparable. The quality of each service encounter therefore, is variable, reflecting the variability of the human interactions and the differing contexts in which the encounter takes place. These characteristics can clearly cause problems of quality control. The inseparability of consumption from production of a service therefore requires careful attention to staff training in order to minimise the potential variability in service quality.

As a result of these characteristics, the traditional 4Ps of the marketing mix have been augmented by three additional Ps, namely physical evidence, people and processes (Zeithaml et al., 2006). Physical evidence provides a pre-purchase indicator of the quality of the service, but also can facilitate the consumption of a service. In the case of buildings and the servicescape, such evidence helps the consumer to form a view of the quality of service prior to consumption as well as forming part of the service experience itself. In contrast to products, service brand fulfilment is delivered through the customer experience during the service encounter, which, in similar ways to corporate brands, depends significantly on the attitudes and behaviours of the service provider's staff and the processes and procedures that control the service delivery. Thus, in order to make the service experience more controllable, services branding theory adds an internal organisational dimension to the management of brands.

First, it focuses brand strategy not just on consumers but also on other stakeholders, particularly staff. Thus, de Chernatony and Segal-Horn (2001), emphasise the need to understand an organisation's values as a foundation on which to build brand values. A strong, positive relationship between a brand and an organisation's staff, referred to by Urde (2003) as the internal brand identity, is fundamental to the delivery of the brand experience. In order to achieve this, some organisations deliberately recruit staff whose values are consistent with the required organisational culture.

Secondly, it focuses brand strategy on the processes that deliver the brand experience by, for example, mapping the operational stages in the service encounter through the development of process blueprints (Shostack, 1984). In some organisations technology is prioritised over staff as the key component of their processes, giving staff less discretion in their behaviour but also less scope therefore, for service failure.

The link between services marketing theory and the place product is made by Warnaby and Davies (1997). To establish this link they transpose the Servuction Model developed by Langeard et al. (1981) into a place product context. In this model, a service organisation is represented by invisible elements and visible elements. The invisible element consists of supporting processes that support the delivery of the service, for example ordering, delivery and billing processes. Visible elements divide into an inanimate component, consisting of the physical environment in which the service encounter takes place, and the people involved in the delivery of the service. The latter includes not only the individual consumer and the service provider's staff, but also other consumers of the service who can influence the quality of the service experience. In the context of places, the invisible elements are replaced by the infrastructural services, for example, public health and security services, infrastructural maintenance and transport. These support the primary services offered by a place such as cultural, retail, financial and leisure (Hankinson, 2004a). The inanimate physical environment is created by the built environment and social milieu in which place consumers engage in the services offered.

Overall, services marketing extends marketing theory into other areas of management theory, notably organisational theory and operations management. The Servuction Model, in particular, takes the focus of brand strategy beyond the perceptual perspective towards the means by which the brand promise is delivered, referred to by Hankinson (2004a) as brand reality.

PLACE BRANDING: A MULTI-DISCIPLINARY FRAMEWORK

It is clear from the diversity of literature reviewed that place branding has been, and will continue to be, studied from several perspectives, some of which take a critical view. However, the primary focus of this review has been on those sections of the literature that help to achieve a better understanding of the place branding phenomenon and provide the basis for improving the management of the process. Although the term branding is not used consistently across the four areas reviewed, each nevertheless makes a significant contribution to this understanding of at least one

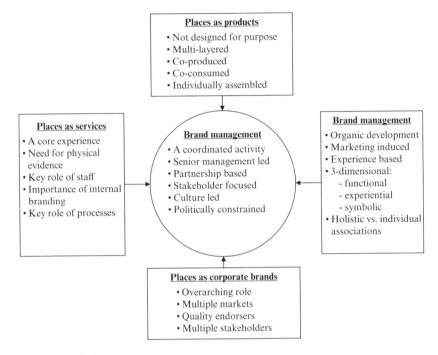

Source: Author's own.

Figure 2.1   Place branding: a multi-dimensional framework

aspect of the place branding phenomenon. However, it is acknowledged that, while distinct contributions have been made by each of the four domains reviewed, overlap also exists, for example services marketing and corporate branding both have their foundations in the broader domain of marketing. The contributions of each of these areas of study together with the implications of these contributions are summarised in a multi-disciplinary framework in Figure 2.1.

Places as Products

Much of the early work on place promotion within the general area of urban policy was focused on the nature of places as marketable commodities offering packages of service experiences for consumption. The place product has developed organically rather than being planned and designed for purpose, a feature that has a profound impact on the development of place brand strategy, making it more akin to rebranding than *ab initio* branding. In many places this characteristic has been used positively by the PBO, for example in the case of historic towns and cities such as Cambridge in England and Bruges in Belgium, where architectural heritage and other historical artefacts have been turned to good advantage. In many other places however, for example in old, industrial cities and towns such as Detroit in the USA and Glasgow in Scotland, it has made branding difficult. Despite this disadvantage many post-industrial cities have reinvented themselves through various processes of urban renewal.

The place product is also multi-layered, consisting of an amalgam of services, each of which is marketed as a product in its own right. This can also work in two ways. Places, particularly large cities, can offer multiple benefits by positioning themselves simultaneously as, for example retail and entertainment centres as well as focal points for commercial and financial activities. In these circumstances, a decision has to be made during the early stages of branding as to the most compatible combination of activities that can form the core brand offer. Because the core offer is co-produced by a collection of autonomous organisations, place branding is required to be partner-based. As co-beneficiaries of a successful place brand, these partners must not only provide funding but also individually deliver services in a way that is consistent with the adopted place brand values. Furthermore, because each place consumer assembles his own unique product experience from the varied selection of experiences on offer, there is a need to influence these choices through selective promotion and careful routing; however, this is never a perfect solution. The problem is made more complex by the co-consumption characteristic of place products. The multi-dimensionality of the place product attracts a variety of consumer groups, seeking their own bundle of benefits. Thus, in certain circumstances, the product experience of one group can be impaired by the behaviour of another group seeking another experience. In order to avoid conflicts of interest, it is therefore important to ensure that the combination of services which comprise the brand offer are compatible, so that the services and attractions offered to one consumer segment will not interfere with the experience of another. Place branding thus, requires careful market positioning.

The Place as an Image

The image component of a brand forms a significant part of all four literatures reviewed here. From a marketing point of view, the induced brand image is the central device whereby a set of functional, experiential and symbolic associations are communicated to target audiences in order to create a holistic image which encapsulates a unique and desirable identity.

In most cases, the objective of place branding is to reposition a place in the mind of the place consumer and to establish a point of differentiation with respect to other places attempting to dominate the same market space. Perhaps some of the best examples of repositioning are the post-industrial cities, which have successfully reinvented their images through a combination of creative marketing communications backed by new investment. As Gunn (1972) points out, many place images are already formed well before the place marketers begin their work. The collections of associations resulting from the arts, history and the media underline once again the fact that place branding is primarily a rebranding exercise that seeks to reinforce, change or augment images which have developed organically. Thus for example, places such as Stratford upon Avon, which is inextricably linked to the poet and playwright, William Shakespeare, must seek to reinforce that key association if it intends to communicate other messages associated with non-tourist market segments.

However, brand equity, the value of the brand, is built, not only by the creation of a unique image, it also requires places to deliver the experiences promised by the brand images they communicate. As a consequence, to be successful, place image creation must be accompanied by investment in the development of both the primary services and the infrastructure required to form the place product experience. For example, this can take place through public/private sector partnerships as in the successful rebranding of Glasgow in the late 1980s and Liverpool early in the twenty-first century, culminating in the European Capital of Culture Award. It can also take place as part of the preparation for a sporting event such as the Olympic Games, which has helped to re-launch cities such as Barcelona, Sydney and very recently Beijing. Such events not only provide significant funding both for infrastructural investment and marketing, but also raise place awareness and provide considerable media coverage of the place and its environs.

Places as Corporate Brands

Because places are co-produced by many independent organisations providing services within its boundaries, the place brand is required to perform an overarching role, providing an identity which links the various service organisations together under a shared set of associations. This is not an easy task but it is nevertheless similar to the task required of large private sector corporations who control a varied collection of businesses. Just as corporate brands, such as Virgin, have a set of core values that unite their various businesses and add financial value to each, so places must find a similar set of values that can unite and add value to the primary services at the heart of their place products. However, one important distinction has to be made here: whereas large corporations have usually grown by acquiring or growing compatible businesses, places have not developed in such a structured way. The consequence of this difference in evolution is that, whereas large corporations begin with a core set of values which guide their growth, places begin with a group of partner organisations who must find common ground. The role of the PBO throughout this process is to ensure consistency in the brand communications by all stakeholders, both collectively and individually.

In addition, both places and corporate brands provide services to different market segments, which frequently include both businesses and consumers. Thus, the set of core values adopted must establish a common meaning across these segments if a strong brand is to be created. Creating brands on the basis of different identities for each segment can lead to market confusion and the dilution of the brand's impact. A central role of the corporate brand is to establish trust amongst its target audiences. This requires the creation of strong quality associations, which have relevance to the multiple markets that its operating divisions serve. In a similar way, places must also communicate associations of quality, which can transcend the varied services making up its product offer. In both cases, target markets may include not only businesses and individual consumers but also other stakeholders who, in the case of places, include funding organisations and government, both national and local. Brand communications must therefore face in several directions, appealing to a frequently diverse set of stakeholders while maintaining a common set of core brand values.

Places as Services

Services provide the core experience of a place; however, services by their nature are intangible. The nature and quality of the service experiences offered by a place therefore have to be communicated using various forms of physical evidence. Such evidence begins with the marketing literature used to promote a place and extends to the built environment. In much of place branding the focus of physical evidence is on the provision of marketing literature and other publicity such as posters, which, through photography, attempt to 'give a feel of the place'. Such print-based promotion frequently represents the limit of place branding activities, particularly in smaller towns and cities. In larger places, such as countries, more expensive promotional media such as television and cinema are frequently used. However, the provision of physical evidence should go beyond promotion. Physical evidence in the form of the built environment for example, is equally important either as attractions in their own right, for example, buildings such as the Guggenheim Museum in Bilbao or the Eiffel Tower in Paris, or as major contributors to the ambience of a place (Hankinson, 2004b). People can also be a part of physical evidence. Because services are at the core of the place product, places must work to ensure that each encounter with service providers' staff supports the overall brand offer. Frontline staff in particular are the deliverers of the place brand and consequently their attitudes and behaviour are central to a successful place brand. Resources therefore, need to be made available for investment in staff development to ensure the adoption of appropriate attitudes and behaviours. For example, in Glasgow taxi drivers have been required to undergo brand training before they are granted a license to operate; awareness of the key attributes of the city forming the core brand identity is developed through a system of workshops.

A further characteristic of services is the central role played by processes, that is the linking of common activities in a logical and efficient sequence. In the case of place branding, this is particularly relevant to infrastructural services such as transport and environmental health services. Transport processes include access to a place as well as movement within it, while environmental health services include processes associated with refuse collection, sanitation and pollution control (a particularly important issue associated with the Olympic Games in Beijing). The provision of efficient process-based services such as these, which either support the primary services at the customer end of the place product or contribute to the ambience of the place product, is a fundamental part of place branding.

The Implications for the Management of Place Brands

It is clear from the literature that there are similarities between place branding and other branding practices. It is also clear that image development is a central activity across all branding activity and it is in this area that place branding had made significant progress. However, it is the nature of the place product and the institutional framework within which place branding takes place that distinguishes it from other forms of branding. As a result of these differences, place branding becomes a coordination process rather than a managed activity; (PBOs), as the lead bodies in developing the brand, have no direct control over either the brand's development or the delivery of the brand experience.

In contrast, PBOs must work in partnership with other organisations to find a common platform on which investment and promotional strategies can combine to develop and maintain a consistent place brand. Common agreement on these must be a priority for the PBO if the brand is to be used to endorse the quality of the key service providers and add value to their brands. Research suggests that as many as 200 such organisations might be involved in this process (Hankinson, 2009). These will include major corporations, hotel, restaurant and retail associations, local government and infrastructural services. Other organisations with a stakeholding in a successful place brand might also be consulted such as residents' associations and the transport companies who provide access to a place. However, as regards PBOs, it may be preferable to work with a relatively small, but broadly based group of compatible, committed stakeholders and to establish long-term partnerships rather than short term partnerships with a large group of similar organisations.

One of the problems facing the PBO is securing the participation of key organisations in branding activities. While a branding strategy can be drafted by the PBO, its subsequent development and adoption ultimately needs to be sanctioned by these key organisations. It is here that the PBO's CEO has a crucial role to play. The partnership-based model of brand management, which is necessary in the building of place brands, requires the CEO to act, not only as the brand champion but also as the person who opens doors in other key service organisations at a senior level in order to build a partnership. Evidence suggests that for this to be effective, the CEO must seek to foster strong relationships between both senior managers with strategic responsibility and operational managers in participating organisations. Research amongst CEOs into the factors underpinning successful place branding identified the need for CEOs to have strong influencing skills and the ability to build strong external relationships.

In addition to this external role, the CEO must also build an internal culture within the PBO around the place brand's values, spreading organisation-wide commitment to the place brand, not only in terms of staff attitudes and behaviour, but also in terms of key organisational processes and procedures. The establishment of a brand-oriented culture such as this may also require changes in the way staff are recruited, trained and remunerated. Organisational culture in support of the brand is at the heart of successful service and corporate branding and its development must start with the organisation leading the place branding. It should then be rolled out to the partner organisations; however, extending this process to partner organisations is more problematic. Amongst private sector organisations, the priority will always be to instil commitment to the organisation's own brand; commitment to the place brand will be secondary unless there is synergy between the brands' values. This can only happen when partner organisations are involved in the specification of the destination's brand values at an early stage in the brand's development. Each partner organisation should then, through a process of internal training and human resource development, ensure that the place brand values are understood and engaged with by all departments, following the lead taken by the PBO. This is a process that will take time to embed, but it can be incentivised through the use of endorsement schemes and licenses to practice linked to training. For example, many places require their partners to commit to the place brand values as part of a brand accreditation scheme. The centrality of these activities to effective delivery of the place brand experience demonstrates the importance of establishing an appropriate institutional framework for the creation of a cooperative network that can take the branding process forward.

Finally, public sector organisations such as PBOs, face the possibility of a political regime change on a periodic basis. What can be achieved from a branding perspective is therefore constrained by the prevailing political climate and therefore subject to change on a regular basis. Such changes can be at national level affecting the institutional framework, for example by switching funding from a tourist board to a regional development agency as has recently happened in the UK and at local level, as a result of changes to local economic strategy. Such constraints are not conducive to branding which is a long-term, strategic activity. First, changes in economic policy can affect investment decisions, which in turn impact on the development of the place product. Secondly, a decline in commitment to branding by elected members of local government can undermine the partnerships which form the bedrock on which the brand has been developed and delivered. Thirdly, changes in funding arrangements can have implications for brand communications, particularly if funding is reduced or made more difficult to obtain agreement on.

CONCLUSION

The overall conclusion from this review is that the development of place branding theory has been multi-disciplinary and written from differing perspectives, some of which have been critical of the practice. However, in contrast to the significant contributions from the domains of urban policy and tourism, the contribution of mainstream product-based branding theory has been limited (principally to image theory). Nevertheless, recent developments in the marketing theory, notably in the areas of services marketing and corporate branding, have the potential to make significant contributions. Notwithstanding this, the nature and structure of the place product combined with the nature of the relationships between the stakeholder organisations involved in developing and delivering the place brand, will continue to require the contextualisation of this theory. The multi-disciplinary framework set out in this chapter must be seen in this context. PBOs seeking to gain from this theory therefore, need to adapt it to the institutional framework within which they are required to operate, working in partnership with other organisations to find a common platform on which product investment and promotional strategies can combine to develop and maintain a consistent place brand. Common agreement on these must be a priority for the PBO if the brand is to be used to endorse the quality of the key service providers and add value to their brands.

3. Is corporate branding relevant to places?

Mihalis Kavaratzis

INTRODUCTION

This chapter takes up the notions of corporate level marketing and branding, which were introduced in the previous chapter, and focuses on the similarities between corporate branding and place branding. The chapter examines two intriguing questions. The first is whether place branding is really branding and whether it can be used as a tool of place development. The ultimate goal of place marketing is to foster local development in order to increase the well-being of the residents of the place. Is branding an effective tool that can be used to that end? The second question is whether place branding is a form of corporate branding. The similarities between corporate branding and place branding have been noted by several commentators (including Kavaratzis and Ashworth, 2005; Hankinson, 2007; Skinner, 2008; Kavaratzis, 2009) and there seems to be an underlying agreement that corporate branding has brought marketing theories closer than ever before to the needs and peculiarities of places (Kavaratzis, 2009). It is useful for the readers of this book to examine the relationship and possible links of corporate branding and marketing to place branding theory and practice. This is done in the second part of this chapter.

IS PLACE BRANDING REALLY BRANDING?

As discussed in the introductory chapter, many authors have noted the popularity of branding and the relevance to places. However, as Braun (2008), among others, identifies, there are different views on what branding is. Braun (2008) contrasts the definition by Kotler (1997) who defines a brand as 'a name, term, sign, symbol or design or combination of them which is intended to identify the goods and services of one seller or groups of sellers and to differentiate them from those of competitors' to that by Schmitt (1999) who claims that a brand is 'a rich source of sensory, affective and cognitive associations that result in memorable brand experiences' (Braun 2008:35). The divergence of the definitions of branding is evident also in place branding and this is only the first of a series of problems touched upon here.

In examining the proposition that places should be treated as brands and therefore place management as place brand management, it is very useful to consider for a moment the opposite proposition (see also Ashworth, 2006). This could be done in two ways. First, the two assumptions on which the whole argument for implementing branding in places is based (see the introductory chapter) could be separated. The fact that places have brand images or, to put it more boldly, that places are brands, does not necessarily mean that place development should be considered as brand development. Secondly, even if it is accepted that brand development and management is what is meant by place branding, it is vitally important to understand branding as an eclectic strategic choice and not a set of promotional tools. Furthermore, it is imperative to develop branding tools that are place-specific and not a simple extension of well known tools that are used for purposes that have little resemblance to place development goals.

Despite the similarities of place branding to corporate branding that have been repeatedly suggested in the literature and will be discussed below, it is not clear in what ways places could be thought of as corporations and, therefore, whether place brands can be treated as corporate brands. It is this line of thought that has led Ashworth (2006) to wonder whether it is possible to brand places, whether it is in fact what we are doing and whether it is the right way to go. It is still useful to think of the place as corporate brand metaphor (also Anholt, 2002). It could be argued that the complexities involved in place branding are much greater than corporate branding (also Anholt, 2008b) and the difficulties more acute. For example, the adoption and projection of a single clear identity, ethos and image by cities is much more difficult (Ashworth, 2006), if desirable at all. 'Cities have many similarities with large commercial corporations but unless these similarities are more important than the dissimilarities of political responsibility and public interest, places cannot be branded in the same sense' (Ashworth, 2006). Applying corporate branding to places demands a treatment of the place brand as the whole entity of the place-products, in order to achieve consistency of the messages sent (Kavaratzis and Ashworth, 2005), which is much trickier than in the case of corporations. At the same time it demands associating the city with 'stories' about it that need to be expressed in the city by planning and design interventions or infrastructure development (Kavaratzis, 2004), both of which demand meeting conditions that are certainly not evident in the corporate marketing environment. Interestingly, one of the strongest and most well known advocates of place branding, Anholt (2008a) makes a very strong case against the appropriateness of the word 'brand' to describe the place branding approach and he suggests the more suitable term 'competitive identity'. The main and utterly correct argument (which also underlies this whole book) is that place branding is 'not about communications but about policy change' (Anholt, 2008a:2) and that 'actions speak louder than words'. Similarly, Kavaratzis (2008) has made two relevant arguments. First, that place branding is not about telling the world that our place is good; instead it is about making our place good and letting the world know that we are trying. Secondly, that place branding does help improve a place's image but this improvement is always based on wide interventions that call the brand to mind rather than on promotion alone.

Anholt (2008b) rejects the idea that it is possible to 'do branding' for a country (or a city or region) in the same way that companies 'do branding' with their products and services, as 'vain and foolish'. As he discusses,

> [i]n short, nobody doubts that places have their brand images, and that those images are critical to their success in the global contest for products, trade, services, talent, finance, investment, culture, respect and profile. It's only when people start talking about *branding* rather than just *brand* that the problems start. It would certainly make life easier for many governments if it were possible to brand places: it would conveniently reduce the success criteria for their economic and political competitiveness to having a big enough marketing budget and hiring the best marketing and PR agencies. But of course the reality is more complex; national images are not created through communications, and cannot be altered by communications (Anholt 2008b:2).

The first question tackled in this chapter could be rephrased as, is place branding the wrong name for the right approach to place development or is it the right name for the wrong approach? It is accepted here, as in the whole book, that indeed the discussion of place branding is not about a simple modification of promotional tools and image-building methods to fit the needs of places. Arguably, all of the chapters included in this book would not belong to such a limited approach towards place branding. The essence lies within strategic thinking and the crucial question is whether branding can provide a useful basis for such strategic thinking when it comes to place development in economic, social, cultural or any other terms. In this sense, it is preferable to accept place branding as a useful metaphor that can be used to find solutions rather than a solution in itself. In conclusion, whether we accept place branding as a simple metaphor or something deeper and more strategic than that, it seems fair to conclude that several of the tools of branding and, perhaps more importantly, its general management philosophy are appropriate for effective place management. Therefore, place branding could well be the wrong name for the right approach towards place development (see also Helbrecht, 1994 for a similar argument on place marketing). If branding altogether is not merely about the intentional communication of a favourable image but is a strategic response to challenges in the environment, then place branding is useful. It also seems fair to conclude, as will be more fully argued later, that corporate marketing is the part of general marketing theory that is closer to the needs and distinctive characteristics of places. This is evident in the existing frameworks or models of place branding that can be found in the literature and are examined in this chapter. Therefore, the next section provides a brief review of corporate-level marketing.

THE CORPORATION AND ITS MARKETING

The concept of corporate branding is a relatively recent development within the marketing discipline although its precursors like corporate reputation or corporate identity have been studied for longer (see also the previous chapter). The study of corporate branding and marketing has been developed and popularised in the last fifteen years (see Balmer 2001; Hatch and Schultz, 2001; Balmer and Greyser, 2003; Balmer and Gray, 2003). There have been many arguments for the need of organisations to develop and manage their corporate brand, together with or even instead of, branding their products. Such branding is broadly understood as the visual, verbal and behavioural expression of an organisation's unique business model (Knox and Bickerton, 2003). The explanation for the increased interest in corporate brands has been summarised by Hulberg (2006) in three main reasons. These are *differentiation* (that is separating oneself from the crowd in an environment where consumers may fail to see differences between products offered), *transparency* (where an organisation's external audience has access to those who are behind the brand, what they stand for and their policy) and *cost reduction* (in which rather than promoting several brands separately, corporate branding creates synergies between brands). Schultz and de Chernatony (2002) argue that a well conceived corporate branding strategy provides a holistic framework for conceptualising and aligning the many different activities through which companies express who they are and what they stand for. Thus it provides a solid foundation for developing a coherent and engaging promise to all stakeholders and it acts as a mechanism to align organisational subcultures across functional and geographical boundaries (Schultz and de Chernatony, 2002). According to Hatch and Schultz (2001), the foundation of the corporate branding process is the interplay between strategic vision (the central idea behind the organisation and its aspirations), organisational culture (the internal values and basic assumptions that embody the meaning of the organisation) and corporate images (the views on the organisation developed by its internal and external audiences). Hulberg (2006) reviews the essential constructs of corporate branding theories, which include: identity, organisational culture, behaviour, values, image and reputation.

An obviously central element in corporate branding theories is multiple stakeholders (e.g. Hatch and Schultz, 2003). Perceptions of an organisation are formed by the interaction and communication with the organisation and one must be aware of the fact that everything an organisation says and does communicates; therefore every single source of communication must be governed by similar messages to assure uniform delivery to all stakeholders (Hulberg, 2006). Another fundamental notion within corporate branding with particular relevance to place branding is corporate identity. Although the definition of the concept is rather problematic (Melewar and Jenkins, 2002), it is believed that a strong identity is very important for transmitting a consistent internal and external image among stakeholders, creating a valuable asset (Simoes and Dibb, 2001). Or as Melewar et al. (2006:139) put it, 'by effectively managing its corporate identity an organisation can build understanding and commitment among its diverse stakeholders'. Balmer (2002) proposes a 'corporate identity mix', which consists of the following components: *strategy* (management vision, corporate strategy, product/ services as well as corporate performance, corporate brand covenant, corporate ownership); *structure* (relationships between parent company and subsidiaries, relations with alliance or franchise partners); *communication* (total corporate communication that encompasses communication between the corporation and its audiences as well as between stakeholders); and *culture* (the soft and subjective elements consisting of the mix of sub-cultures present within, but not always emanating from the organisation). Melewar and Jenkins (2002) provide a different but not dissimilar model, which breaks down corporate identity into the areas of communication and visual identity, behaviour, corporate culture and market conditions.

More recently Balmer and Greyser (2006) introduced the wider concept of corporate level marketing, offering their suggestion on a corporate marketing mix. As the authors emphasise, corporate marketing is more of a philosophy rather than a function, therefore the elements of the corporate marketing mix should not be seen as elements for a department of the company to orchestrate but rather as informing an organisation-wide philosophy. The 6 Cs of Corporate Marketing and the key statements that underpin each of them are (Balmer and Greyser, 2006):

- *Character* (tangible and intangible assets of organisations as well as activities, markets served, philosophy: what we indubitably are).
- *Culture* (internal collective feeling derived by the values, beliefs and assumptions about the organisation: what we feel we are).
- *Communication* (channels of communication with customers and other constituencies, ideally taking into account the effects of word-of-mouth and media/competitor commentary: what we say we are).
- *Conceptualisations* (perceptions of the corporate brand held by customers and other stakeholder groups: what we are seen to be).
- *Constituencies* (meeting the wants and demands of stakeholder groups taking into account that many customers belong to other groups also: whom we seek to serve).
- *Covenant* (the promise made by the corporate brand which leads to the expectations associated with it by stakeholders: what is promised by us and expected of us).

It is outside the scope of this chapter to go into more details on the corporation and its marketing; instead the next section focuses on the possible links to place branding.

THE RELEVANCE TO PLACES

As mentioned above, there are evident similarities between corporate branding and place branding and the relationship of these two forms of branding has been examined in the literature, mostly in terms of lessons that can be learned from corporate branding. The similarities between corporate and place branding have been summarised elsewhere (see Kavaratzis, 2009) and relate to their multidisciplinary roots, the multiple groups of stakeholders that they address, their high level of intangibility and complexity, their need to take into account social responsibility and accountability, their need for long-term development and the multiple identities of the object of both these forms of branding. Hankinson (2007) provided five guiding principles for destination branding based on corporate branding concepts. He argues that 'there are sufficient similarities between these two types of brand to allow useful lessons to be drawn' and suggests that efficient destination branding depends upon a strong, visionary leadership, a brand-oriented organisational culture, departmental coordination and process alignment, consistent communications across a wide range of stakeholders and strong, compatible partnerships.

In a similar vein, Hankinson (2009) examined 'recent literature with regard to corporate brands in particular, [which] suggests that they have several characteristics that align them with destination brands and that managing destination brands might therefore be much like managing corporate brands' (p. 98). The characteristics identified refer to the requirement to manage interactions with multiple stakeholders with potentially conflicting objectives, the communication with stakeholders through a variety of contact points, the strong overarching role adding value through endorsement across a variety of business activities and the requirement to be the focal point for several consumer segments simultaneously (Hankinson, 2009). The literature review leads Hankinson (2009) to identify five critical antecedents of successful destination branding (also briefly outlined in the previous chapter): stakeholder partnerships, brand leadership, departmental coordination, brand communications and brand culture. From a managerial point of view these antecedents imply specific tasks that need to be fulfilled in order for successful destination branding to be attempted. *Stakeholder partnerships* are multidimensional partnerships based upon relationships between compatible organisations in terms of their goal, their power, the compatibility of their respective brands and the relative strategies pursued by each member. *Brand leadership* is the key to brand commitment and it is suggested that it is necessary to coordinate efforts at a senior level, therefore ultimate responsibility for the brand should lie with a team of senior level managers who act as brand champions. *Departmental coordination* goes beyond the basic need to coordinate the various departments' responses to marketing information and intelligence to include the coordination of inter-departmental processes and behaviours around the creation, development and protection of the brand. *Brand communications* refer to the variety of ways in which a corporation communicates with its several groups of internal and external audiences though a multiplicity of contact points and practices in order to build trust through consistency of execution. Finally, *brand culture* is understood as the alignment between organisational culture (values, beliefs and basic assumptions) with the values embedded in the brand vision so that they become part of the customer's image and experience of the brand.

The relevance of corporate-marketing level concepts to places becomes apparent in the above discussion and more so if a closer look is taken at the, so far fragmented, suggestions of the literature in terms of place branding frameworks. This is the purpose of the next section of this chapter.

REVIEWING PLACE BRANDING FRAMEWORKS

As stated earlier there is an evident confusion between city branding and promotion, caused by the perceived lack of control over other elements of the marketing mix (Virgo and de Chernatony, 2006). This misunderstanding has misled most contemporary city branding practices into the exclusive use of promotional tools such as slogans and logos or, at best, advertising campaigns. However, a strategic and responsible view on city branding includes many more areas of activities. Although it is true that considering the popularity of place branding, 'very little has been written about how place marketing and in particular the branding of places should be managed' (Hankinson, 2007:241), there have been suggestions of place brand management frameworks. This section attempts a short description of relevant frameworks and begins the process of a synthesis that might eventually lead to a more generally accepted framework of how to develop and manage city brands.

The first framework is the theoretical framework of Kavaratzis (2004). The framework describes city-brand communication through different variables, which have both functional as well as symbolic meaning. It distinguishes between intentional and unintentional communication:

1. Unintentional Communication relates to the communicative effects of a city's actions and marketing measures when communication is not the main goal. It is divided into four broad areas of intervention: Landscape Strategies (including urban design, architecture, public spaces in the city, public art and heritage management); Infrastructure Projects (projects developed to create, improve or give a distinctive character to the transport, communication, cultural, tourism and other types of necessary infrastructure; Organisational Structure (the effectiveness of the city's governing structure including organising for marketing, Public Private Partnerships, community development networks and citizens' participation in the decision making); the City's Behaviour (the city leaders' vision for the city, the strategy adopted, the financial incentives provided, the quality of services and the number and type of events organised).
2. Intentional Communication is the formal communication that most commonly takes place through well known marketing practices like advertising, PR, graphic design, logos etc.

Rainisto (2003) proposed a general framework of place branding concentrating on the marketing of places as business locations and in particular the activities of inward investment agencies. The framework consists of nine success factors of place marketing and branding practices. According to this framework, the core building stones of place marketing (and most important success factors) are: Planning Group (the organ responsible to plan and execute marketing practices), Vision and Strategic Analysis (the insight of the place about its future position), Place Identity and Image (a unique set of place brand associations, which the management wants to create or maintain), Public-Private Partnerships and Leadership (the capability to conduct complex processes and obtain the organising power). These are factors that a place can actively influence and that represent the organising capacity of the place. Another four success factors assist the above to meet the challenges in the environment where place marketing practices are performed; these are Political Unity (agreement about public affairs), Global Marketplace, Local Development and Process Coincidences (the occurrences of notable events during the marketing process).

Anholt (2006) describes a framework for evaluating city brands called the city brand hexagon that is used to create the Anholt-GMI City Brands Index. The six components of the hexagon are Presence, Place, Potential, Pulse, People and Prerequisites. The *Presence* refers to the city's international status and standing – how familiar people are with the city. The *Place* component refers to the physical aspects of the city – how beautiful and pleasant or otherwise the city is. The *Potential* considers the opportunities the city has to offer in terms of economic or educational activities. The *Pulse* examines the existence of a vibrant urban lifestyle or lack thereof; how exciting people think the city is. The *People* component examines the local population in terms of openness and warmth and also looks at safety issues in the city. Finally, the *Prerequisites* deal with the basic qualities of the city; the standards and price of accommodation and public amenities. This framework has been developed as a means of evaluating the effectiveness of branding but it is a particularly helpful tool for guiding the branding effort, in that it distinguishes between the broad areas of local policy making that will ultimately influence the judgement of the city's brand.

A different view is offered by Hankinson (2004a) who distinguishes between four branding perspectives, namely: a) brands as perceptual entities, b) brands as communicators, c) brands as relationships and d) brands as value enhancers. He provides a model of place brands based on the conceptualisation of brands as relationships, in which the brand is construed as having a personality that enables it to form a relationship with the consumer. The starting point is the core brand (the place's identity and a blueprint for developing and communicating the place brand), which can be defined by the brand personality, the brand positioning and the brand reality. The effectiveness of place branding relies on the extension of the core brand through effective relationships with the various stakeholders. These relationships are grouped into four categories: a) Primary Service Relationships (services at the core of the brand experience, such as retailers, events and leisure or hotels); b) Brand Infrastructure Relationships (access to services, brandscape/built environment, various facilities); c) Media Relationships (organic and marketing communications); and d) Consumer Relationships (residents and employees, internal customers, managed relationships from the top). 'The extension of the brand from the core to include primary services, the brand infrastructure, media and communications and consumers is best described as a ripple effect in which brand relationships are gradually extended through a process of progressive interaction between the network of stakeholders'. (Hankinson, 2004a:115)

More recently, the same author (Hankinson, 2007) suggested another framework that underlines the leading role played by the Destination Marketing Organisation (DMO). The development and management of the destination brand is described as a process dependent on the effectiveness of brand leadership by the DMO. The process begins with the DMO deciding on a vision for the brand and a strategy for brand-building. First the brand needs to be built internally from the top by embedding its values to the internal culture of the organisation (Internal Brand Identity). The brand 'rolls out' to partner organisations, attempting to build strong alliances and partnerships based on compatibility (External Brand Identity). Afterwards, the brand is communicated and the brand experience delivered (Consistent Brand Communications), with the DMO ensuring effective communication with all stakeholders (Multiple Stakeholders).

Trueman and Cornelius (2006) undertook a thorough review of relevant literature and identified several, if not too many, approaches to the topic of place branding providing a useful analysis of the differences in their focus and, therefore, in the results and suggestions. Integrating the results of this literature review with the example of the city of Bradford, the authors suggest a 'place branding toolkit' which includes five fields of measures that can be taken, termed the '5 Ps' of place branding: *Presence* (on the one hand the appearance of architecture, icons and the built environment, on the other hand the emotional landscape connected to the local social fabric); *Purpose* (in the levels of various boundaries that exist in the city, for instance neighbourhood vs. city or other social boundaries); *Pace* (the speed at which the place responds to internal and external market conditions); *Personality* (which is made up by presence, purpose and pace as well as the visual impact of the built environment); *Power* (or empowerment of change, without which local communities are unlikely to support regeneration or adopt ownership of city brands). The authors include for each 'P' relevant tools that a city can use to successfully cope with the demands of managing each of those areas of intervention and demonstrate this with an application of their toolkit to the city of Bradford. The relevant tools that they suggest are:

- Presence: iconic symbols (that offer a clear differentiated visual image), ordered and multi-layered identity (that caters for the different needs and aspirations of the main stakeholders) and visibility (the visual presence in the street environment).
- Purpose: distinct boundaries (that facilitate the link between the brand and specific locations), brand ownership (a measure of civic pride), multi-cultural society (that facilitates regeneration and new ideas) and clear communication channels (that reinforce messages and cohesion).
- Pace: public-private partnerships (that balance the perspective and mitigate tensions).
- Personality: the emotional landscape (that provides a reality check and clarifies evaluations of the city's aspects).
- Power: social purpose and empowerment (that reinforces brand presence and trust).

TOWARDS PLACE BRAND MANAGEMENT?

The common ground of the frameworks described above as well as the lessons that they adopt from corporate-level marketing concepts have been examined in detail elsewhere (see Ashworth and Kavaratzis, 2009; Kavaratzis, 2009). Suffice it to note here that the frameworks seem to have in common several elements that may lead to integration. It is also worth noting that these common elements in one way or another relate to notions developed within the corporate branding literature. The important common elements of the frameworks, which could also be thought of as proposed elements of a comprehensive place branding framework, can be summarised as follows. First, there is a need for a widely accepted vision for the city's future that will guide all efforts and for a clear strategy to realise that vision (*vision and strategy*). Secondly, there is a need to receive feedback, agreement and support of employees and to spread brand orientation through the city's management and marketing itself (*internal culture*). Activation of local communities must follow, as there is a need to prioritise the needs of local communities (residents, entrepreneurs, local interest groups) and involve them in the strategy and brand delivery. Then, the common ground between relevant stakeholders within the city (local chamber of commerce, trade associations, locally based corporations) and outside (regional/national governments and associations, neighbouring cities, international level) needs to be explored through the seeking of synergies. The next need to be addressed is that for basic infrastructure, necessary for the function of the city as a place to live, work, visit and invest in, highlighting the communicative value of such infrastructure. Aligning the brand promise with the natural and built environment of the place is another precondition and interventions are necessary of both functional and symbolic character, particularly (but not only) in central parts and main entrances and corridors (*cityscape and gateways*). Fundamentally important for the creation, development and protection of the place brand is also the need to provide opportunities to targeted individuals (in the fields of employment, education, services, leisure, lifestyle etc.) and companies (financial or tax incentives, favourable labour conditions etc.) consistent with the city's brand. Finally, creative and effective brand communications are necessary to address the need for consistent communication and promotion of existing and new elements of the city and its brand building. All these elements are better thought of as 'substantial, strategically informed, symbolic actions' (Anholt, 2008a:5) and they are at the same time components of the place story and the means of telling it (Anholt, 2008a).

The issues mentioned above as lessons from corporate branding inform the theoretical development of place branding in a manner more comprehensive and solid than in the past. Most of these issues are examined in more or less detail in several of the chapters that follow. It is useful to remember that most of them are not new ideas within the armoury of place managers and not even new suggestions in the relevant literature. The need for a vision for the place and its future, for instance, has been identified as a distinct need in the earliest literature of place marketing (e.g. Ashworth and Voogd, 1990a; Kotler et al., 1993). Equally old in the place marketing discussion has been the need to involve the multiple and radically different stakeholders in the whole place marketing endeavour. The usefulness of the 'place as corporate brand' metaphor lies in the fact that these known ideas can be better understood in a strategic context through the notion of corporate branding and can be better integrated with place-specific notions in the same context. Corporate level marketing, being a notion much closer to the origins of marketing and, at the same time, exhibiting significant similarities to place branding, does provide useful advice and ideas that can be implemented within places. The tools of corporate branding demand a large amount of adjustment before they can be used in place branding and places cannot be thought of as one complex type of corporations. In other words, place branding is neither the same as corporate branding nor a particular type of it. However, corporate branding can be thought of as the basis on which to develop a place-specific form of branding and can provide a preliminary framework of place brand management.

It is suggested here that place brand management could be based on a synthesis of the place branding frameworks reviewed above, building on their similarities and integrating their complementary suggestions. It is blatantly obvious that any attempt to offer a place brand management framework should be tested in practice to ensure applicability. It is also fair to state that the place branding discipline might just not be ready yet to make theoretical suggestions that would have chances of being universally accepted (therefore the need for this book and, hopefully, other books that will follow). It is with these in mind that this chapter attempted this integration of frameworks and an initial suggestion of place brand management elements. Several of the elements suggested here along with their implications, will be discussed further (and more fully) in the chapters that follow and their relevance and contribution will be evaluated in the concluding section of the book.

4. Place marketing, local identity and branding cultural images in Southern Europe: Nea Ionia, Greece and Pafos, Cyprus

Alex Deffner and Theodore Metaxas

INTRODUCTION: IDENTIFYING THE CITY/PLACE MARKETING PROCESS

The role of city marketing has become increasingly important in Europe, mainly aiming at three general target markets: residents, tourists, and businesses/investors. Today it has become a necessity for a plurality of goals, uses and/or instruments, including global competition of cities, tourist attraction, urban management, city branding and urban governance. Since the 1990s many cities, especially in Europe, have used promotion policies to support their images and competitive position (Ashworth and Voogd, 1990a; Kearns and Philo, 1993; Kotler et al., 1993; 1999; Braun, 1994; Gold and Ward, 1994; Duffy, 1995; Ward, 1998; Avraham, 2000; 2004; Urban, 2002), a process that is especially noticeable in the contexts of globalisation (Short and Kim, 1999) and entrepreneurialism (Hall and Hubbard, 1998).

It can be argued that there are three main 'national' schools of place marketing: a) the UK/US which is the most widely used (Morrison, 1989; 2001; Kearns and Philo, 1993; Kotler et al., 1993; 1999; Gold and Ward, 1994; Ward, 1998; Murray, 2001; Anholt, 2007); b) the German, which is mainly practice oriented (Konken, 2004; Zerres and Zerres, 2000); and c) the Dutch, which is the most theoretically enriched (Ashworth and Voogd, 1990a; 1994).

In marketing terms the product (Goodwin, 1993), or 'good' (Metaxas, 2003), in place marketing is a place, often a tourist destination (Buhalis, 2000), tourism product (Meler and Ruzic, 1999; Morrison, 1989; 2001: 288), or destination product (Oppermann, 1996; Murphy et al., 2000).

Ashworth and Voogd (1994) define city/place marketing as:

. . . a process whereby local activities are related as closely as possible to the demands of targeted customers. The intention is to maximise the efficient social and economic functioning of the area concerned, in accordance with whatever wider goals have been established. This definition significantly shifts the secondary definitions of product, customers and goals compared to conventional marketing.

City marketing can be considered, despite many views to the contrary, as an element in urban planning (Barke, 1999; Deffner and Metaxas, 2006b) and, especially, regeneration (Paddison, 1993; Smyth, 1994) and governance (Harvey, 1989). Moreover, the need of place marketing to be informed as a strategic process has been pinpointed by many scholars (Ashworth and Voogd, 1990a; 1994; Kotler et al., 1993; 1999; Nykiel and Jascolt, 1998/2008; Berg and Braun, 1999; Warnaby et al., 2005). Particular attention has been given in general, and specifically in this chapter, to culture and tourism.

THEORETICAL FRAMEWORK

Place Marketing in the Field of Culture and Tourism

The performance of cultural policies as tools for urban economic development has expanded in several sectors, such as tourism, sports, recreation, the arts and the media (Bianchini, 1993:29), leading, at the same time, to powerful cultural/creative industries, including a variety of activities, such as fashion and design, architecture and townscape, heritage, local history, eating and entertainment, and generally a city's identity and external image (Pratt, 1997; Deffner, 2000; Kong, 2000). The expansion of this approach at a higher spatial level and/or on a larger economic scale leads to the assumption of the existence of a creative city (Landry, 2000; 2006). However, these considerations are not necessarily linked to the reformulations of social class, nor particularly to the adoption of Florida's fashionable, albeit US-based, approach regarding the existence of a 'creative class' (Florida, 2002).

The international experience indicates a focus on tourism and culture and shows an extensive variety of initiatives that concern urban and economic regeneration, by using particular strategies and tactics e.g. the cases of Sheffield (Bramwell, 1998), Apulia in Italy (Novelli, 2003), Pamplona and Holstebro in Spain (Kotler et al., 1999), Alonnisos and the National Marine Park of Northern Sporades in Greece (Loukissas et al., 2002). All these cases use some specific actions as tools in order to achieve their main goals. These actions are: a) identification of the environmental strengths and weaknesses of the places; b) identification and evaluation of particularities and distinctive characteristics of the places; c) use and implementation of market research analysis; d) development of promotional policies; and, e) development of a partnership between the actors in the places.

The significance of culture is also observed, not only as the object but also in the approach of place marketing, where place marketing contributes to a sense of place and should be linked more to place development (Murray, 2001). In this process, a crucial role should be played by history especially as transformed into heritage (Ashworth and Tunbridge, 1990; Ashworth and Larkham, 1994; Graham et al., 2000; Alsayyad, 2001), which, like many things, can also be marketed (Deffner and Metaxas, 2006b; Misiura, 2006).

Unlike culture and tourism, the relationship of sports (the third main component of leisure) to city marketing is not so clearly delineated, and the notable exceptions (Berg et al., 2002) verify the rule. The contribution of tourism and culture must be related to the proposal and the implementation of urban policy actions, a focus on the satisfaction of the needs and demands of potential target markets, the contribution of citizens towards achieving a better quality of life, the construction of a place's competitive advantage, and the promotion of a cultural identity and the branding image of the place, based on its distinctiveness.

The Relationship Between Place Image and Place Identity

The creation of an attractive and competitive place image has been singled out as a major necessity, especially since the nineties. International literature highlights several cases of place images and the efforts to reconstruct, or to create from scratch, such an image (e.g. Rotterdam – McCarthy, 1998; Prague – Hammersley and Westlake, 1996; Berlin – Cochrane and Jonas, 1999) or as tourist destinations (Croatia – Meler and Ruzic, 1999; India – Chaudhary, 2000; Hong Kong – Choi et al., 1999).

Referring to Europe, Simpson and Chapman (1999) assert that cities (especially the historic ones), are recognised as valuable resources within the increasingly competitive and integrated European economy. Harris (1997) argues that cities are the biggest dynamic centres of economic change in international-global economies. The creation of a positive city image constitutes an extremely important element in economic regeneration (Hall, 1998; 2001:115). In this approach, cities are seeking the creation of the most competitive and attractive image in order to increase their market share in a globalised economy. Cities like Rotterdam (as a business centre, Jansen-Verbeke and Recom, 1996) and Singapore (as an information city or 'intelligent island', Mahizhnan, 1999) and Bradford (as an industrial area, Hope and Klemm, 2001) seek to develop cultural and tourist policies in order to attract potential target markets and to strengthen their economic development.

Following the definition of Kotler et al. (1999:160), the image is a sum of beliefs, ideas and impressions that people have of a place. The images represent a simplification of a large number of assumptions and pieces of information connected with the place. Selby and Morgan (1996) argue that images are constructed by the amount, source and objectivity of the available information regarding a city/place, especially in the case of tourist destinations.

On the other hand, a city's identity relates to its historical background and to the particularities that traditionally characterised that city. According to Barke and Harrop (1994), the 'identity' of a place may be regarded as an objective thing. It is what the place actually likes. Pritchard and Morgan (2001), examining the relationship between culture, place identity and tourism representation, state that 'the representations used in destination marketing are not value-free expressions of a place's identity – instead they are the culmination of historical, social, economic and political processes'. Twigger-Ross and Uzzell (1996), in trying to explain the role of place and identity processes by using Breakwell's model (1992; 1993), support the view that cities/places, like individuals, have specific character and distinctions.

The relationship between place image and place identity could be summarised as follows: the place identity concerns those distinctive characteristics that historically more or less provide the place with a character. The most important thing is whether this character is a strong or a weak one. The creation of the place image is a supportive tool in order to secure two things: a) the strong identity of the city and its ability to stay strong and distinctive in a continuing process (Twigger-Ross and Uzzell, 1996); and, b) the ability for a weak identity to become strong and competitive through the creation of effective images for cities. This process characterises strategic planning, and Kotler et al. (1999:160) refer to it as 'Strategic Image Management' (SIM). Shaping the vision constitutes the first step in the strategic planning implementation that a place has to follow in order to construct its identity and to produce its image as a 'final provided good'.

The Vision and the Distinctiveness of a City/Place

The most important issue is that the vision of each place, as well as the development objectives and strategies, depend on its local distinctive characteristics and particularities. In addition to the core elements of a place, its positive characteristics need to be promoted simultaneously, since consumers make decisions based not only on functional quality but also on the representational and emotional quality of a place (Nuttavuthisit, 2007).

The 'final provided good' is the image of the place/city that is applied to the selected target markets. The production of this 'good' is not something random: it is a continuous process with particular development stages. The image of the place is related to its distinctive characteristics. Each one of these characteristics constitutes a 'distinctive good'. The image of a place is more or less a puzzle of 'distinctive characteristics', each of which needs a different strategic approach (Metaxas, 2003), and the production of place image as a 'good' is an integral part of place marketing.

In recent years, what has actually been observed is a focus on place branding (Kavaratzis, 2004; 2005; Kavaratzis and Ashworth, 2005; Anholt, 2006). Branding is a wide process that does not substitute for the marketing process but provides a distinct focus on the communicative aspect of all marketing measures (Kavaratzis, 2004). Branding, as part of marketing, relates more directly to local identity and local distinctive characteristics, including heritage.

Constructing Branding Images

The American Marketing Association defines a brand as a 'name, term, sign, symbol, or a combination of them, intended to identify the goods and services of one seller or group of sellers and to differentiate them from those of competition' (Kotler and Gertner, 2002). According to Morgan and Pritchard (2002:60), branding is perhaps the most powerful marketing tool available to policy-makers and marketers, while the demand for the most effective place brand-building strategies has never been greater, and for many places with only limited resources, difficult choices must be made as to which brand strategies to implement (Rein and Shields, 2007).

Constructing a brand constitutes an extremely crucial process. According to Morgan and Pritchard (2002:69), the construction of a brand is based on the planning and the performance of five important phases: a) the market investigation (competitors and consumers trends); b) the development of the brand identity; c) the communication of the vision; d) the brand implementation; and, e) the feedback process. In particular, these phases are parts of the place marketing process as a whole.

A higher spatial scale of branding is nation branding, which is quite an organised field and is also linked with public diplomacy (Anholt, 2007). City branding is defined as the planned image or brand of a city and it constitutes a challenge for urban planners (as well as architects) in the effort of cities to distinguish themselves whilst responding to the increasing pressure of competition in the context of a globalised culture (Hauben et al., 2002). Apart from economic functionality, the cultural and sociological aspects of branding are also important, since it is by means of the double 'effect of differentiation *and* collectivity, competition *and* certainty, that brands are able to be successful in an economic sense' (Mommaas, 2002:34).

The focus on culture and tourism that was observed in place marketing is also observed in place branding, either referring to the entertainment economy (Evans, 2003; Hannigan, 2003) or events (Kolb, 2006). The communication of a branding image to a potential target market has long been regarded as an important marketing activity (Gardner and Levy, 1955; Moran, 1973; Park et al., 1986). A destination brand can be developed in a variety of ways, mainly in advertising, through direct marketing, personal selling, brochures and websites, as well as through the cooperation of destination marketing organisations (DMOs), via journalists or event organisers (Morgan and Pritchard, 2002:59). In the 1980s, there were several highly successful marketing campaigns that focused on a consistent communication proposition. New York's 'I love NY' and the 'Glasgow's miles better' campaigns are two of the best known (Morgan and Pritchard, 2002:64).

As far as tourism is concerned, many destinations, irrespective of their spatial scale (countries, regions, cities) or size, are adopting branding strategies similar to those of commercial companies with brand names, in an effort to differentiate themselves and to connect, not just emotionally, with potential tourists (Morgan et al., 2002/2004). The actions relating to place marketing, hallmark events and branding focus on the concept of creativity. Creativity is a dynamic tool for urban innovation and imaginative action, focusing on culture, and contributing to success in various contexts. Some of the foundations of creativity are: the existence of an organisational culture (e.g. organisational capacity), fostering a strong local identity, initiatives in urban spaces and facilities, and networking dynamics and associative structures. Branding indicates the need for individuality and emotional connection with the environment in the context of globalisation. Cities should have depth, originality, and a distinct character though the materialisation of choice, diversity, and distinguishing features (Landry, 2000). Thus, branding contributes to the construction of local identity.

THE CULTMARK PROJECT

CultMark (*Cult*ural Heritage, Local Identity and Place *Mark*eting for Sustainable Development) is an INTERREG IIIC project. CultMark applies a place marketing strategy with a cultural approach. This means that it emphasises the cultural dimension of marketing, as well as the promotion of the cultural resources of each place, both of these in connection with the planning of demonstration actions. The innovative characteristics of this project are reinforced by the use of the two concepts of 'creativity', and 'destination branding'.

The main aim of CultMark is to create a final successful image for each city/region partner, as well as the study area as whole. The main objective is the development and implementation of innovative place marketing strategies, based on the elements of local identity and the cultural assets of the partner areas, in order to contribute to their sustainable economic and social development. Its secondary objectives include: the promotion of heritage as a significant factor in local and cultural development, the promotion and improvement of the investment climate of each area, the global promotion and support of the image of each area, the connection between place marketing and spatial development as an innovative approach to planning, the promotion and support of the representation of common developmental interests, the promotion and support of local knowledge and skills, the development of common and individual demonstration actions taking into account the particularities of each area, the support of the provision and diffusion of knowledge and know-how to actors and encouraging the development of entrepreneurial skills.

The implemented demonstration actions in each place include:

- Nea Ionia: Promotion of Silk Museum, Olympic City image and legacy, local cuisine/gastronomy (tsipouradika), Asia Minor traditions, painting, Rock and Blues festival;
- Kainuu: most northern castle in the world, local cuisine, crossroads of civilisations;
- Chester or Dee Estuary: leisure canals, Boat Museum (Ellesmere Port & Neston Borough Council);
- Rostock: industrial and maritime traditions, Hansesail 2005, Olympics bid 2012, wind turbines (kinetic art);
- Pafos: signing of St Paul's trails, info-kiosk at old harbour, promotion of Aphrodite Festival.

In this chapter, two cases of CultMark partners are presented: the case of the Nea Ionia municipality in the prefecture of Magnesia in Greece, and the region of Pafos in Cyprus. The analysis focuses on the presentation of the vision, the image that represents the 'final provided good', the proposed promotional strategies and tactics and the implemented promotional policies.

THE CASES: NEA IONIA, MAGNESIA, GREECE AND PAFOS, CYPRUS

Profiles

The Prefecture of Magnesia, having a central geographical position in Greece and being almost equidistant from the two major urban centres of Athens and Thessaloniki, constitutes a very important junction. The urban agglomeration includes the municipalities of Volos, Nea Ionia and other smaller areas, and it has a population of about 130 000. Volos and the wider area have been developed as manufacturing and industrial centres, especially in the last three decades. The economy of the city is based on the industrial and service sectors.

An important advantage in Nea Ionia's attempt to develop tourism is the construction (due to the 2004 Olympics) of a modern, organised and large (in both size and potential) sport centre around the Panthessalikon Stadium, and the consequent free international promotion of the city. This constitutes a comparative advantage against other cities that, like Nea Ionia, do not have a tourist destination profile to promote. The elements that could lead to tourist development should be focused on:

- The staging of special sports events after the Olympics (this actually happened in the cases of European Gymnastics and the Volleyball Championship);
- The promotion of the great arched Mycenaean tomb in the 'Kazanaki' area, that could become the 'heart' of a popular archaeological site;
- The promotion of the local cuisine.

Pafos is located in the west of Cyprus. The whole city of Pafos is included in the official UNESCO list of World Heritage Sites. For the last fifteen years, tourism has been a major source of income in Pafos. Tourism development has been increasing but remains quite controlled. The environmental protection measures, the special morphology and its many ancient sites, provide Pafos with the opportunity to become one of the most popular tourist destinations in Cyprus. The Pafos area has beautiful mountain villages, where life has remained unchanged over the years, and where the customs and traditions of Cyprus have been kept alive.

Pafos has recently experienced a rapid growth in commercial and business activity, with the development of a number of well-designed shopping centres in the tourist area, Kato Pafos (the lower part), and in the city centre. Pafos is well provided for in the fields of banking, financial and consulting services. All the important enterprises have a branch in the city and surrounding area of Pafos, which gives an indication of the importance of the area, especially after the recent boom in tourism.

Methodology and Primary Research

Following the strategic planning process, the whole project based its analysis on a variety of primary market surveys, personal interviews with local actors and decision-makers, in order to identify the potential target markets and to propose particular development strategies and tactics for each place. This chapter uses evidence from two surveys, as presented in Table 4.1, that relate to local actors and decision-makers in the two places.

Table 4.1   Primary data research

Steps	Method	Purpose	Sources
The identification of the vision	● *Questionnaire 3* Interviews and survey-questionnaire analysis (open-ended questions and Likert scale 1–5) to 'key' local actors and decision makers in each place (sample: 30 individuals per place) [period: January to March 2005]	Identify the factors that constitute advantages in culture sector Identify the vision and the image of each place	Cultural Sector Report (June 2005)
The identification of the image as a final provided good	● *Questionnaire 2b* A survey-questionnaire analysis (open-ended questions and Likert scale 1–5), to 'key' local actors and decision makers in each place (sample: 30 individuals per place) [period: June to September 2004]	Identify and evaluate the degree of place capacity to satisfy the demands of the target markets	Final Provided Good Report (December 2004)

Source: Cultural Sector Report (June 2005) – Final Provided Good Report (December 2004).

Vision and Determinants that Satisfy the Vision of the Two Places

According to the evidence of the 'Cultural Sector Report' (CultMark, 2005), experts and decision-makers in Nea Ionia envisage a city that is economically robust, socially balanced and pays due respect to both the natural and the cultural environment. On these grounds, they consider that a well-planned development, which takes care of the environmental problems (including traffic) and provides the necessary cultural infrastructure (museums, theatres, galleries or other spaces to house culture), will support the further development of the city as a tourist destination and attraction. The local cultural characteristics of the people (mainly refugees from Asia Minor), the beauty of the natural environment of the wider area, and the available sports infrastructure (mainly developed for the 2004 Olympics), constitute some of the main assets of the place. The vast majority of the respondents argue that it is quite possible for such a vision to become a reality in the future.

The vision of Pafos is for a cultural and natural heritage area able to attract high quality tourism all year round, whilst at the same time improving the quality of life of the locals. It is argued that what is required is the development of an appropriate cultural infrastructure (e.g. new theatre, galleries, etc.), the maintenance and protection of archaeological areas, the improvement of the Archaeological and other Museums, and the organisation of events of worldwide significance (such as the status of European Capital of Culture). It is generally agreed that such a vision is not difficult to accomplish.

With regard to the factors that contribute to the accomplishment of the city vision, there are two that score highest: the participation in European development programmes in cooperation with other cities/places, and the acceptance of the vision by the local community (Table 4.2 and Figure 4.1). The diagnosis and evaluation of the distinctive characteristics of each development sector for Nea Ionia is a crucial factor that could contribute towards achieving the vision. Also the significance of partnership developments between local authorities, universities and citizens, within the framework of a cooperative marketing strategy, is also crucial in order for the vision of the city to be satisfied. Ultimately, the ability of local authorities to adopt and implement innovative activities carries quite a high degree of importance vis-à-vis the vision of the city. All other factors are seen as of medium importance, apart from the analysis of the internal and external environment, which is regarded as of low importance. Of course, all these factors can operate successfully when all the internal actors and forces of the city represent common interests and develop common activities, taking into consideration that the vision of the city concerns all groups equally.

Table 4.2   Factors that contribute to the accomplishment of the vision

Factors	NEA IONIA	PAFOS
The planning and the implementation of particular city development plan (CDPL)	2.8	4.6
The identification of particular main development goals (DEG)	2.5	4.8
The analysis of city internal and external environment (based on particular methods, such as SWOT analysis) (SWOT)	2.0	4.2
The diagnosis and the evaluation of city-distinctive characteristics in each development sector (DICHA)	3.0	4.2
The planning and the development of partnerships between the local authorities and the business community (PARTNER1)	2.5	5.0
The planning and the development of partnerships between the local authorities and the academic or research centres (PARTNER2)	3.0	3.8
The planning and the development of partnerships between the local authorities and the citizens (PARTNER3)	3.3	4.0
The participation to specific European development programmes in cooperation to other cities (PROG)	3.8	4.0
The development of a systematic collection of data and information supporting the decision-making process (DATA)	2.8	4.4
The adaptation and the implementation of new innovative promotional policies by local public authorities (PROM)	3.2	4.6
The representation of common interests for city development by the local authorities, the enterprises and the community (RCIN)	3.0	4.6
The level of capacity and the level of knowledge of the local public authorities to plan and to implement development policies (LACAP)	3.0	4.6
The understanding of the community that the vision of the city is a common interest (VISION)	3.5	5.0
average	*3.0*	*4.4*

Note: 1: min, 5: max.

Source: Cultural Sector Report – *CultMark* project (December 2005).

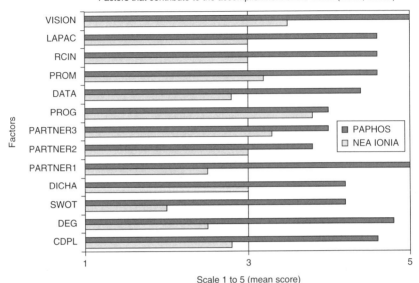

Source: Author's own.

Figure 4.1   Factors that contribute to the accomplishment of the vision

In Pafos, as far as the factors that contribute to the accomplishment of its vision are concerned, respondents unanimously place the development of partnerships between local authorities and the business community at the top of the scale, as well as the acceptance of the vision by the local community. Other factors that score very highly (but not unanimously) are the existence of development goals, the participation of the community in the development of the vision, and the level of capacity and knowledge of local authorities to plan and implement development policies. All the other factors are deemed to contribute to the accomplishment of the vision to a high degree. These include the existence/provision of a development plan, the analysis of the internal and external environment (e.g. SWOT analysis), the identification of distinctive characteristics, the development of partnerships between local authorities, research centres and the citizens, the participation in European development programmes in cooperation with other places, and the systematic collection of data and information required for comprehensive decision-making. Consequently, the average is very high (Table 4.2). This fact leads to the conclusion that in Pafos, a well-organised effort to develop cooperative actions in order to satisfy its vision has already been implemented by the relevant actors and decision-makers.

The two places share the same wider objective, looking forward to economic prosperity, social cohesion and a high quality of life for their citizens. The development of the cultural sector can substantially contribute towards this end. It can improve the quality of life and enhance the overall attractiveness of the place, thus advancing tourism. As expected, however, this general objective is tailored differently by each place in the attempt to form a vision that better suits its specificities, conditions, needs and history. Nea Ionia and Pafos have a clear orientation towards leisure and tourism and, from a rather narrow perspective, seek to develop the cultural sector (mainly infrastructure) and use it as a vehicle for the enhancement of their position as tourist destinations.

Constructing Branded Cultural Images of the Two Places as 'Final Provided Goods'

The image of Nea Ionia comprises two elements, the traditional and the modern. On the one hand, it is a city that seeks to keep its links with its distinctive traditions and cultural heritage (the first inhabitants were refugees from Asia Minor in 1922), and on the other, it strives to become modern and economically robust, confronting the same problems of urbanisation that most Greek cities face (i.e. congestion, pollution, etc.). The image of Nea Ionia is a multiple-tourism good, based on heritage, sports and food, a combination of distinctive features that characterise the city. This combination is a very difficult one, since it requires particular promotional actions and consequently particular sub-promotional maps. Of course, the combination of the 'final provided good' offers the opportunity for the selected target markets to receive multi-dimensional final goods, combining several activities. In this case, the creation of specific promotional packages that include all the aforementioned factors will be one very positive action. Of course, this is something that depends on the identification of the particular target markets that the city of Nea Ionia wishes to attract. Local experts agree that the factors that are related strongly to the effective promotion of a city's image are: the high quality of the natural environment, local community hospitality and the provision of open and green spaces.

Pafos is a well-known resort and tourist destination with a rich historical heritage and high environmental quality. The particular elements of this image highlight the city as: a well-known tourist resort, a city rich in historical and archaeological sites, a city with beautiful scenery and high standards of hospitality and a city with a low incidence of crime and with a high quality environment. For Pafos, the creation of the 'final provided good' is based on the analysis and evaluation of the culture and tourism sectors. The main development axis is the application of the 'special events' area and the creation of special goods and services deriving from a mix of culture and tourism. Pafos needs to penetrate into international event tourism: with the main axis of development and competitiveness being the Aphrodite festival, it is seeking to improve its 'event image' and to become attractive compared to other places.

Promotional Policies Related to the Place Branding Image

As regards promotional policies, local experts in Nea Ionia agree that none is implemented to a high degree. Of the six with medium implementation, the one that scores highest is the creation of a website for a specific event that takes place in the city (although there is quite a divergence of opinion among the respondents on this issue) (Table 4.3 and Figure 4.2). The other five are the creation of a website for the city, the creation of city image guides, the creation of particular actions and promotional packages for specific target markets, the participation of the city in European culture-related networks, and the promotion of the city image through links with other cities and countries. The policies that are marginally implemented are the development of sponsorships, the existence of strategic marketing or public relation plans, and the active participation of the city actors in the development of a city image promotional process.

In the case of Pafos, promotional policies show an above-average degree of implementation. There are five that score highly: the creation of a city website and city image guides (both of which are unanimously at the top of the list), the development of promotional packages for specific target markets, the creation of strategic image-marketing plans, and the participation in European/international exhibitions, fairs, etc. (which shows a considerable divergence of agreement). All the rest are regarded as being of medium significance in their implementation, apart from the existence of information centres and the creation of promotional CD-ROMs, DVDs and videos, which, surprisingly for a tourist destination city, score low (in fact, having the lowest score).

The two places have certain similarities in terms of the wider image they are striving to develop. This is perhaps due to the fact that they have the same problems, needs and objectives. The basis of their image can be found in the local distinctive characteristics, whereas their development can be seen as an attempt to reconcile history, traditions, industrial past, etc. (the 'old') with modern requirements and way of life (the 'new'), in order to achieve sustainability. Although Nea Ionia realises the importance of a

Table 4.3   Degree of implementation of promotional policies in relation to the place branding image

Promotional Policies	NEA IONIA	PAFOS
Creation of a website with particular links to the cultural sector of the city, or other sectors (business environment, services etc.) (WEBSITE1)	2.8	4.0
Existence of a particular website of special events that your city is known of, with a variety of information for the visitors (WEBSITE2)	3.2	3.4
Creation of city image guides, focus on the culture, tourism and business environment of the city (GUIDE)	2.7	4.0
The existence of a newsletter which is published from a local authority organisation and it is distribute to the city community groups (citizens, enterprises, hotels, restaurants etc.) (NEWSLETTER)	2.3	3.4
The existence of information centres with specialised staff (INFOCEN)	2.0	2.4
The creation of CD-ROMs, DVDs and videos, which provides information to the potential target markets (CD-DVD)	2.2	2.4
The use of advertising campaigns in the city but also at a regional, national or European level (ADVCAM)	2.0	3.2
The use of advertising in magazines or newspapers in local level or national level (MAGAZ)	2.0	3.4
The participation of the city in European or international exhibitions, fairs, festivals, musicals or theatrical performances, etc. (INEVENT)	2.3	3.6
The creation of particular actions and promotional packages for specific target markets (visitors with special interests, disability groups, students, etc.) (PACKAGES)	2.5	3.8
The participation of the city to European networks that promote and support the image of the cities, with special reference to culture (NETWORKS)	2.5	3.2
The existence of particular package of sponsorships (SPONSOR)	1.8	3.0
The promotion of city image through links with tourist and culture organisations and agents in other cities and countries (PARTNER)	2.7	3.4
The creation of a strategic image management and marketing plan (SIM-MP)	1.8	3.8

Table 4.3   (continued)

Promotional Policies	NEA IONIA	PAFOS
The active participation of city actors and organisations (museums, theatres, tourist agents, etc.), to establish common strategies and tactics for the city image promotional process (ACTORS)	1.8	3.2
The development of cultural business activities, through the production and the promotion of products, which characterise the image and identity of the city (CIPROD)	2.2	3.2
The creation of a strategic public relation plan, aiming at the most effective distribution of the image of the city as 'good' (PRP)	1.8	3.2
The creation of a specialised working group which will evaluate, organise and implement all the aforementioned actions above (SPECIALISTS)	2.2	3.2
average	*2.3*	*3.3*

Note: 1: min, 5: max.

Source: Cultural Sector Report – **CultMark** project (December 2005).

well-developed and -promoted city image, it seems hesitant to take appropriate action. Meanwhile, Pafos tries to build on its well-known advantages (natural environment, history, tourism, etc.) in order to experience further growth and prosperity.

Proposed Marketing Strategies for the Two Places

The identification of the marketing strategies should satisfy the development objectives of each place. Kotler et al. (1993; 1999) point out two crucial questions concerning strategies: what advantages do we possess which suggest that we can succeed with the strategy and, do we have the resources required for successful implementation of the strategy? Porter (1980) proposes two basic strategies that could be implemented in the case of place marketing: differentiation and focus strategy. The first strategy is related to the awareness of the competitive advantages and the uniqueness of the place, while the second focuses on a specific target market, which the place should cover and satisfy particular needs. Deffner and Metaxas

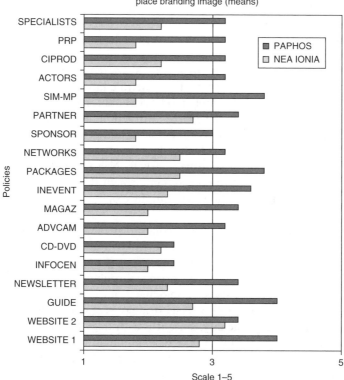

Degree of implementation of promotional policies in relation to the place branding image (means)

Source: Author's own.

Figure 4.2 *Degree of implementation of promotional policies in relation to the city/place branding image*

(2006a) propose the penetration and the cooperative marketing strategy. In the first one, the place image penetrates a new target market, promoting and supporting the local goods that already exist, while the second strategy requires the planning and implementation of promotional actions, through the representation of the common interests of the internal actors.

More specifically in the case of Nea Ionia, the study proposes the implementation of a focus strategy, by taking into account that Nea Ionia wants to promote three main types of tourism (cultural, sports and food), and so should choose the appropriate strategies for each type and each target market. Based on its distinctive characteristics and the advantage of having been an Olympic location, Nea Ionia is trying to acquire a strong position in the area of sports and cultural tourism. Taking into consideration that the vision of Nea Ionia is based on the identification of distinctive characteristics and the strong cultural identity, the focus strategy could satisfy the vision and the development objectives for the following reasons:

- The city tries to increase its market share regarding specific tourist markets at national level and to penetrate into the same markets at European and international level. So, the enforcement of its tourism economy is based on the effective attraction of these target markets and the total satisfaction of their needs and perceptions.
- The creation of a competitive advantage based on the analysis and the evaluation of these target markets. Nea Ionia should focus on its specifics in order to plan and implement the appropriate actions necessary to secure the successful development of its promotional policy.
- The vision of Nea Ionia is to become an attraction pole, promoting a multi-dimensional image to the potential target markets. The implementation of a focus strategy provides the opportunity for the city to acquire knowledge and experience through this process, which in turn allows it to satisfy its development objectives.
- The implementation of a focus strategy is closer to the vision and the objectives of the city, since it is a strategy that is proposed for small cities, with a low level of recognition, low ability to implement a variety of promotional policies and also an internal weakness in developing effective partnerships between the internal actors.

In the case of Pafos, the study proposes the implementation of a combined strategy. Concerning the cultural sector, Pafos has to follow a focus strategy based on the promotion of special events (as the main development axes) and also the penetration into specific target markets. More particularly:

- The worldwide cultural reputation will be stronger through the organisation of these events. At present, a considerable effort is taking place regarding the Aphrodite Festival. A tourist-marketing office exists, but it is essential that a place marketing perspective be applied to the planning and implementation of particular place-promotion strategies and tactics. The implementation of this strategy aims at those organisations that agree to participate in the special events that the city has the capacity to organise.
- The creation of a competitive advantage is also crucial. The implementation of this strategy requires the existence of qualified staff,

a good Public Relations Plan, and the development of alternative methods, such as brainstorming.

In the area of tourism, the region, in accordance with the general national tourism strategy, has to follow a penetration strategy, investing in a variety of special tourist products and aiming to become an attractive tourist destination for a large market. Based on the promotion of distinctive characteristics and the provision of high-level customer services, this strategy is related to the satisfaction of the vision and the development goals of Pafos, for the following reasons:

- the creation of branding based on the provision of services and tourist facilities. Pafos has the capacity to follow international tourism trends and to create new tourist products and services, combining the sectors of tourism and culture.
- this leads to the awareness of Pafos as a top tourist destination, at European and international levels with regard to developing mass tourism activities.

CONCLUSIONS

Place marketing is a strategic process contributing to urban/regional development and urban/regional competitiveness. To this end, place marketing can operate effectively, mainly through the promotion and support of the image of a place as a 'final provided good'. This image relates both to the vision and the locally distinctive branded characteristics of each place. This chapter used two examples from Mediterranean countries (Nea Ionia, Magnesia, Greece and Pafos, Cyprus) and the data of the INTERREG IIIC *CultMark* project, in order to reinforce the argument that place marketing should have a primary focus on tourism, while, at the same time, tourism (and/or destination) marketing should have a focus on place marketing.

Comparing the ability of the two places to accomplish their vision, it can be argued that Pafos seems to be effective in terms of planning, setting up principal objectives, performing situation audit analysis, organising efficient partnerships between local authorities and businesses, implementing practical methods of information and data collection, and, finally, managing to understand the main point that the vision of the place is a common interest concerning all the active groups of the community. It can be argued that up to now Pafos has followed the Strategic Planning process, while Nea Ionia remains behind in this area. Regarding the degree of implementation of promotional policies in relation to place branding image the view is almost the same. The implementation of strategic planning steps leads Pafos on the implementation of various promotional policies to a higher degree compared to Nea Ionia: the use of advertising campaigns, the development of specialised tourism packages for specific target markets, the existence of sponsorships, the development of a strategic image and marketing plan, but also the elaboration of an advertising plan.

Two main points have to be mentioned if an explanation is wanted referring to the comparison of the two places. First, Pafos is a well-known tourist destination, located in Cyprus, which is also a well-known tourist destination in a very competitive tourism and cultural area such as the Mediterranean. This fact leads to the necessity for Pafos to become competitive through the development of strategic actions and the use of branding. By contrast, Nea Ionia is a small area, with limited tourism. Furthermore, Nea Ionia lacks a strategic planning process, which is the basis of an effective place marketing plan. Secondly, Pafos follows a national tourism policy. Cyprus is a small island-state and like other small island-states focuses on the tourism/culture economy. This fact leads these island-states to the development of marketing strategies in which small islands must emphasise the significance of market research and segmentation for a better understanding of tourist trends and demands. On the other hand, Nea Ionia is also affected by the Greek national tourism/cultural policy but to a very small degree in comparison to Pafos. This situation affects also all the local groups, regarding their ability to plan, evaluate and perform effective marketing actions. Pafos is more efficient because local authorities and decision makers participate at a national strategic process, thus strengthening their local communities and their capacity.

In any case, the two places have certain similarities in terms of the cultural image they are striving to develop. The construction of their identity, and consequently their branding, is based on the shaping of their vision and the local distinctive characteristics and can be seen as an attempt to reconcile heritage, i.e. history, tradition, industrial past, etc. (the 'old') with modern requirements and way of life (the 'new'), in order to achieve sustainability.

ACKNOWLEDGEMENTS

We would like to express our thanks to the JTS INTERREG IIIC East and to the partners of Nea Ionia and Pafos for the use of the delivered material.

5. Branding Madrid: from 'Madrid Global' to 'global Madrid'

María Cristina Mateo and Gildo Seisdedos

INTRODUCTION

The attempt to position a city on an international level is a trend shared by the majority of cities, in particular those that aspire to enter the category of global cities. Madrid is the capital city of Spain. Its population is 3.2 million although the Madrid Metro Region has more than 6 million people. The per capita GDP is 53400 USD, 137 per cent of the EU average. Economic growth in recent years has been very strong – 4 per cent a year in the 2000–07 period. However, thanks largely to the planned renewal of the city, Madrid is quite efficient and sustainable and, in many ways, a model of urban excellence.

Madrid is the European Union's third city in population size, and has in the last eight years enjoyed the benefits of a dynamic economy, which paradoxically was accompanied by a much slower development of its image abroad. Rankings where Madrid scores highly, effectively illustrate this divergence, as it is evident in those rankings used by specialist groups like entrepreneurs (European Cities Monitor, 2007) or in those that analyse more objective aspects of cities, such as financial solvency (Standard and Poor's, 2006); quality of infrastructure, transport and communication (International Olympic Committee, 2008); the preparation of the workforce and the degree of economic diversification (DATAR, 2005) or the city's specialisation in advanced services for businesses. Madrid is, however, largely penalised in less specialised rankings that measure more subjective aspects for a less specialised audience. Madrid is downgraded in rankings such as those that measure what is understood as the strength of a city's brand, as it is perceived abroad (Anholt-GMI City Brands Index, see Anholt, 2006). In this regard, even if Madrid has a higher and a more solid competitive performance, it is surpassed by cities that possess a stronger brand. We shall attempt to describe further the reasons why this is happening.

Madrid had favourable objective conditions compared to other cities in a similar situation. In order to overcome this situation, the City Council set up an office, with the sole purpose of reinforcing and monitoring the city's international positioning: the Office for Strategic International Action, *Madrid Global*.

This office is responding to a new approach to city marketing: Madrid maintains its tourist promotion and attraction of inward investment, but in parallel to these actions, this office has begun to develop a new generation of policies directly focusing on the strengthening of the city's image through campaigns and activities directed at opinion leaders, urban diplomacy and policies searching for alliances with other international bodies and other cities.

This chapter reflects on the diagnosis, which motivated Madrid's decision to set up 'Madrid Global', and equip it with this latest generation of urban promotional tools. The chapter will also describe the process of the creation of the office and the vision it responds to, as well as the type of instruments used, and programmes executed.

A NEW GENERATION OF POLICIES FOR THE INTERNATIONAL POSITIONING OF CITIES

When cities become aware that they are complex organisations, operating in a competitive environment, and that the design of successful urban strategies is paramount, then the deployment of city marketing tools gains in importance and meaning (Ashworth and Voogd, 1990a). This process was favourably influenced by the onset of globalisation and its inherent forces, which modified the time and place barriers that confined our cities to the margin of inter-territorial competition (Borja and Castells, 1997).

The application of marketing to cities has been a rapidly growing phenomenon and, perhaps for this reason, its adoption has been incomplete and superficial to the degree that city marketing was equated with urban promotion (Kavaratzis, 2004), again committing the same corporate error of confusing marketing and sales (Ward, 1998). Nevertheless, at least conceptually speaking, the application of city marketing implies the selection of the right market segment. Following from this, stems a very different strategy aimed at a specific target group, on the basis of knowing their needs, the nature of their choices on the one hand, and the city's strengths, on the other.

Moreover, although attracting investors and tourists has been the object of strong competition between cities, the attraction of residents and creative citizens, the fight for the attraction of talent, has also been recently added (Florida, 2002). With this perspective in mind, city marketing has evolved into the design of an adequately priced urban product, and its effective and attractive communication to a specific group of residents, investors and tourists (McCarthy, 1960).

In this perspective the key is to identify the common ground available amongst all different groups in order to present them with a unique offer, in order to occupy a specific market point in the mind of the clients. A similar approach is currently developed by the departments in charge of the promotion of tourism, and attraction of investment, who identify the city's strengths for both tourists and investors, and at the same time, exercise a certain level of influence in the field of urban design. This has led to the planning and construction of specific urban features, such as the development of convention bureaus, iconic buildings, innovative business centres or centres for the development of cultural activities (Seisdedos and Vaggione, 2004). Moreover, other interesting and complementary approaches have arisen, which emphasise the communicative aspects brought about by the development of a brand concept and which centre around the building of a set of clear identifiable messages, with urban positioning as the sole objective (Kavaratzis, 2007) and *Madrid Global* is, as we shall describe further, a good example of these. Such approaches do not aim at mass targeting, nor do they use mass advertising campaigns. Instead, they 'sell' the city, by means of developing specific messages and niche actions. In this regard, their messages depend on the precision with which their target is chosen. For this, public relations and urban diplomacy are key activities in the task of choosing the right stakeholders and opinion leaders to whom to address their messages. Moreover, the choice of media and the degree of originality and exclusivity, tend to form a part of the actual message (McLuhan, 1987). This new model, compared to those based around mass marketing referred to above, can be described as in Table 5.1.

The policies and the instruments developed by *Madrid Global* to

Table 5.1   Blended marketing approach

Driver:	Mass	Pinpointed: Accuracy and Precision
Target selection:	Segment based	One to One
Type of Relationship:	Clients	Partners
Tools:	Advertising	Public Relations, Publicity, Urban Diplomacy
Organisations:	Tourism Bureau Investor Office	Madrid Global

Source: Authors' own model.

position the city internationally are clearly those of a new generation of city marketing tools, as we shall describe next.

WHY POSITION MADRID INTERNATIONALLY?

Madrid is Spain's capital but from an international viewpoint its positioning has been weak, partly affected negatively by this role. Indeed, its perception has been associated with the values of an administrative capital resulting in a distorted image, far removed from its competitive reality. This is, however, a problem shared by some other capital cities, as we shall describe next.

Peripheral cities even within the same country as that of the capital city, often occupy a superior position in spite of being called 'incipient global cities' by the Globalisation and World Cities Group (Beaverstock et al., 1999). This is perhaps due to the fact that historically their geographical position has contributed a greater visibility, and consequently they have been alerted at an earlier stage to the benefits of pursuing an international positioning strategy. In this regard, as Tables 5.2 and 5.3 show, whereas Madrid is considered a global city of an incipient character, according to GaWC World City, other cities classified as 'World cities' such as Sydney, Rome, or Barcelona, are better placed than Madrid in rankings which measure the level of perception and recognition, such as that of the Anholt-GMI City Brands Index.

As discussed earlier, Madrid is not alone in this respect, it shares the problem of not having the image it deserves with other cities such as Sao Paulo, Moscow, or Toronto, which despite having more potent local economies and more powerful political influence than Rio de Janeiro, Saint Petersburg or Montreal, are less well known and less relevant in terms of their city brands' potential and presence (Begg, 1999). In this regard, Dubai is much more positively perceived than Abu Dhabi despite, or maybe owing to, the fact that it is neither the capital of the Emirates, nor possesses large oil reserves and therefore has developed a series of re-branding initiatives (such as 'islands of the world' etc.), which seem to have influenced its international perception positively as regards the level of media interest that the city generates.

In the case of Madrid several factors could explain this gap between perception and economic performance. First, its performance has very recently changed. Madrid stopped being the economic centre of the country only in the late 1990s. From the eighteenth century, Spanish economic growth was mostly centred around Barcelona and Bilbao, leaving Madrid to play the role of a political and administrative centre. Secondly,

Table 5.2   The Anholt-GMI City Brands Index (2006)

1	Sydney	11	Amsterdam	21	Munich
2	London	**12**	**Madrid**	22	Tokyo
3	Paris	13	Montreal	23	Boston
4	Rome	14	Toronto	24	Las Vegas
5	New York	15	Los Angeles	25	Seattle
6	Washington DC	16	Vancouver	26	Stockholm
7	San Francisco	17	Berlin	27	Chicago
8	Melbourne	18	Brussels	28	Atlanta
9	**Barcelona**	19	Milan	29	Dublin
10	Geneva	20	Copenhagen	30	Edinburgh

Source: Taylor (2005).

Table 5.3   Taxonomy of leading cities in globalisation (GaWC)

GLOBAL CITIES
Well-rounded global cities
i.   Very large contribution: London and New York. Smaller contribution and with cultural bias: Los Angeles, Paris, and San Francisco
ii. Incipient global cities: Amsterdam, Boston, Chicago, Madrid, Milan, Moscow, Toronto

Global niche cities – specialised global contributions
i.   Economic: Hong Kong, Singapore, and Tokyo
ii. Political and social: Brussels, Geneva, and Washington

WORLD CITIES
Subnet articulator cities
i.   Cultural: Berlin, Copenhagen, Melbourne, Munich, Oslo, Rome, Stockholm Political: Bangkok, Beijing, Vienna
ii. Social: Manila, Nairobi, Ottawa

Worldwide leading cities
i.   Primarily economic global contributions: Frankfurt, Miami, Munich, Osaka, Singapore, Sydney, Zurich
ii. Primarily non-economic global contributions: Abidjan, Addis Ababa, Atlanta, Basle, Barcelona, Cairo, Denver, Harare, Lyon, Manila, Mexico City, Mumbai, New Delhi, Shanghai

Source: Taylor (2005).

Madrid is, since the 1978 constitution and the arrival of democracy, the capital of a radically changed, and new Spain. A political change guided by the country's entrance to the European Union in 1986 has, over the last two decades, also led the country to become an economic success. The country's strong growth, above the European average, provided for job creation, and the generation of a growth of businesses primarily located in Madrid. These companies looked to internationalise, and grew in a country whose infrastructure was mostly financed by European Community funds. Such infrastructure led to the urban regeneration of cities that were endowed with modern and efficient infrastructure. In fact, some of the best examples are found in Madrid, with its metro system, suburban trains, new airport terminal, and high-speed train network, all of which have reinforced Madrid's central geographical position as a strength, and competitive advantage.

Thirdly, the association of Madrid with the national brand Spain, was not perceived as modern and competitive until recently, which has also affected Madrid's image negatively. Madrid has often been associated with stereotypical aspects of Spain consisting of icons such as flamenco, bulls, siesta and football, compared with other Spanish cities such as Bilbao or Barcelona that are widely perceived as innovative and dynamic.

However, as stated above, Madrid is now the capital of a different Spain, and the association between Madrid and Spain can play a different, richer and more advantageous role, which Madrid needs to proactively embrace. It is an incipient global city, according to the classification of Globalization and World Cities work group centred in the geography department at Loughborough University (Beaverstock et al., 1999; Taylor, 2004), recovering its character as both economic and political capital, and Europe's third city in size of population. These facts have been key factors in the possibility of Madrid City Hall imagining an internationalisation strategy, focusing on closing the gap between perception and reality, a strategy built with non-conventional tools.

MADRID GLOBAL, BACKGROUND AND DEVELOPMENT

In order to understand *Madrid Global*, it is important to identify a series of factors, which in the context of the changes experienced by the city, as described above, contributed to its birth, namely a successful economic environment, both in Spain and in Madrid, which led to a series of long overdue urban developments on the one hand. These include the underground, a new airport terminal (Barajas Airport accommodates up to

70 million passengers a year and is third in operations and fourth in the number of passengers in Europe), a high speed train, and the renewal of Madrid's ring road, the M-30. Also immigrants have been attracted. Between 2000 and 2007, the proportion of immigrants in Madrid's population went from 2.99 per cent to 17 per cent. This contributed to making Madrid the second city in Europe after London, as far as the share of the population aged 15 and over with tertiary education. This has also contributed to having a well-qualified and relatively inexpensive labour force; a real competitive advantage for the city. Thus, Madrid has acted as a talent magnet: ninth in the European Ranking as regards a highly skilled workforce of graduates and post-graduates. Alongside such a process of development, the Madrid City Council initiated a series of measures aimed at renovating the city in order to prevent Madrid from becoming an unmanageable, unpleasant and problematic city during its growth. This effort was multidimensional and affected many of Madrid's urban infrastructures: airport, highways, roads, streets, pedestrian areas, mass transport systems, parks and housing. This set of policy measures intended to endow Madrid with conditions to make it fit for the twenty-first century: such as good internal and external connectivity, and environmentally conscious measures that improved people's lives. In recognition, at the 2007 World Leadership Forum in London, Madrid was awarded the Best European City Award together with a special award for the best urban regeneration programme.

Thus, in all performance indicators during the 2000–07 period, Madrid started to appear as a miracle of growth, and this awakened a lot of interest from within the rest of Spain and from abroad. Madrid started to be a noticeable entity: 'We identified that Madrid was of interest to others, and when foreign authorities came over and saw the state of renewal of the city, we could see that they hardly believed their eyes!' (interview with Ignacio Niño, CEO, *Madrid Global*). The scope of what was accomplished and the time-scale in which it was finished – all deadlines were met – provide evidence of an efficient use of resources committed to making Madrid a more liveable city – a city that offered a new model of renovation to the world, something that in theory was to put the city in a very new competitive position.

It is fair to say that the city had transformed itself from 2003 up to the early part of 2007 hand in hand with what would be considered an incipient city marketing perspective. Thus, during that period the local administration of Madrid dealt with aspects such as tourism promotion and investment attraction aimed at two very specific targets: tourists and investors, respectively. These tasks were implemented by two departments within the Madrid City Council: the Tourism Department, and the department in charge of the Economic Development of Madrid, which operated within a city marketing framework, and maintained a presence in trade shows and disseminated promotional material: brochures, web pages, etc. Their main objectives were to attract what they had identified was their target public. In other words, during that period, success for the City Council meant attracting tourists and investment to Madrid. This approach was successfully implemented owing largely to the development of an internationalisation plan carried out during the same period. This laid out the road ahead by stressing the weaknesses and strengths of Madrid compared to other globally recognised leading cities in the world, such as London, Paris or New York, which according to the Anholt-GMI City Brands Index 2006, are ranked second, third and fifth, respectively, as regards people's perception. Incidentally, Madrid is placed in the twelfth position in that ranking.

Furthermore, all that has been mentioned above took place in the midst of debates around the increasing importance of cities, as it became evident in the OECD International Conference, entitled: 'What Policies for Globalising Cities? Rethinking the Urban Policy Agenda', co-organised by Madrid City Council in March 2007 (where Madrid understood the importance of leading world debates about cities) and in the increasing number of conferences, and city summits on the topic. An example of this increasing protagonist role of the city is the invitation made by the organisation of the Shanghai World Expo 2010 to cities invited to be present at a World Expo for the first time. Indeed, cities rather than countries were becoming, and continue to be, agents of change and reference in issues as decisive as climate change:

> Cities and their leaders are now armed with the knowledge and the desire of their constituents to strive for cleaner sources of energy, more effective urban transport systems that reduce dependence on private cars and more energy efficient building (. . .) At the same time as higher energy prices are helping to increase the density of cities, innovative mayors with foresight are also pushing this agenda with uncommon vigour as we have seen through associations of mayors in the United States, the UK and many other countries. (Adams, 2008)

Within such a context, the Madrid City Council representatives saw the need to promote the city internationally by taking further advantage of the prospects of enhancing the reach of its own organisation through the help of public private partnerships, similarly to what other cities, such as London or New York, were already doing: 'In the States, city administrators were already working this way with a view to build cities successfully because they knew that they needed the support and involvement of the private sector' (Ignacio Niño, CEO, *Madrid Global*). Therefore, *Madrid Global* was set up as the Mayor's first government decision, after the local elections in May 2007, and modelled itself on 'NY City Global Partners'.

It is fair to say that *Madrid Global*'s birth in the summer of 2007 aimed at closing Madrid's gap between perception and reality. Indeed in a globalised twenty-first century any city aspiring to become a global metropolis had to have a global and international vision in its direction, management and strategy. To this end, *Madrid Global*, the Office of Strategy and International Action was set up as an independent office under the umbrella of the Mayor's Cabinet, inside the Area of Studies and External Relations, in the Area of *Vicealcaldía* (Vice-Mayor's office), within an approach which soon required the integration of a range of wider disciplines such as urban diplomacy, communication, strategic marketing and branding itself. These are the norm in the management of commercial brands like Nike or Coca-Cola, but were relatively new to a local administration environment in Spain.

However, all such offices have teething problems. This was the case during the first year of existence of *Madrid Global*. It followed a chronological evolution that did not always follow informed criteria. It started applying marketing initiatives, namely, those of promotion and city marketing, aimed at competitive niche development characterised by what has been described as, 'cluster building and more intense public-private partnership' (Kavaratzis, 2007). It moved gradually more into those of city branding, adopting progressively more advanced steps of a fairly strategic nature aided by an advanced model of urban diplomacy. At the request of representatives from Europe and the USA, who had purposely come to see the new infrastructures of Madrid, *Madrid Global*'s top officers gave presentations on models of governance to Spanish and several Latin American cities. It also used tools such as the setting up of trusts and chairs: *Fundaciones* and *Cátedras* respectively, which allowed it the degree of flexibility and dynamism that the task of branding the city required.

In conclusion, from initially not fully identifying its needs, after one year of existence, *Madrid Global* had started to grow into a good reference for many local administrations intending to brand their emerging cities. The next section describes in more detail how this was achieved.

MADRID GLOBAL'S VISION

The focus of this chapter is on *Madrid Global*, because it acts as a case study in as far as it exemplifies the challenges of treating city branding in a similar way to commercial branding, because both deal with people's mental constructions within a framework, but different to that deployed by private enterprises for branding their products. From the moment *Madrid Global* was set up within Madrid City Council, it followed a new approach to its work, within the broader framework of city branding, by attempting to manage an image of the city, which would act as the vision coordinating all efforts. '. . . the significance of the image of the city in the attempt to influence it could well be an effective way to coordinate marketing efforts; . . . the desired image of the city could provide the necessary target for marketing activities to aim at' (Kavaratzis, 2007).

Indeed, *Madrid Global* had the goal of positioning Madrid as a global city, third capital in size in the European Union, a cultural referent for the Latin American world, with deeply rooted links with the Mediterranean and the Middle East (Spain, until the fifteenth century, was dominated by the Arabs for eight centuries), and the city's current name is Arabic, a common background, positively viewed by both Spanish and Middle East representatives. In addition it was to be viewed as a model of urban management, due to the city's successful recent urban renewal, (all of which would make it of interest to emerging cities in Asia). In order to do that, it needed to be aware of its place in a globalised arena in which other cities, academic institutions, international organisations, private companies, the media, and opinion leaders, needed each other, and were inter-dependent and together could establish a network of partnerships.

The next sections of this chapter will therefore focus on the way *Madrid Global* started using a range of tools to do city branding, understood openly from a communicative perspective: 'as an attempt to influence the context in which messages are communicated' (Kavaratzis and Ashworth, 2007). These tools, briefly described, have a continuous focus on the establishment of partnerships in order to allow *Madrid Global* to handle the positioning of Madrid as a brand in three different ways:

1. Moving from mass marketing to targeting specific segments, and to developing a network that assumes that building allies and partners is crucial.
2. First establishing and then managing a new network of allies, and, simultaneously strengthening the existing network of public diplomacy partners, hence paving the way to a dynamic approach to understanding urban diplomacy.
3. Discerning through the above mentioned partnerships, strategic initiatives that will contribute towards Madrid's international positioning. Indeed, articulating Madrid's positioning in the world through the network of partners requires choosing the right allies, and the right initiatives, as the options are almost infinite.

General Coordination

D. G. of International Relations

D. G. of Strategy and International Development

D. G. of International Projection and Partnership

Source: Madrid Global

Figure 5.1 Madrid Global *organisational chart*

Moreover, for such an articulation to be effective, it needed to be mirrored by the office itself, and this is why *Madrid Global* is composed of three departments which reflect such vision, namely: *Dirección General de Estrategia Internacional* – Strategy and International Development Area, which monitors the positioning *Madrid Global* is working towards; *Dirección General de Relaciones Internacionales* – International Relations Area, which establishes alliances with cities, international institutions and diplomacy; and *Dirección General de Proyección Internacional y Partenariado* – International Projection and Partnership Area that establishes alliances with the public and private sector to gain their interest with a view to finance the different initiatives in progress, such as funds to support the Olympic bid or the participation of Madrid in the Shanghai World Expo. In addition, there is a general coordinator, *Madrid Global* CEO, who overviews the development of each area and identifies any overlapping and potential synergies between all of them.

At present, *Madrid Global* is at a stage where it has the required structure to accomplish its goal, so now is the time to start communicating internationally through the partnerships developed in order to achieve the above objective. Thus, at present *Madrid Global* is engaged in the development of the details of its future strategic plan that supposedly comprises the management of the city image through a list of initiatives and partnerships worth implementing. Indeed, this is the case, as *Madrid Global* is adamant that it is only through these associations that it can articulate the initiatives that will position Madrid successfully. Moreover, it will only be at the end of its operational time frame: four years (the length of an electoral period) when *Madrid Global*'s success can be measured. This will be done by way of examining the quality of the partnerships achieved, in addition to a constant monitoring of the attention received by the city through rankings, articles and reports.

BUILDING PARTNERSHIPS

It has been stated that in order to position a city internationally, it needs to be treated as a brand, since 'people understand cities in the same way as they understand brands' (Kavaratzis, 2007:703), and this assumption requires bringing together a set of disciplines, which through a succession of increasingly more and more sophisticated stages, has evolved into new ways of resolving matters, based on the notion of building varied partnerships, in order to stretch the local administration's limited reach. In fact a range of initiatives demonstrate how city branding is implemented by *Madrid Global*. Existing strategic projects such as the presence of Madrid in the Shanghai World Expo 2010 (where Madrid will build a real life example of a sustainable social housing block), and the creation of bodies like: 'Madrid Global City 2010 Fund', which will be described later, as well as initiatives such as the British Council Open Cities project, or 'Madrid Cluster in Public Infrastructures and utilities', clearly illustrate *Madrid Global*'s interpretation of city branding as one focused around the construction of an image for the city that needs to be communicated to the partners it is associated with. Moreover, the partnerships that initially were primarily protocol (institutional visits, twinning between cities etc.) became multifaceted and longer term, transforming into a rich set, consisting of private companies, opinion leaders from a range of fields, media partners and even other cities, thus establishing a network of mutual support and interest.

Thus, as described above, in order to establish a network of allies it is crucial to choose the right partners as these will largely determine the initiatives which will have an effect on Madrid's international positioning, as well as in the regions of influence. The following sections of the chapter therefore, specifically describe the partnerships chosen by *Madrid Global*, as well as the ways in which they were built and the reasons why they were chosen.

Strategic Projects

Participation in Shanghai World Expo in April 2008

In May 2008 Madrid was chosen as one of only 15 cities in the world (out of 188 proposals, only 15 projects were selected for the Simulated City Block), to have the opportunity to build a pavilion in the Shanghai World Expo 2010, whose claim is 'better city, better life'. This has translated into the acceptance of two of the projects proposed by Madrid: a distinctive pavilion (a real social housing building, 'House of Bamboo') that received the 2008 RIBA European award, and an eco-boulevard in the public space

('Bioclimatic Tree'). In order to fully develop the initiatives, Madrid will use the enhancing capabilities of a 'trust', the Madrid Global City 2010 Fund.

However, above all, participating in the Shanghai World Expo was also a key to building alliances. These were inside the City Council (Madrid-Global and the EMVS, *Empresa Municipal de la Vivienda y Suelo de Madrid*, responsible for the building of the House of Bamboo); those on behalf of different sectors of the City (Environment, Urbanism, Public infrastructures, and Culture) and with R&D leading institutions such as the Energy and Environmental Research Centre (CIEMAT), and the IE Business School. In addition there were private companies (through a sponsorship programme), together with international institutions and opinion leaders. Furthermore, its presence in Shanghai 2010 will contribute to gaining an optimum level of communication of Madrid's leadership in urban management and infrastructures aided by the network of allies developed with a set of similar interests, in a part of the world that will work as a global magnet, namely Shanghai.

2016 Olympic bid
The Madrid 2016 Olympic bid is based on several fundamental premises which aim to show the International Olympic Committee and the sporting world that Madrid deserves to organise the Olympic and Para-Olympic Summer Games of the XXXI Olympiad, because the city and its inhabitants are ready and want it. Madrid's motivation is intrinsically linked with these values, which are epitomised by the 'Madrid 16' logo and strap line: 'Feel the experience – it's in your hands'.

Thus, whereas Barcelona 92 represented a before and after in Spanish sports, the results and preparation of Spanish athletes have improved considerably since, and so has the infrastructures of the city bidding for the hosting of the games. That is why the Olympic and Para-Olympic Games in Madrid can be considered as a step forward. For Madrid the motivation to host the Games seems rooted firmly in the belief that the values of the Olympics can and should be the catalyst to promote social cohesion and

Source: The Madrid 16 Foundation

Figure 5.2   Madrid 2016 logo

proclaim the transformation of the city, and the country, Spain. In this respect, when Madrid was bidding for the 2012 Olympic Games against cities such as London, Paris or New York, the IOC's evaluation gave Madrid the top qualification in categories such as 'people's support, sports infrastructure, infrastructure and the environment'. In the current bid the IOC has granted Madrid an even higher score than earlier, reaching second place after Tokyo, ahead of Chicago and Rio.

For *Madrid Global* therefore, this bid (the sponsorship programme is carried out by *Madrid Global*'s 'International Projection and Partnership Department') is a unique opportunity to convey the city's message: the games can be held in Madrid because it is a city with high scores in distinct areas, such as 'popular support, sports infrastructure, infrastructure, and the environment (as in the IOC's review). Concurrently it is an exceptional opportunity to create a close relationship with a range of private partners with whom to build the city further, and in particular with the top sponsors of the bid, the so-called: 'Madrid 2016 Club', who are engaged with the City Hall through links which go beyond the bid itself. Indeed, even in the context of global events, the focus for *Madrid Global* is on the partnerships developed, as these are longer term than the events themselves.

Place–product co-branding initiatives
Undoubtedly the City Council cannot strengthen its international visibility on its own, hence the need for allies and partnerships well beyond the context of a particular occasion, such as that of the global events. Therefore a strong association with world-renowned commercial brands is also necessary because of their long-term nature. Indeed, there are cities that are already taking advantage of the benefits of their city being a co-branding element, in a relationship that is to the benefit of both the commercial brand and the city in question. This is the case, with for example L'Oréal – Paris, Rimmel – London, or Custo – Barcelona. While there are various degrees of visibility regarding this association, Madrid has hardly exploited any of them. This is largely due to the lack of brand values associated with the city.

However, there are increasing efforts to build on this association. To this aim, *Madrid Global* has started working very closely with a well-known forum of recognised Spanish brands: the FMRE (Leading Brands of Spain Forum) which comprises many widely recognised Madrid brands. These brands act as ambassadors in that they often carry the city's name and brand values associated with the city to the four corners of the earth, which could consequently help building the city's brand. Thus, brands like *Real Madrid* football team, or the *Instituto de Empresa*, a world-class business school based in Madrid, promote positive aspects of interest for the city, and that is why *Madrid Global* has signed agreements with both of them.

The centenarian *Real Madrid* football club, which uses in its own name the word 'Madrid', is for this reason and for its worldwide recognition, an invaluable ally. Similarly, the IE Business School, with which *Madrid Global* is also associated, conveys the idea of intelligence – in the sense of talent attraction – and innovation, which are key messages that the city of Madrid is trying to promote. However, there is still a large untapped potential in this relationship, especially regarding luxury brands that have the city name in them, such as *Loewe Madrid*, the luxury fashion and accessories house, born in the heart of Madrid in 1846, or *Carrera and Carrera Madrid* (jewellery). Although they are not mass-appeal brands, and instead convey messages of luxury, elegance and fun, these attributes are key for initiatives held in parts of the world where high visibility could be beneficial to both the commercial brand and the city brand, and should be therefore explored further by *Madrid Global*.

Madrid Cluster in public infrastructures and utilities
As stated above, during these years Madrid has captured the advantages of globalisation by becoming the third metropolitan area in Europe, attracting foreign investment and talent while experiencing a dynamic economic growth, making the best of the positive business cycle in Spain, especially in terms of job creation. Moreover, it is little known that Spanish companies, most of them based in Madrid, hold a 42 per cent world market share in infrastructure projects, followed by China's 13 per cent and France's 10 per cent, and that 5 of the top 10 private builders of public infrastructure are multinational companies based in Madrid. Also the world's largest solar power plant will be build in Arizona in 2011 by one of the top companies in this cluster using technology born in Madrid. However, not much is said about this, partly due to Madrid not having a positive place-of-origin image, until recently.

Because of all the above, and to promote what has been called Madrid's Cluster in public infrastructures and utilities, *Madrid Global*, and the IE Business School, seek the support of scientific and technological research centres, and private companies to create the first 'Madrid Global Chair in International Urban Strategies', in early 2008. The Chair aims at conveying to emerging cities the message of Madrid's urban leadership. Indeed, it was thought that promoting the Madrid Cluster in the midst of a process of fast urbanisation around the world would place the city in an advantageous position in urban management matters, as it would offer a relatively well-developed solution to recent urban problems.

Note: Open Cities is a British Council project in partnership with cities around the world.

Source: Open Cities.

Figure 5.3   Open Cities logo

Open cities
Open Cities is a British Council project led by Madrid and Belfast City Councils, with the participation of other European cities (Bilbao, Cardiff, Dublin, Vienna, Gdansk, Malmo, Sofia, and Dusseldorf) in order to see what cities can do at the local level to be more open and attractive to migrants and internationally mobile populations. The objective is to put forward a portfolio of best-practice case studies and a set of guidelines for city policies, aimed at developing an index of openness, which started with an initial definition of Openness that included 8 factors and 40 indicators. There was an International Conference held on this in Madrid in February 2008. There is a website which has information and updates and a logo that has been developed for cities qualified as 'open' to use.

Madrid Global recognised that Open Cities was a great opportunity to communicate that Madrid is a leading city, concerned about its openness and, most importantly, that it was a unique opportunity to partner with international organisations, such as the British Council and the EU (which provide funding for the project), as well as experts who help to manage it, and with whom *Madrid Global* is collaborating further, as well as with other cities in the network. Indeed, this was the main reason to purposely express an interest in participating in the initiative with the British Council.

First Meeting for the exchange of ideas between young urban Europe and Asian leaders
Asia is one of the regions where Spain and Madrid have had less visibility, and where fewer partnerships have been created until recently. *Madrid Global* has been working towards a key initiative for the establishment of Madrid as a partner of reference for Europe and Asia. This is the type of

geo-strategic role that Madrid strives to play. To this end, in November 2008 *Madrid Global* together with *Casa Asia* (Asian House) and the Asia Europe Foundation ran a week-long programme for the exchange of ideas between young urban leaders from the ASEM countries (the Asia-Europe Meeting). These people, aged 20–40 years, are required to have expertise in public administration, business, the arts, politics, the media or the academic world. The programme was developed around a series of modules related to urban strategies, to their implementation, and contribution towards urban development. Moreover, the running of this programme is hoped to help communicate the leadership of Madrid in urban management whilst strengthening the relationship with key international Asian organisations such as ASEF, *Casa Asia*, and the representatives of ASEM's countries.

Japan Plan

The Japan Plan is another example of attempting to gain strategic presence in Asia. It had two stages. The first from 2005 up to 2007 was about attracting tourists to Madrid as numbers had started to decrease due to the high level of theft. Thus, in comparison to the previous year, in the year 2006 there were 103 942 Japanese visitors to the city, which represented an increase of 40 per cent. The second stage, from 2008 to 2011, aims at raising the knowledge of Madrid in Japan. While the project started in the Economy Department of the City Hall, it became a task of *Madrid Global*, because its present dimension is closer to the establishment of partnerships (with the Japanese Embassy in Madrid, JETRO: Japan External Trade Organisation, and Japanese trade associations in Madrid), and towards the building of wider programmes of exchange in disciplines such as culture and the arts, in the hope that they can cause an impact in Asian cities of global reference, like Tokyo.

As described above, all the initiatives have attempted to show the way they have largely responded to the pursuit of partnerships, which are key for the implementation of *Madrid Global's* strategy, together with participating in large global events where partnerships also play an important role. Indeed, the engagement with academic and research centres such as the IE Business School, the CIEMAT, private companies of the sector, together with the identification of commercial partners such as *Real Madrid* have helped convey Madrid's international image overseas, as an open and efficient city, thanks largely to the image of the partners themselves.

However, it is perhaps evident that during this first year of existence, *Madrid Global* has not implemented a proactive partnership strategy. Instead, the engagement with partners and consequent joint activities has originated from an ad-hoc response to opportunities at hand, with the exception of Open Cities, mostly in pursuit of a common objective, the building and communicating internationally of Madrid's leadership in urban management, leaving perhaps other aspects of the communication (its arts heritage, for instance) behind.

Moreover, *Madrid Global*'s more proactive and directed alliances with Asian institutions in Madrid as well as those overseas are examples of partnerships of a more targeted nature, aimed at gaining an impact in a part of the world where Madrid has not naturally had much presence before. For this the message around its leadership in urban management was also critical.

It is therefore fair to say that from now onwards, *Madrid Global* will need to plan very carefully its future partnership strategy if it wants to further its goals. In this regard, it will be crucial to identify the prospective partner's long-term requirements, and operational synergies, in order to align common goals, and identify prospective and complementary roles.

CONCLUSIONS

This chapter has described the new approach followed by the city of Madrid towards the branding of the city as an attempt to close the gap between the theory and practice of city branding. To this aim, we have described the reasons that on the one hand have pushed Madrid's local administration to develop a new strategy, and on the other, the urban vision which informs the city's strategic international positioning, as well as the *raison d' être* and structure of *Madrid Global* – City Hall's office in charge of this task – together with a series of implemented initiatives.

Madrid Global started initiatives of city positioning when it became evident that after an early diagnosis, the city's high score in indicators of competitiveness were not equivalent to those related to its international perception. Thus, any city with a weak international image would be jeopardising its international positioning, and even its own competitiveness. This diagnosis led to the birth of *Madrid Global*, and the subsequent development of new city branding tools which in particular attempted to build a series of partnerships, focusing perhaps too intensely on building and communicating one particular aspect: Madrid's leadership in urban management, in parallel to those most specific to city marketing; namely, city and investment attraction, implemented by other areas of City Hall.

Indeed, whilst either approach is equally necessary, there are differences between them concerning their objectives and the type of initiatives. Thus, Madrid City Hall has continued to develop initiatives aimed at specific segments – tourists, investors and residents – using mass advertising, as if they were clients that one needs to convince. However, these type of initiatives, although effective when attempting to improve the number of tourists, or attracting investment, have a limited effect as regards building solely a city's image and monitoring its positioning.

Moreover, the interesting aspect as regards the case of Madrid City Council is that it has blended the above approaches with those of a different and a more innovative nature, closer to the type of initiatives within the remit of public relations, and urban diplomacy, that *Madrid Global* has applied. Therefore, the emphasis lay on establishing a partnership approach for which the identification of the right partners is crucial.

First of all, by stating its positioning objectives, through a geographical, cultural, economic and urban-developmental dimension, Madrid strove to be a global city, the third capital in the European Union, a cultural referent for the Latin American world with deeply rooted links with the Mediterranean and the Middle East and a model of urban management, all of which would make it of interest to emerging cities in Asia. In doing this, *Madrid Global* was perhaps limiting itself, as this meant concentrating on building and communicating its leadership in urban matters, but at the same time, was avoiding resorting to commonplace strategies. Thus, such dimensions acted as a unique plotting device, which helped it navigate through the myriad of potential initiatives. In the future, nevertheless, a proactive partnership strategy can lead to identifying further partners, such as the already mentioned *Loewe, Madrid*, which can endow the city with further communicative features, also of interest for its international positioning.

Secondly, as stated, the type of initiatives that both *Madrid Global* and other areas of the City Hall implemented, were entirely different. Whereas tourism and investment attraction departments resort to activities of mass appeal, whose indicators of success are the number of visitors expected and/or the level of investment attracted, *Madrid Global*'s initiatives did not target the public. Instead, they intended to communicate the desired positioning of the city in a selective process that established who to partner with in order to implement strategic projects. The key for *Madrid Global* was, therefore, the target partner rather than the initiative itself, as it was the former who largely defined the initiative. Needless to say, any city branding approach dealing with a city with a weak perception such as Madrid, suffers from shortcomings. First of all, in a task where partnerships are key, following a proactive longer-term strategy is paramount and this has not happened during this first year. Also, it is often difficult to combine the efforts of topics that were not necessarily set up under the same organisational structure.

Inherent in this, is the relative excess of focus on projecting the image of the city around one aspect, namely its leadership in urban management. The difficulty here lies perhaps not so much on *Madrid Global*'s side, which has identified the need for a more rounded approach, but on how to coordinate all the efforts made around such an image when there are so many different areas involved within the City Hall. The time and energy invested to establish such an alignment are therefore often larger than the expected results. This is something that Madrid City Hall has not fully solved yet, and it is an important challenge for the successful coordination of all the marketing efforts of the city, which should not solely fall under the auspices of one single area or department, especially when there are several areas involved from different perspectives in such efforts.

Another issue to consider is the level of expertise and motivation required to accomplish the task of branding a city. Thus, as described above, the range of disciplines tackled by city branding is wide, including the economy, marketing, sociology, architecture, etc., and the professionals needed for it have to be sufficiently motivated to work only for a specific city, rather than in often better paid projects of a more varied nature such as those of consultancy.

Finally, the way these projects are perceived by the citizens is also critical in itself. The general public often sees the city administration's efforts as banal, unnecessary and led by a political agenda. It is therefore paramount to ensure that a good communication plan is drawn up, one in which citizens' views are incorporated.

To conclude, it will be of interest to observe the progress of *Madrid Global*'s work and its pursuit of a successful city branding strategy through the monitoring of Madrid's position in city indices, media coverage, and above all scrutinising the nature and quality of its partnerships. Thus, if in a few years time Madrid's image helps to coordinate all the initiatives and efforts, and if its positioning is clearly perceived internationally as a global city and third capital in the European Union, and there are media stories and reports by international opinion leaders that confirm its position as a cultural referent for the Latin American world and a referent for emerging cities in urban management, the success will be fully evident.

6. Managing Otherness: the political economy of place images in the case of Tuscany

Nicola Bellini, Anna Loffredo and Cecilia Pasquinelli

INTRODUCTION

Discussions about image and branding policies are usually placed in the framework of 'place marketing' and marketing literature helps in defining the features, components and main characters of image and of its relationship with local identity. We suggest, however, that managing images is also a political process with significant impact in supporting and shaping the scenario (perceptions and expectations) for innovation and economic policies (Bellini, 2004). The argument is supported by two different and complementary case studies from Tuscany (Italy).

The first one discusses the case of areas that show a divergence from the dominating pattern of social and economic development in the region. It is shown that 'managing otherness' is more than a communication problem and may reveal underlying ambiguities: at the same time, a request for supporting structurally disadvantaged areas and the affirmation of an alternative identity and of alternative development patterns. The second case study shows a different kind of 'otherness', concerning new industries and emerging social groups. Discussion shows that the branding process may imply a competition between images in order to control the representation of the past, present and future of an area. This competition aims at influencing the policy agenda by manipulating the gaps between image and identity.

THE THEORY

The Lessons from Marketing

Place image (the image of a region, of a city etc.) has come to the attention of both scholars and practitioners mostly within the framework of place marketing in its three main variations defined by its target (inward investors, tourists, residents) as well as with reference to country-of-origin effects on product image (Kotler and Gertner, 2002; Rainisto, 2003; Jaffe and Nebenzahl, 2006; van Ham, 2008). It is certainly a concept with a longer history, but it is marketing that has framed it in a consistent way and, above all, has tried to operationalize it. Place branding has been defined as the practice of applying brand strategy and other marketing techniques and disciplines to the economic, social, political and cultural development of cities, regions and countries. Marketing has thus provided 'a philosophy of place management' (Ashworth and Voogd, 1994:39) and place branding has attempted to transfer into local economic development not only some communication techniques, but also the identity-building power, the linking value and the emphasis on experience that 'post-modern' scholars attach to brands (Kavaratzis and Ashworth, 2005; The Communication Group, 2006; Kavaratzis, 2007; Anholt, 2007). Without doubt, marketing has either strengthened or introduced some serious biases in the way we look at place images. The emphasis on distinctiveness and competitiveness has reflected an obsession with urban and regional 'entrepreneurialism' as well as with an easily misconceived 'customer orientation'. Furthermore marketing implies a competitive, quasi-mercantilist view of regional and local development that is increasingly unrealistic (or at least, partially misleading) in the network-like, 'coopetitive' scenario of today (cf. Kalandides, 2007a). Lastly, branding tends to be seen as a technocratic activity, representing the belief in the virtues of professionalism in public management, as opposed to old-fashioned politics.

On a more technical side, the dominance of marketing approaches aimed at attracting economic actors, such as tourists and inward investors, has led to emphasize strong, seductive images ('a special place to be'). The new priorities in the 'knowledge economy', and especially the emphasis on attractiveness with regard to residents belonging to certain social groups (such as the 'creative class'), imply to re-focus attention on the quality of everyday life and of the 'ordinary place'. Marketing lessons are nonetheless fundamental also from a policy perspective. As marketing teaches us, image is bound to have important effects which can be dangerous when they are not monitored or when they are not dealt with:

- image reflects and synthesizes the experiences and visions of individuals and groups, from which it derives. Two aspects co-exist: the *evaluative* component which reflects our experiences and what we perceive as real, and the *preferential* component which portrays the desires and motivations, in short, what we wish the area to be like (cf. Ashworth and Voogd,1990a:77 et seq.);
- image communicates and shapes expectations with respect to what the area can or should give to individuals. This concerns not only explicit expectations (those which, even though they are not necessarily realistic, clearly define problems and solutions), but also those – much more difficult to manage – which are implicit (taken for granted or which are not subject to discussion), or even fuzzy (as they are schematic, ideological, emotional, and not based on a clear understanding of what should be done concretely and how);
- image is a filter that influences the perception of the area, the quality of life and services, the level of development and the (individual and collective) expectations about the future. It obviously also filters communication: a positive image reinforces the credibility of messages, whereas a negative image reduces their credibility; a positive image allows minor problems not to be emphasized, but can result in underestimating emerging threats, whereas a negative image on the other hand can lead to the dramatization of marginal questions but can also raise attention in time by emphasizing weak signals;
- image is self-reinforcing through the activities of actors that conform to the expectations and through their subjective evaluations based on the relationship between perception and expectations (Figure 6.1). When an image has been consolidated, it is likely to be self-fulfilling.

From Marketing to Policy

In our view, marketing is no substitute for policy. Still marketing can be functional to policy, especially when we consider it in a governance perspective. By the term 'governance' we mean a variety of guidance mechanisms, not necessarily restricted to public actors, whereby social processes are consciously directed in situations of interdependence. The concept that allows best to describe and understand the practical meaning and implications of governance is 'policy network'. We define policy networks as '(more or less) stable patterns of social relations between interdependent actors, which take shape around policy problems and/or policy programmers' (Kickert et al., 1997). Policy networks are therefore alternative to traditional ways of government (and, to a large extent, also to contemporary

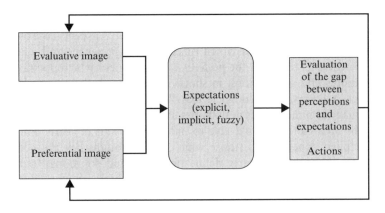

Source: Author's own.

Figure 6.1   Image, expectations and feedback mechanisms

approaches of 'new' public management). The management of policy networks can take place at two different levels, using substantially different sets of tools. On the one hand, the structure of the network can be influenced, for example, through the composition, the number of actors, its openness, the internal rules, the introduction of new actors and the exclusion of some of the present actors, etc. Branding policies seem indeed highly dependent on the level and quality of available social capital: on the effectiveness of consensus-building, interactive procedures; on a substantial degree of inclusiveness and on the actors' restraining from opportunistic behaviour (Ward, 2000; Rizzi and Scaccheri, 2006).

On the other hand, at the cognitive level, it is possible to influence the perception, the views and expectations, to anticipate the exclusion of diverging ideas and views, to facilitate interaction and to promote a common language, to induce collective reflection and to prevent cognitive *lock-in* etc. Therefore the toolbox of industrial and innovation policies also includes a set of 'second generation' policy instruments, which impact on the cognitive dimensions of local networks in the attempt to govern their evolution through the formation of perceptions and expectations and which incorporate the management of regional/city images through branding (cf. Bellini and Landabaso, 2007).

This is especially true when policies deal with complex processes like innovation and economic development, which are characterized by risk, uncertainty and information asymmetries. Making sense of the place where we live and work, as well as of its present reality and future perspectives, is then essential:

. . . what is critical is how this information is processed, via mental processes of cognition, to form stable and learned images of place, which are the basis for our everyday interactions with the environment. It is the mental maps that individuals create that allow them to navigate through complex reality, because 'our surroundings are often more complex than the sense we make of them'. Branding deals specifically with such mental images. Place branding centres on people's perceptions and images and puts them at the heart of orchestrated activities, designed to shape the place and its future. Managing the place brand becomes an attempt to influence and treat those mental maps in a way that is deemed favourable to the present circumstances and future needs of the place (Kavaratzis and Ashworth, 2005:507).

The political relevance of place branding is twofold. First, the image of an area (region, city) reflects its identity. As such we are not dealing with objective, technical data, but with a social, historical and highly subjective (and sometimes even artificial) construct, which consists of the total of affective and rational images produced by individual actors or by groups of actors. These images show the values that the various groups connect to the area, to its characteristics and its identity. 'In defining their discourses of inclusion and exclusion that constitute identity, people call upon an affinity with places or, at least, with representation of places, which, in turn, are used to legitimate their claim to those places' (Ashworth and Graham, 2005:3). It is in this way that groups take possession of a geographic space, synthesizing their view of the area in stereotypes and 'labels' and creating 'myths' through the selective narration of the social, economic and historic characteristics of the area. Through appropriate governance processes this may lead to increased social and political cohesion about related policies, constructing a sustainable 'brand purpose' (Anholt, 2007).

However 'different people, at different times, for different reasons, create different narratives of belonging. Place images are thus user determined, polysemic and unstable through time' (Ashworth and Graham, 2005:3). When different images coexist at a certain time, there may then be a competition between images in order to control the representation of the past/present/future of a territory and therefore the policy agenda.

Secondly, in dynamic contexts there may be coherence or incoherence between 'image' and 'product' as a result of conscious manipulation. In some cases, a prevalence of preferential over evaluative components is generated in order to anticipate a change in a reasonably nearby future, which some social groups want to strive for: a 'better' area (city or region), more livable and/or wealthier and/or more modern than it effectively is. The imagery therefore overlaps and expresses the vision that those groups envisage and to which they are committed (cf. Hospers, 2004; 2006).

In other cases evaluative components are misleading. Situations of political and cognitive lock-in in 'post-paradigmatic' areas can generate stereotypical images referring to historic production structures. These images are outdated and – which is worse – can hamper innovative changes. Emerging industries and social groups are not recognized or dismissed as transitional, non-credible and non-reliable phenomena.

THE IMAGE OF TUSCANY

Features and Components

By all standards Tuscany has a strong, high-profile and widely recognized image. According to a recent survey (Cavalieri, 2001), more than 90 per cent of German consumers know the brands 'Toscana' and 'Firenze'. 'Firenze' is also known by 75 per cent of consumers in US and Japan, while the recognition of 'Toscana' is lower, but still relevant (more than 40 per cent). In some countries the familiarity with Tuscany identifies social and even political groups. In British and American literature (as also reminded by movies such as 'A Room with a View', 'The English Patient' and 'Stealing Beauty') Tuscany is a sort of exotic dreamland where the beauty of landscape and art takes away inhibitions and frees the souls, so that visitors discover their own feelings, emotions and sensuality. In German political jargon the expression '*Toskana-fraktion*' is used to indicate a number of left-wing intellectuals, sharing a custom of spending holidays in Tuscan countryside and therefore suspected of mixing revolutionary ideals and hedonistic behaviour.

Tuscany's image is primarily linked to tourism. The tourist image of Tuscany is an unparalleled blend of intellectual and emotional components. History, culture and the past shape the region's image from the Etruscan Coast to the medieval villages and the renaissance cities. Thanks to its glorious past, a sense of nobility, greatness and magnificence is conveyed to the visitors: 'Tuscany: noble and great region'. Cities like Siena define themselves as a 'strip of land rich in coat of arms and nobility' and their distinctiveness is described as 'aristocratic exclusiveness'.

The reference to art is obvious, due to the extraordinary, internationally recognizable assets inherited from history with 'brands' such as Leonardo da Vinci, Michelangelo, Giotto, Brunelleschi, Piero della Francesca etc. Tuscany's streets are 'Houses of the Memory' of eminent figures in the history of knowledge, such as Dante Alighieri.

Complementary to history is Nature, that perfect symbiosis man–nature that is detectable in the famous Tuscan landscape: 'The ideal place to spend your holiday time'. The mix of nature and history makes Tuscany 'genuine': 'A glow of genuineness that surrounds everything with perfumes of Tuscany'. Within this overall 'Green Tourism' approach, man–nature interactions are varied. They are related to sport and to the availability of biking and walking itineraries, allowing for 'Slow Tourism'. So, for example, the White Streets in Siena are presented as the icon of tourism in Tuscany, because they are streets without cars, where people walk for hours. More recently promotion placed new emphasis on thermal baths, as connected with relaxation and health: 'Tuscany: the region of well-being'.

A fundamental field of interaction between man and nature is food. In Tuscany there is an obvious link between green, slow tourism, on one hand, and wine and food, on the other. Along Tuscany's 'Wine Roads', innumerable opportunities to 'taste local culture' are available to the educated gourmet: 'About a territory, as ours is, we can say that's sufficient shaking it to make good food and products fall down. . . if you shake it a little more, you make theatre fall down'. Wine is 'the flag bearer of Tuscany in the world', 'the faithful image of Tuscan culture and tradition'. Nature, food, art, a human dimension of living distant from stressful contemporary world make up for a sweet life, the *dolce vita* (an expression usually kept in the original Italian) (Cavalieri, 2001:35). Moreover, Tuscany does not change. In some cases 'timeless images' are proposed, but more often the reference to key phases of Tuscan history is explicit. The preservation of the 'real Tuscany' through centuries is presented as a fundamental value: 'Time seems to have stopped'. Visiting Tuscany is experiencing history. In the case of Siena, the rite of the 'Palio' game brings history into real life: 'Siena is an itinerary that joins past and future'; 'A scrap of history that shows up in the present'. Food and wine also show their deep historic roots, as they are connected with traditional know-how of rural areas: 'Oil production goes back to seventh century BC'; Sangiovese was the grapevine of the Etruscan people; etc. Food and wine speak about history.

The Weaknesses of a Strong Image

The Tuscan case proves the 'weaknesses of strong images'. Tuscany's images can be confused and ambiguous as much as they are obvious and stereotypical. This is clearly shown by the many 'missing links' that are often revealed between different place brands: is Florence in Tuscany? is Florence the same as Tuscany? where is the leaning tower of Pisa? Tuscany's identity runs serious risks of 'commodification' (cf. Simon, 2005:32 et seq.), as shown by the emergence of alternative tourist locations labelled as 'the new Tuscany'. According to the New York Times, the Italian Region *Le Marche* may be 'the next Tuscany', with advantages compared to the real one such as being less crowded, not yet discovered ('secret'), quiet and unused to tourism, while offering similar postcard features (converted farmhouses, small and picturesque Italian towns, traditional products and wines, rolling vineyards, hills, golden grain fields topped by crumbling castles, simple people rooted in the territory, rural life, sunflower fields etc.). It is suggested that this is an 'Authentic Italy that's vanishing from other parts of his homeland'. It is 'what Tuscany was': 'This is what Tuscany must have felt like 10 or 20 years ago, before it was discovered by tour groups and their omnipresent buses, carrying thousands and thousands of travellers who flock there each year to try to recreate the pleasure of "Under the Tuscan Sun", a Tuscany so crowded with British expatriates and second-home owners that that country's press calls it Chianti-shire. . . Tuscany is an increasingly challenging place to have an intimate encounter with true Italy'.

Significant challenges come from other countries. Again the New York Times finds 'The Tuscan Life' in Croatia and its cheaper second-home market. According to this report, 'the government would like the region to resemble a mix of Tuscany and Provence. . . somehow more honest and much more user-friendly. (. . .) We heard this was the New Tuscany. But you can't get places in Tuscany like this any more'. In Bulgaria (namely in Veliko Tarnovo Region, Gabrovo Region and Lovech Region), a growing real estate market, rurality, nature, a unique culture in vibrant old towns, exquisite landscape, rural traditions, timber-and-stone houses legitimate an active real estate agency to be named 'The New Tuscany Ltd'. Also in Alentejo (Portugal) and Priorat (Catalonia) being 'like Tuscany' is a positive element to be emphasized in area marketing.

To sum up, the idea of being 'like Tuscany', the 'new Tuscany', the 'next Tuscany' seems to be spreading rapidly. Adding to a more or less vague physical resemblance to the original, all 'other Tuscanies' seem to provide an increasingly generic, globalized 'authentic experience' based on some 'uniqueness of culture', a 'theme park' that gives tourists the 'feel of Tuscany'.

TUSCANIES

Not Just Florence

'Tuscany' is also unable to represent the different 'Tuscanies' (Cavalieri, 1999). The variety of landscapes and societies that make up the present Region of Tuscany is hardly reflected in the 'strong image' that is known worldwide. Thus we often find the need to define or brand parts of the region as the 'other Tuscany'.

Firenze/Florence is the dominating brand, standing out of the crowd of the other Tuscan images. Quality, centrality, excellence, traditions, taste, culture as well as the mix of urban features and countryside fascination (the 'Chianti-shire') make this city a high-value 'oasis' compared to the rest of Tuscany (as suggested by local place marketing). Only 50 per cent of German consumers know about other Tuscan cities: Siena, Pisa, Lucca. Only 8 per cent of Americans and Japanese know about other cities, namely Siena and Pisa. Due to the successful development of the local airport as gateway for an increasing number of international visitors, the image of Pisa is very often one with the image of Tuscany. In their schedules, major international airlines prefer to name the airport not Pisa, but 'Pisa Florence' (Ryanair), 'Pisa/Tuscany' (Delta) or 'Pisa (Tuscany)' (Easyjet).

Then, there is the 'other' Tuscany. As a communication device in tourism marketing, 'other' is used to suggest the opportunity to look for alternative/minor destinations, that are still unknown, not yet discovered and crowded by major flows of tourists: little medieval towns, wine areas not as celebrated as Chianti etc. But 'other' does not necessarily reflect positive values: it may mean separate, distant, backward, discriminated...
At least two areas in the Region are 'other': Lunigiana in the North and Maremma in the South. The latter case is discussed in the following pages.

Maremma

The Province of Grosseto (Figure 6.2) occupies the southern extremity of Tuscany and is the largest province of Tuscany (4504 sq km). The number of inhabitants (220 742 in 2006) makes it one of the provinces with the lowest population density per square kilometre (49 inhab./sq km). The Province administers a total of 28 towns spread over hilly inland areas, isolated mountains (such as the eastern part occupied by Monte Amiata) and, near the coastal zone, a plain better known as 'Maremma', which is crossed by rivers, interrupted by promontories (rocky coastlines) and characterized by wetlands and marshland. The southern islands of the Tuscan Archipelago (such as Giglio and Giannutri) are also part of the Province.

The provincial economy shows characters and performance that clearly differ from the rest of Tuscany, a Region that, starting from the second half of the twentieth century, has joined the North of Italy as one of the most advanced areas in the country (Table 6.1).

Already in 1969, a renowned economist, Barucci, concluded a report on the local economy by stating that 'also Tuscany has its South. A great part of this depressed Tuscany is Grosseto' (Barucci, 1969). IRPET

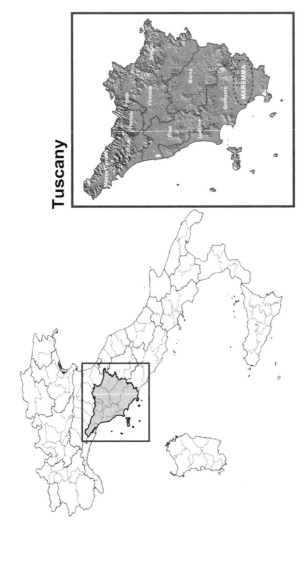

Source: Regional Institute for Economic Planning of Tuscany. Copyright held by author.

Figure 6.2 The Province of Grosseto in Italy and Tuscany

Table 6.1   Added value in the economic sectors in the Province of Grosseto – 2003

Sectors	% in the Province of Grosseto	% in the Region of Tuscany
Agriculture, forestry and fishing	*5.90*	1.70
Fashion industry	*1.20*	6.20
Mechanics	*1.10*	4.60
Other manufactures	*7.00*	12.30
Construction	*5.10*	4.70
Trade	*24.40*	18.50
Services	*33.10*	32.80
Public administration, education, health, other services	*22.20*	19.20
Total	*100.00*	100.00

Source: IRPET 2005.

(2003), the regional research institute for economic planning, openly stressed the diversity in an official report entitled *'La Provincia di Grosseto: l'altra Toscana?'* (Grosseto Province: the other Tuscany?). In the report Grosseto's 'otherness' is based on economic grounds: a development model different from the 'classic' model followed by the rest of Tuscany ('pre-industrial . . . or rather non industrial'; statistical economic indexes (population, employment rate, income. . .) that are consistently lower than the rest of the region; distance from the core of regional development (the Arno valley axis), emphasized by the lack of adequate infrastructures.

The growth of the economy in Grosseto is constrained by major structural deficits. Most often Grosseto ranks last in Tuscany with regard to infrastructures: setting an index equal to 100 for Italy, the province of Grosseto reaches 48.8 for the road network (Tuscany = 100.6), 77.1 for the rail network (Tuscany = 128.5), 71.3 for the airports (Tuscany = 100.4) and only 33.6 for the port network (Tuscany = 128.8). This infrastructural gap (that worsened in the last fifteen years) makes Grosseto, despite its geographical position, a kind of 'island' within an otherwise advanced region. The demographic trend shows an ageing population, with a consequent reduction in productivity: the category over 64 rose from 20.6 per cent in 1991 to 24.9 per cent in 2005, leading to a reduction in weight of the working age population (15–64 years) from 68 per cent in 1991 to 64.1 per cent in 2005. The viability (and identity) of an economy still based on rurality is clearly in danger when 45 per cent of farmers are over 65 years old and 96 per cent of entrepreneurs are over 60.

Table 6.2   Employment in the high-tech sector in the Province of Grosseto

%	Grosseto	Tot. Region	Tot. Italy
% HT employment on total employment of the Province of Grosseto (1991)	*3.4*	4.2	5.9
% HT employment on total employment of the Province of Grosseto (2001)	*3.0*	4.6	6.1
% change of the HT employment 1991–2001	*–9.7*	16.6	11.3
% change of total employment 1991–2001	*2.4*	4.7	8.0

Source: Istat.

Table 6.3   The openness of Grosseto economy

	2003	2004	2005
Grosseto	*9.2*	*8.5*	*7.8*
TUSCANY	*39.6*	*40.2*	*41.2*
ITALY	39.5	41.0	43.0

Source: Istituto G. Tagliacarne.

Parallel to this, Grosseto shows a serious gap in all innovation-related indexes, especially compared to a dynamic high-tech Tuscany. Grosseto has no university, but just a small teaching branch of the University of Siena, and only a few, minor research centres. R&D expenditure as percentage of local GDP is estimated to be only 0.22 (as against 1.06 for Tuscany and 3.50 for Pisa, ranking first in the Region). Employment in high-tech companies is at the bottom end in the ranking of Tuscan provinces and even shows a negative trend between 1991 and 2001 in sharp contrast with the rest of the Region (Table 6.2).

Looking at more fashionable indices does not improve the outlook for Grosseto. With respect to the 'Creativity Index' *à la* Florida, Grosseto ranks 40th in Italy (63rd for talent, 54th for technology, 30th for tolerance), while Firenze ranks 5th and Pisa ranks 13th (Tinagli and Florida, 2005). Last but not least, the development of the Province is affected by the low openness to the international economy (Table 6.3).

The uncertain urban characters of the city of Grosseto are one of the main features of the area and, according to some, one of the most serious handicaps for its economic development. The weaknesses of Grosseto have deep roots in history. Until the Italian unification (1861), Grosseto never had a real autonomy nor a local noble class (being therefore 'directed' by outsiders from the neighbouring city of Siena or from Florence). Even when becoming provincial capital within the new Kingdom of Italy, the city maintained its non-urban, predominantly rural characters. It was considered an uncomfortable place to live and work. When the summer heat was at its peak, public offices were moved to a neighbouring village, with a better climate.

The rural character was further emphasized during Fascism for political and ideological reasons. Grosseto and its province were often referred to as the example of the 'sound' rural Italy. As Mussolini himself put it in 1930, 'within five or ten years, all of your province must be ploughed by roads, hundreds of houses must rise and will rise to host the rural population'.

After War World II, Grosseto remained what was defined as a 'city notwithstanding' ('*Città malgrado*': Elia, 2003). The city grew essentially by attracting people from the countryside, but never worked as a real 'melting pot' and never gave birth to some kind of new identity. Other migrations to Grosseto and its province were on the contrary directed from outside: the people from Veneto region to settle in the reclaimed areas of Maremma; the military personnel in the barracks of the city of Grosseto; and now also tourists themselves in their 'second houses'. At the same time, intellectuals and the potential members of new elites have been flowing away from the city to look for greater opportunities in bigger towns.

Being the 'Other Tuscany'

Thus, the image of Grosseto Province is shaped by the wide, intact, rural spaces of Maremma, the area surrounding the city. Traditionally the landscape has been the dominating element emphasized by travellers. One of the masterworks of Italian cinema ('Il sorpasso', 1962), a kind of 'road movie', has passed on the image of a land to travel through, to be looked at from a car's window. 'This is a land where man has lived in respectful admiration for centuries', a land where nature has dominated man, rather than the other way around.

The main icon is provided by the *buttero*, a local cowboy bravely facing wild nature. A statue was dedicated to him in the rail station square, welcoming travellers arriving to the city (Figure 6.3). The myth has survived the end of his economic role. Old stories narrate about the legendary challenge of the *butteri* to the American cowboys, touring Italy with Buffalo Bill in 1890. To be a *buttero* is a way of life: still today the *buttero* symbolizes the values of hard work and respect for traditions.

A very powerful image of the area derives from a book written in 1957 by a local writer, Luciano Bianciardi (Bianciardi, 1957). In this peculiar

Source: Nicola Bellini.

Figure 6.3   The statue of the buttero

work (indeed an essay in a novel's style) the author sketches an animated discussion between 'erudite' locals about the origins of the city of Grosseto: '. . .in our city there were learned, erudite and intellectual people who were looking for its origins'. 'Medievalists' set the birth of the city exactly in 1138 when Grosseto became a diocese. On the contrary, 'archaeologists' believed in an undoubted and illustrious Etruscan origin: 'Our city was born in the heart of the Etruscan civilization, who was set up here for the healthy air, richness of forests and fertile lands'. Provocatively, to the younger generation, 'determined to break with tradition', the year of its foundation was 1944: 'The origins of the city? The year of its foundation? But it was 1944, no doubt. Before that time, it did not exist, the Americans had established it. . .'.

In the same essay a young American visitor suggests that Grosseto looks very much like his own town, Kansas City, a town 'open to the wind and to the foreigners', 'not resembling any other Italian town'. Such imagery has been very successful, although one can hardly figure out anything more distant from the standard Tuscan stereotype. Grosseto/ Kansas City is a borderline town, with an uncertain identity. Grosseto, like Kansas City and unlike the 'great Tuscany', is a 'cowtown': simple, small, isolated, unsophisticated. Grosseto, like Kansas City and unlike the 'noble Tuscany', forgets its past and concentrates on recent history, when its city status was recognized. To sum up, Grosseto, like Kansas City, is an open city, meaning there is a lack of 'owners' of its identity.

Grosseto is 'periphery'. In fact the idea itself of being a periphery is cultural and psychological much more than 'objective'. It is related to the new dependence of Grosseto from Florence, first in the age of the Grand Dukes of Tuscany and later (since the 1970s) with the establishment of the Regional government. From a mere geographical point of view, there is no such thing as the marginality of Grosseto, that is located right in the centre of the country (see again Figure 6.2). For example, the 'need' for a local airport is often argued on the basis of the excessive distance from the regional airports of Florence and Pisa (160 km). At the same time Grosseto is only 170 km distant from the main Italian airport and international hub, Rome Fiumicino. Clearly marginality is more a matter of perceptions and stereotypes rather than an objective reality.

Grosseto is the 'other Tuscany'. The 'otherness' of Grosseto has more than one meaning: 'being atypical and being peculiar are also the juxtaposed terms by which the local society and its elite have portrayed themselves in their relationship with the external world' (D'Agnelli, 2003). Possibly the most consistent effort to re-build an identity based on pride and diversity has been realized during the two terms of Alessandro Antichi as mayor of Grosseto (1997–2005). This controversial, conservative, anti-communist lawyer defeated the left-wing government of the city by emphasizing the reaction to the widespread feeling of decline and by proposing a new rhetoric of development (in his words, 'a new renaissance'), based on the otherwise lost local identity. He was also a provocative and imaginative manager of symbols and icons, including monuments and cultural events. One famous photograph portrays him as a defiant, proud (but also modern and bourgeois!) replica of the *buttero*, while taming a cow (Figure 6.4).

Differences may then also reveal a new, positive and dynamic development model based on a greater weight of rural environment and therefore (especially in a post-industrialist, environmentalist approach) on a new tourism relying on 'a network of environment, natural resources, rural dimension, rural and artisan products of high quality'. Maremma is the land of escapes: not only for the frustrated metropolitan inhabitants looking for a slice of slow life, but, e.g., also for social experimenters like

Source: www.alessandroantichi.org.

Figure 6.4   Mayor A. Antichi

the founders of the Christian community of Nomadelfia (a community where private ownership is abolished according to the myths of early Christianity).

Therefore Maremma can also be opposed to classic Tuscany in a positive sense. Classic Tuscany would offer cities of art, the most celebrated monuments, but also noisy and inattentive crowds of tourists and glittering outlets, while 'the other', 'unexpected' Tuscany would offer uncongested landscape, rural values, high quality environment, naturalistic and historical values: in other words, a different, greater authenticity, 'un-sophisticated genuineness' that gives 'emotions'. These are indeed the Leitmotiv of tourist marketing:

> Meant for those who love to travel, in search of colours, fragrances, sounds, flavours of the Maremma: a land you must live, love and visit. The traveller who wishes to awaken his emotions with a lifestyle linked to traditions and nature,

has only to come to Tuscany, in the fascinating Maremma region. Maremma is a lifestyle. . . consisting of the sea, nature, archaeology, craftsmanship, sport, good food. . . and much more. Today, more than ever, the Maremma is the perfect choice for the romantic traveller.

Nature here is not an asset nurtured by history and consciously shaped in accordance to a specific identity. Rather it is the result of a limited industrial development in the past. Wide spaces are then offered as an opportunity to investors. According to official brochures, the 'first reason' to invest in Grosseto is that the area has had a 'peculiar development' compared to the rest of the Region, leaving the natural aspect almost intact and 'untouched' by excessive industrial and urban settlements: 'this offers today the possibility to design new investment projects without being constrained by previous situations'.

The local discourse echoes the different meanings of this 'otherness'. The *maremmani* like to show the pride of their being different, but the political debate seems to be obsessed by the problems of being 'periphery', with a kind of (sometimes unjustified) inferiority complex that is a ready-made alibi for all failures in solving the economic and social problems of the area.

Thus, another icon of Grosseto is the 'Canapone', the nickname of the last granduke of Tuscany, Leopold II and also of its beautiful statue in the main square of the city (Figure 6.5). This granduke had a special paternalistic 'affection' for this area and indeed was committed to the solution of its main problems, starting with malaria. In his testament he refers, almost poetically, to Maremma as 'the first sick region, needing help, and yet so beautiful and rich of hopes'. The locals rewarded this love with a statue that portrays him, dressed up like an ancient roman, raising a distressed, sick lady with an act of pity and encouragement. To contemporary eyes, this is also an icon to the sense of frustration of the area and to the expectation of external help as the most likely solution to local problems.

BRANDING FUTURE TUSCANY

Images of the Regional Industry

Tuscany is a strong brand in tourism, but not for industry and not even for the food industry. The 'region-of-origin' effect is weak. According to the above quoted survey, only 60 per cent of German consumers link some food product to Tuscany (mostly wine and oil); among American and Japanese consumers this share drops to 7 per cent. As far as the fashion

Source: Nicola Bellini.

Figure 6.5   The 'Canapone'

industry is concerned, only 12 per cent of German consumers and 3 per
cent of consumers in the US and Japan know some Tuscan *griffe*. By far
the brand that is most clearly identified as Tuscan is Gucci. Prada and
Ferragamo are recognized as Tuscan only by a small minority. Moreover,
among the brands that are mentioned as Tuscan there are also non-Tuscan
brands such as Armani and Benetton, showing how the Tuscan image
easily disappears into the stronger 'made in Italy' brand. No connection

emerges between other major made-in-Tuscany brands (e.g. the *Vespa* motorscooter) and the region.

Even when we move from general consumers to professional buyers, only 60 per cent of the sample recognize a positive value in a 'made in Tuscany' product compared to a 'made in Italy' product. Many of the positive factors attached to the Tuscan origin of the product are mere repetition of the traditional factors characterizing 'made in Italy' products (Cavalieri, 2001:19 et seq. and 28 et seq.). To some tourists (like the Japanese), rather than a place of origin of prestigious products, Tuscany is an excellent location for shopping (Cavalieri, 2001:36). The Tuscan economy, therefore, seems to be able to exploit the high visibility of the Tuscany brand only in a very limited measure. Can a strong image give a substantial contribution to cognitive, social and political lock-ins? The case of Tuscany seems to suggest that this is possible. The tourist image of Tuscany is intimately consistent with a popular vision of the future development of the Tuscan economy that assumes the exit from the manufacturing sector as unavoidable and – in fact – desirable. According to this post-industrial vision, tourism, services, agri-food industries and other environmentally sustainable enterprises should substitute manufacturers in creating value and sustaining income levels.

This vision has been increasingly influential, although never made it to 'get hold' of the political agenda. Regional and local governments have mostly confirmed their allegiance to 'industrialist' visions, even in front of the crisis of the few large corporations present in the Region. This has happened with two (complementary, but sometimes juxtaposed) variations: the belief in the alternative model of development provided by smaller companies in the 'industrial districts' vs. the belief in the evolution towards a neo-industrial scenario, characterized by service-manufacturing integration, high levels of R&D activity and an increasing role of high-tech companies.

Both industrialist visions had images of Tuscany that could be conveyed to the general public. On the one hand, the industrial district vision built a powerful intellectual myth of an alternative economic model, mixing cooperation and competition, capitalist growth and social stability. Only in one case, i.e. the city of Prato, one has openly made reference to and emphasized the role of manufacturing tradition as a constituent part of the image of the city. More recently, due to the ups and downs of the economy, the general perception of industrial districts has been more frequently linked to crisis and de-industrialization rather than to success and growth.

On the other hand, the neo-industrial vision has developed its own brand, 'ArnoValley'. The obvious reference to Silicon Valley is here combined with the fact of the geographic concentration of high-tech activities Universities, research centres and some 3000 companies in the area between Florence and Pisa, along the river Arno. The name 'ArnoValley' was first used provocatively by a Tuscan economist in an interview. Rapidly it spread across local and national newspapers, with no intentional planning or monitoring. As a consequence also no distinctiveness or authenticity were communicated and the most simplistic analogies with the Silicon Valley myths were suggested, notwithstanding the warnings of many about the excessive optimism of such messages. In 2002, a formal agreement between the City Councils of Florence and Pisa and the government of the Tuscan Region put the ArnoValley label on a programme promoting a more robust and networked business community for the Tuscan high-tech. Among the most noticeable initiatives were the publication of a report on the 'Net Economy in Tuscany' that raises some public debate and the start of a website 'ArnoValleycommunity.com', with the aim of contributing to the establishment of a business community. At the beginning the idea looked quite successful and the Community appeared to be an effective way to give visibility to the high-tech industry in the area, also by providing an interface to politicians and other business interests. In 2003 a study was commissioned in order to design the possible institutionalization of the ArnoValley Community. The report, following a thorough consultation of all stakeholders, suggested to link the ArnoValley brand to the Tuscany brand, which is 'unique and easy to be sold'. It also proposed the establishment of an 'ArnoValley Association' as animateur of business aggregation and of concrete projects, arguing communication was 'not enough and, if [ArnoValley did] not tackle business problems pragmatically, it [would not have left] any signs' (Marenco, 2003:12). And yet at the end of 2003 the project entered a fatal deadlock. The association was not founded, the ArnoValley Community website was progressively abandoned and is now no longer updated.

Why is this the case? ArnoValley never took off because it was inherently a very weak initiative, unable to build a significant 'brand purpose' (Anholt, 2007), that entered a vicious circle of irrelevance and ineffectiveness and appeared to most stakeholders as not bringing any real added value. The process was carried out quite poorly, both technically (because of the prevailing role of communication and public relations experts) and above all politically. The constituency of the local political elite remained rooted in the traditional industries and their territorial clusters. Unsurprisingly political support turned out to be more lip-service to then fashionable catchwords than actual commitment. The Region never assumed full financial and strategic responsibility, leaving the leadership to the two City Councils. These had a very loose coordination: the two municipalities designed distinct and separate initiatives and governance arrangements in order to pursue their own objectives under the broader coalition's aims. The municipalities also suffered from not being at the appropriate scale of jurisdiction, not representing other smaller, but not less active municipalities (such as Pontedera and Empoli). Their own commitment was also very much dependent on the personalities involved and clearly declined when the political leaders of the project left their jobs. Other competing projects were allowed to emerge with no greater success or scope of action (e.g. the so-called *Progetto California*), but for sure not helping communication and community-building efforts.

The result was a weak and vague brand identity proposition that was rejected by more established and stronger identities. Actually, the need to dialogue with the deeply rooted Tuscan identity was often overlooked. Especially during the first stage, instead of reducing the conflicting potential in order to harmonize contemporary and traditional assets within an 'umbrella identity', the high-tech was superficially communicated as a 'potential economic miracle' able to 'radically upset the traditional productive and social fabric' of Tuscany. This promise was accepted with scepticism by the industrial and political establishment and in fact proved to be undeliverable when the new economy bubble burst. The bluff was revealed and ArnoValley finally delegitimized. In conclusion, also due to the weak perception of the need to brand industrial Tuscany, the strength of the traditional image succeeded in preventing the emergence of new ones, that could reflect the vision of more dynamic industries and social groups.

Heritage and the Forgotten Past

The role of cultural heritage here comes into play, showing how different images and visions are built upon a very selective narration of the region's history and shared values. Facing the inability to sustain a 'dissonant' discourse on regional heritage (cf. Tunbridge and Ashworth, 1996), the emphasis on a romantic, anti-modern, 'natural' image of Tuscany, the obsession with 'preserving the past' and the stubborn reluctance to modern additions has been clearly instrumental to the post-industrial vision of regional economic development. Thus heritage has failed to contribute to the regional innovation culture, i.e. to the shaping of those institutions (norms, values, formal, informal) that have a significant influence on the perceptions of actors involved in innovation process (Didero et al., 2008).

The dominant manipulation of heritage as entertainment for tourists, typical of the 'cities of art' (as distinguished from the 'cities of culture': Sacco et al., 2008) is based on forgetting. When nature is indicated as the strategic resource of future Tuscany it is easily forgotten how little of the Tuscan landscape is 'natural' and how often it is, on the contrary, a classical case of *Kulturlandschaft*, with man-shaped hills, lines of cypresses and pine forests along the coast. When authenticity is based on history (i.e. the longer its history, the greater the authenticity), it is easily forgotten the huge amount of process and product innovations that are supporting the quality and competitiveness of the local 'authentic' food industry.

An excellent example is wine. Like (and more than) other food products, the link to the geographical origin is essential. As mentioned before, in Tuscany this has also a historic dimension: being rooted in history makes the product and the experience connected to it more 'authentic'. But not all Tuscan wines have a history. Outstanding wines with spectacular commercial success are in fact 'new products' and have created 'new' wine areas, in no way more 'noble' than wine areas are in Northern California or other extra-European regions. The best known case is the Sassicaia wine, produced in Bolgheri since the 1960s. Producers in areas like Bolgheri itself, Val di Cornia or the Pisan Hills have been constantly innovating production technologies, introducing new grapes and varieties, exploiting new lands, bringing in non-Tuscan entrepreneurship and capitals and even 'scandalous' modern winery architecture. Of course, marketing concedes that wine-making science has evolved, but, whenever possible, distinctiveness and quality are presented as based not on contemporary creativity and knowledge, but on available historic antecedents (including Romans and Etruscans).

As one scholar of high-tech development problems in Tuscany once reminded his readers, 'Galileo used to live here' (Bianchi, 1996). Yet it is surprising to notice how rarely the brand 'Galileo' is used, even in his hometown, Pisa. Leonardo da Vinci, another icon of modern science, is much more frequently remembered (and reminded to tourists) as an artist than as a scientist.

Also forgotten are some fundamental characters of Tuscan history, such as the intimate link between modernity and beauty and between culture and economic development that was the essence of the golden age of the Medicis. Beauty is communicated as a mostly aesthetic fact and visitors often are left in total ignorance about the tremendous technical challenges and outstanding skills behind some of the greatest works of art. In Pisa, only the dramatic events concerning the stability of the Leaning Tower have drawn attention to the fascinating technical complexity of that building.

The strength of this collective mood is reflected in Florence, a 'high culture district' (cf. Lazzeretti, 2003) with a dramatic inability to express and communicate innovation. As one inhabitant once put it in a private conversation, 'we should expect to be ordered to go out dressed up in medieval costume'. The most modern landmark in the city is the Santa Maria Novella railroad station, a masterwork of modernist architecture, built in the 1930s and actually imposed on the city by the Fascist regime. With the exception of some linkages to modern creativity, mostly in the field of fashion, Florence is today a frozen city, in sharp contrast with the characters of contemporary creative cities (Hospers, 2004) providing a reminder of the fact that 'the most successful heritage cities are those of sufficient size to offer numerous amenities, including heritage, but not dominated by it' (Graham, 2002:1014). The recent debate about the new entrance to the Uffizi Museum and the innovative proposal by Arata Isozaki (finally cancelled in 2004) has led the distinguished art historian Irving Lavin (2005) to comment about 'the bitter irony that is behind the conservative mood that dominates in Florence – right in Florence! – and suffocates the spirit of adventure and innovation that created the city we all love and admire, where the notion itself of modernity was born. The Cathedral itself, and especially Brunelleschi's dome, would be surely prohibited today (. . .) Florence has become a stone-made Disneyland'.

The 'Other Tuscany', Once Again

Unsurprisingly, Tuscany shows a great difficulty in managing umbrella brands, as serious inconsistencies easily emerge in messages conveyed to different targets (e.g. tourists vs. foreign investors). Inward investment attraction needs to communicate an image that is substantially different from the tourist one: a society with a strong productive tradition; a diffused entrepreneurial culture; the network of institutional partners for guidance, support, assistance; the pervasiveness of infrastructures, its accessibility also due to the importance of regional airports; the excellence of its universities and research centres. Even speaking of 'quality of life' may be difficult. To tourists it is related to relaxation, 'stopping time', isolation, silence, and a break with modernity (from cars to e-mails). To investors and their workers it obviously relates to accessibility, connections, urban excitement, progress and modernity.

Tensions emerge. The emphasis on history clashes with the need to communicate an orientation to the future. While some industries (like textile, clothing, shoe-making and other fashion-related manufactures) may more easily make reference to the past, this is perceived as difficult for modern industries, like the automotive, electronics, biotech or chemical industry. Contrasts are then dramatized. The 'New Deal of the Tuscan System', from traditional manufactures to high-tech, looks more like a jump forward, a surprising outcome rather than an obvious bridge between past and future: 'The time runs unexpected roads. In Tuscany.'

Furthermore modernity seems to threaten genuineness. Modern features in farmhouses (like swimming pools) need to be explained as not 'artificial', but expression of a humanized approach, that makes living comfortable by our standards today, as they were centuries ago for the people of the past.

An additional, even more dramatic tension exists between industrial landscapes and the Tuscan landscapes as communicated to tourists. As it is often the case with advertising, communication reveals rather than downplays these tensions. For example, playing on the double meaning of the word 'natural' (related to nature, on the one hand, and right, ideal, obvious, on the other) place marketing suggests that Tuscany is 'The natural choice of your business location'. More evocative analogies are sometimes attempted. For example see Figure 6.6, a group of cypresses should portray the quality of local social capital and the attitude to networking among economic actors (like in the 'industrial district'). In the end, high quality and excellence seem to be the only truly horizontal features of Tuscany that are able to support umbrella brands effectively. Quality and excellence concern lifestyle, society, landscape, education, food and wine, environment, traditional products (fashion, jewellery, textile), new products. Irony helps: 'also an imperfection may make one extraordinary, as in 'In Tuscany' (see Figure 6.7).

Again, due to the strength of tourism's stereotypes, important features of the Region, such as the presence of a high-tech industry, need also to be labelled as the 'other Tuscany', suggesting a problematic relationship with the identity of the Region. The President of the Region, visiting Japan in early 2007, referred to Research and Technology in Tuscany as 'the other face' of the Region, an unknown face, to many an unexpected one ('Tuscany as you didn't expect'), that deserves to be 're-discovered': 'Leonardo was a great scientist too and we want to demonstrate that still today we are an advanced technology and research land, not only of style, wine and tourism'.

CONCLUSION

This chapter has emphasized the many weaknesses inherent in Tuscany's strong image. Branding Tuscany is a technically challenging task not only because of the inertia of the many stereotypes, but also because of the many policy implications that are 'hidden' behind brands. In particular we notice that a strong brand can be as effective in linking and including

Anche i singoli fanno sistema. In Toscana.

Source: www.investintuscany.com.

Figure 6.6   Promotion images of Tuscany 1

Anche un difetto può rendere eccezionali. In Toscana.

Source: www.investintuscany.com.

Figure 6.7 Promotion images of Tuscany 2

as it is in excluding regional sub-areas as well as social groups. Of course, otherness may be considered either in its negative or in its positive signifi- cance. However, the stronger the collective image, the greater should be the attention to branding, as a way to legitimize new social groups, emerg- ing industries and alternative models of development.

7. Place-making or place branding? Case studies of Catalonia and Wales

Assumpció Huertas Roig, Annette Pritchard and Nigel Morgan

INTRODUCTION

Whilst it is widely acknowledged that branding has the potential to play a key role in destination development, the relationship is not always straightforward or well understood. Branding has been applied to consumer products for well over a century but the idea of places pursuing formalised brand strategies only originated on any scale in the 1990s. Whereas earlier 'image-building' marketing activities in the 1980s by cities such as New York and Glasgow (encapsulated by the slogans 'I love New York' and 'Glasgow's miles better') foreshadowed such strategies, a strategic approach to place branding as we understand it today was pioneered at a national level in Australia, Hong Kong and Spain (Baker, 2007). Then major US cities like Seattle, Las Vegas and Pittsburgh embraced it, responding to a need to compete more effectively, to create a strategic decision-making framework and to increase accountability to their stakeholders. Many destinations now see place branding (which may encompass aspects of tourism, investment, exports, culture, sports, events, education and immigration) as a major instrument of management. The Destination Marketing Association International, the world's largest official destination marketing organisation designates the development of a brand strategy as one of the critical items needed for accreditation in its Destination Marketing Association Accreditation Program (Baker, 2007).

In today's competitive globalised marketplace, branding has been described as 'the most powerful marketing weapon available to contemporary destination marketers' in their efforts to combat increasing product parity, substitutability and competition (Morgan et al., 2002:335). Place branding strategies require a longer-term commitment than a mere image-building campaign, using public-relations and advertising as they usually seek to build a sense of purpose and vision, aligning the agendas of

116

tourism and investment promotion agencies, exporters, policy-makers and cultural organisations in a long-term development strategy. The concept of place branding has gained a high profile in recent years as different countries, regions and cities compete with each other to gain a foothold in a complex and changing market. Kotler and Gertner postulate that brands not only 'differentiate products and represent a promise of value', but also 'incite beliefs, evoke emotions and prompt behaviors' (Kotler and Gertner, 2002:249).

Brands endow places such as countries, regions and cities with consistency and credibility as well as a communication link with consumers. However, the application of branding to such places can prove difficult and involves certain limitations. Places have multiple personalities, target many different audiences and can engender a high degree of emotional attachment. For instance, many places are now attempting to move beyond using branding strategies to attract tourists and are seeking to use them in their efforts to establish themselves as business and investment centres and to attract new residents. This means that a place brand must embrace multiple positions, strategies, segments and audiences. For this reason, the branding of them is less easy to control, more complex and multi-dimensional than product branding and partly as a result, place branding is less developed than product branding (Tasci and Kozak, 2006). Destination branding strategies for tourism markets often contradict or even damage wider place branding strategies for the same nation or region (Anholt, 2004). For example, many have argued that images of Scotland and Ireland as quaint, old-world places whose inhabitants are charming, friendly and unsophisticated may appeal to tourists but are counter-productive to attempts to attract investment (e.g. Pritchard and Morgan, 1996). Destination branding is thus a highly complex activity that is further complicated by the reality that a destination or territory is not 'created' by marketers but is an existing, living reality that evolves and is based on communities, histories, cultures and identities.

For commentators such as Gerard (quoted in Olins, 2004:18) branding cannot be applied to a destination, whether this be a city, region or country as he argues that a product can be re-branded but that a territory cannot. For Gerard, organisations change and re-invent themselves, but regions and countries do not change, they are intransformable and their realities are permanent. However, we would argue that since socio-cultural contexts are continually changing places are not immutable but ever-evolving and as a result most place branding strategies attempt to reflect the realities of such changing national, regional and territorial identities and cultures. Thus, in tourism terms, virtually every destination attempts to position its unique culture at the forefront of its branding strategy and this has been the case with many territories which exist within larger European nation states, including: Brittany, Scotland, Wales, Lapland, The Tirol and Catalonia (Tresserras, 2008). The values that these brands represent and on which they are based are those of an 'intangible cultural heritage', defined by UNESCO (1998) as including traditions, oral expressions, entertainments, social rites, rituals and festivals, particular knowledge and practices as well as the skills associated with traditional crafts. In such cases, these tourism positioning strategies may also reflect wider political and cultural moves for greater regional/territorial autonomy as each of these above mentioned regions/countries are territories (and therefore also sub-brands) within larger national entities (namely France, the UK, Finland, Italy and Spain) and in some cases themselves include cities with established brand reputations (e.g. Edinburgh, Cardiff and Barcelona).

Our particular focus in this chapter is on an in-depth, comparative analysis of the Wales and Catalonia destination brands in order to explore the relationships between these country/regional brands, their suprabrands of the UK and Spain and their capital/regional city brands of Cardiff and Barcelona. It analyses the Wales and Catalonia strategies and explores their implications for their related place brands with their multi-layered identities. In particular, the chapter examines the place-making impacts of such branding activities that are profiling particular stories of place, culture and nation. It concludes that in the case of Wales, tourism is playing a key role in the newly established Welsh Assembly Government's drive to create greater international distinctiveness for Wales and together with a range of para-diplomatic activities can be seen as part of a wider nation-building project.

WALES AND CATALONIA: THE SOCIO-CULTURAL CONTEXTS

This research focuses on a comparative analysis of the Wales and Catalonia destination brands using a communications perspective in order to explore the relationship between these brands and territorial identity. Wales and Catalonia are not single entities, they are both part of larger states (United Kingdom and Spain) and their respective capital cities of Cardiff and Barcelona have significant roles to play in Welsh and Catalan social, cultural and political life and in the branding strategies of Wales and Catalonia. The aim of the chapter is to: i) examine the extent to which both regions can be considered as brands built on culture; ii) explore the relationship between these two territory brands and their umbrella brands of the UK and Spain and their city brands of Cardiff and Barcelona. Wales and Catalonia were chosen as the case studies as both share many characteristics: both have languages and cultures which make them distinctive within their respective states, tourism is important to the economy of both and both have relatively newly established semi-autonomous governments (the Welsh Assembly was established in 1999 and the new Statute of Autonomy was passed in Spain in 2006): both are seeking to communicate the distinctive nature of their respective territories internationally.

Wales, Scotland, Northern Ireland and England form the UK. The structure of the UK tourism industry is rather complex and VisitBritain (established in 2003) exists to promote Great Britain overseas and to coordinate the marketing of England domestically. The powers to promote overseas tourism to Scotland and Wales was devolved to the Scottish and Wales Tourist Boards in mid-1990s (tourism in Northern Ireland was already devolved and the Northern Ireland Tourist Board had been created in 1948 under separate legislation) and on 1 April 2006, the Welsh Assembly abolished the Wales Tourist Board and transferred its staff and functions into the Assembly within which it now operates as Visitwales (www.visitbritain.com). Tourism is relatively more important to the Welsh economy than it is to the UK as a whole. It is worth £3 billion annually, accounts for seven per cent of its gross domestic product and employs nine per cent of the workforce, compared to five per cent across the whole of the UK (www.visitwales.com; www.visitbritain.com). Wales has a range of assets, which underpin its tourism appeal and its diverse natural environment (particularly its coastline and mountains) is the main factor in attracting UK and European visitors (WTB, 1994). Wales' other principal tourism asset is that it is a distinctive country with its own language and culture. At the present time, Wales is being separately and simultaneously branded in the UK and in its key overseas markets. The Welsh language and culture is being used by Visitwales (the tourism marketing arm of the Welsh Assembly Government) as a key marketing advantage in overseas markets where visitors are seeking a 'new', culturally diverse experience (WTB, 1994; Pritchard and Morgan, 1996; 1998). Conversely in the UK, it is the natural environment that forms the main basis of Wales' marketing appeals and consumers are gradually being 'introduced' to the possible attractions of Wales' distinctive culture and language in marketing activities (Pride, 2008).

To fully understand why these quite different strategies are being pursued it is important to place contemporary political, economic and investment strategies in their socio-historical context and this has been done extensively elsewhere. Pritchard and Morgan (2001) reviewed how the historical construction of Wales as a social and cultural landscape explains the pattern of its current tourism marketing and there is no further need to rehearse their arguments here. Wales was governmentally unified with England in the 1536 Act of Union but has since remained culturally distinct within the UK with the Welsh language being the most obvious symbol of its cultural distinctiveness. However, whilst Wales' distinctive culture and language have provided a crucial branding platform in its overseas markets for some time, it is only since Wales achieved devolved government in 1999 that they have begun to feature in Wales' domestic marketing to the rest of the UK. Thus, whilst it continues to pursue separate activities domestically and overseas, Visitwales is currently developing a domain or overarching brand that will eventually drive all its brand strategy, communication and positioning (Pride, 2008). This initiative is intended to bring together one positioning for the three key aspects of Wales as a place for: tourism; investment/business development; to live and work. The overarching positioning is united by one tone of voice, one logo and one common set of brand values. These are based on Wales as a country of original thinking and communicate the spirit of real, honest people and 'human' places, whilst conveying a sense of a country which has always challenged convention and authority. The brand values therefore are: honesty, integrity, originality and challenge; Wales is the 'real alternative'. This tourism branding strategy closely aligns with the wider activities of the Welsh Assembly Government, which Haf (2008) argues reflects the fact that Wales is building a new civil society, which seeks to incorporate a range of identities and has a profile at three key levels – within Wales itself, within the UK and within the European Union (Haf, 2008). Indeed, the Welsh Assembly Government's activities to raise Wales' international profile have accelerated year-on-year since devolution, particularly in the areas of economic development (trade and investment), cultural projects and tourism. Royales (2008) has identified the following as crucial to this: i) the key necessity to promote Wales overseas to attract investment and boost economic development; ii) the desire of the current Assembly government to finance cultural projects which project Wales onto the world stage (such as the Millennium Centre in Cardiff Bay); iii) the personal interest in such initiatives of Wales' First Minister Rhodri Morgan.

Interestingly, in contrast to the Catalonia experience, the attitude of the UK central government has been quite relaxed towards these initiatives by the Welsh Assembly Government (Royales, 2008). However, since the new Statute of Autonomy was passed in August 2006, Catalan nationalism has caused considerable controversy and division in Spain. This controversy was fuelled during the intense negotiations over the development of the new Statute of Autonomy, which is the prime institutional law of Catalonia. During the process (2004–06) there was considerable debate over the definition of Catalonia as a nation and the financial aspects of the settlement. The fact that Catalans wanted to be a nation created such controversy among Spanish citizens that many became highly critical of Catalan society and there were even popular campaigns to boycott Catalan products in the rest of Spain. Nevertheless, the current Catalonia brand was created in 2002 by the previous government, which was nationalist and centre-right. The current government decided not to change it, as brands need to have some durability if they are to succeed and at the same time, the current government also believes in creating a distinctive image for Catalonia based upon its culture.

METHODOLOGY

Analyses of visual material such as websites are highly problematic because issues of 'representation', 'interpretation' and 'sampling' are all highly contested in visual research and a number of scholars have writen extensively on the reading and analysis of visual texts (e.g. Jenks, 1995; Pink, 2001). The visual plays a crucial role in the production, practice and performance of tourism and visual culture and visual design has now emerged as an important area of tourism study (e.g. Crouch and Lubbren, 2003). Typically, researchers employ methodologies that utilise either semiotic or critical discourse analysis, approaches that both provide a critical framework for understanding how 'visual structures realize meaning [just] as linguistic structures do' (Kress and van Leeuwen 1996:2). Semiotic approaches allow the researcher to understand the mechanics or poetics of texts whilst critical discourse analysis is an interdisciplinary approach to the study of any text, which views language as a form of social practice and focuses on the ways social and political domination is reproduced by text and talk (Fairclough, 1995).

This study of visual material combines content analysis with critical discourse analysis. Content analysis has long been a particularly useful research tool as it is ideally suited to quantify and classify the content of tourism messages. In this case the official websites of Visitwales (www. visitwales.com) and Catalunya Turisme (www.turismedecatalunya.com) are analysed as the Internet and new information technologies play a key role in the communication of destinations and their brands. They are an important source of information, and also offer advertising, marketing and commercial applications. Moreover, they have interactive resources that provide services and attract the users' attention and from the communications perspective websites have been described as the future of marketing communications, because they have the potential both to provide high levels of information and to create virtual product experiences (Klein,

2003). Destination marketing organisation websites have two functions. First, to build brand image, and secondly, to obtain a direct response from users (Hollis, 2005). As Cho and Cheon (2005) state, websites have different missions in communication, namely, public relations, promotion, or advertising. For these reasons and the importance of Internet in the tourism sector, we decided to analyse destination brands through a content analysis of their websites.

The analyses of images and videos use codes, with the object of discovering the dominant message. Each photograph is seen as a polysemic construction with multiple meanings. In this research we have also analysed how the images represent what they want to symbolise. The second method of analysis used in the study is the analysis of social networks, using the Visone program. This represents graphically the relationship between the values associated with the brand. Visone, like other similar analytical programs, is designed to present data in a visual form. This particular program can analyse and display visual text in the form of a network of meanings. It is, therefore, particularly suitable for illustrating values and symbols which are associated with a brand. The Visone program is developing models and algorithms to integrate and advance the analysis and visualisation of social networks. Social network analysis is a methodological approach in the social sciences using graph-theory to describe, understand and explain social and other type of structures. The Visone software is an attempt to integrate analysis and visualisation of social networks in research (Brandes and Wagner, 2004). Consequently, most of the tool is about methods of drawing graphs specifically adapted to facilitate the exploration of visual data and here we use this program to investigate the relationships between the different place brands of the UK, Wales and Cardiff, and Spain, Catalonia and Barcelona.

THE RELATIONSHIPS BETWEEN THE BRANDS OF WALES AND CATALONIA

The first point to note in the comparison between the Wales and Catalonia brands is that neither of them are territorially based. Rather, they stem from the tourism agency or body that promotes these destinations, thus the website for Wales is that of Visitwales and for Catalonia it is Turisme de Catalunya or Catalunya Turisme. Although the word 'tourism' is sometimes omitted from the logotype, the brands are those of the above mentioned tourism agencies. This effectively creates a barrier to the development and dissemination of destination brands, which cannot belong to a single institution but to a whole community. Brand creation involves the participation and consensus of both public and private institutions, and the citizens themselves, who then make it their own. This is the reason why in the near future the Catalan Tourism Institution plans to create their own brand. Then, the Catalonia brand will not be an institutional brand, but a territorial one. The objective of Catalan Tourism Institution is to encourage the adoption of the Catalonia brand by all the key public and private tourism sector stakeholders.

The Wales website does give a brief explanation of which body the brand represents – the tourism department of the Welsh Assembly Government. In contrast, the Turisme de Catalunya website does not mention the institution itself. It does, however, provide information about the marketing and strategies employed by the institution, which the Wales website does not. The Turisme de Catalunya website also gives information about awards for the promotion of tourism, the most recent tourism campaign in Catalonia, the Strategic Plan for Tourism in Catalonia for 2005–10, and even includes a study on the image that current and potential tourists have of Catalonia. It is, therefore, the website of an institution about which it does not provide information, even though it gives details about many marketing and promotional activites carried out. In this sense, it is different from the Wales website. A graphic and symbolic analysis of the brands and logotypes reveals a similar approach in both cases. The logotypes of the Wales and Catalonia brands represent territorial identity, the flag and the country (Figure 7.1). In both cases, the design of the symbols derives from the countries' flags, which clearly reflect a national reality and identity.

The Visit Wales logotype is a red dragon, which is the Welsh flag. The *Y Ddraig Goch* dates back to the period when Wales was part of the Roman Empire. According to historian Carl Lofmark, it is more than likely that the red dragon was inherited from the Roman legion II (Augusta) stationed in Caerleon. The Catalan logotype is a modern interpretation of *La Senyera*, the Catalan flag. *La Senyera* symbolises bravery and the defence of Catalonia, based on a popular legend. It is curious that both Wales and Catalonia should choose the same strategy for their logotypes. Nevertheless, it is entirely coherent with the symbolism that brands generally attempt to create. Both Wales and Catalonia focus on their identities, but in different ways, although the purpose of the branding strategies are to differentiate Wales from the rest of the UK and Catalonia from Spain. In addition to the concepts of difference, originality and uniqueness, which both countries have in common, they also endeavour to convey a sense of identity. Both brands base their identity on their unique cultures, including language, history and cuisine and the highlighting of their culture is very much part of the tourism strategies of both Wales and Catalonia.

Logotype of Visit Wales

Flag of Wales

Logotype of Catalonia

Flag of Catalonia

Source: Visit Wales & Turisme de Catluyna.

Figure 7.1 The logotypes and flags of Wales and Catalonia

Indeed, the Wales Tourist Board (WTB), which was the forerunner of Visit Wales was created in 1969 to manage the country's marketing effort and was charged with protecting and enhancing the Welsh culture in all its activities – a commitment which was exclusive to Wales and not part of the remit of any other UK national tourist board. As its mission statement suggested, the WTB sought 'To sustain and promote the culture of Wales and the Welsh language' (WTB, 1994). Indeed, it recognised that 'The Welsh language and cultural traditions of Wales are vital to the future of Wales as a country. . . [and] in a tourism context' (WTB, 1994:91). Thus, the WTB committed itself to '. . . draw together all kinds of activities, cultural as well as historical, to create a strong image, especially abroad. . .. It is our aim to show the visitor that Wales is a bilingual country' (WTB, 1994).

Despite this common approach to branding, there are factors which differentiate the two brands. The Catalonia brand is currently more comprehensive than the Wales brand and it seeks associations with many more values and characteristics (Figure 7.2). For example, Catalonia associates itself with the idea of a region full of diversity and contrasts: seaside and mountains, avant-garde and traditional, adventure and relaxation, rural and cosmopolitan, modern and old, active and peaceful, sweet and savoury, serious and fun, leisure and work, continuity and innovation.

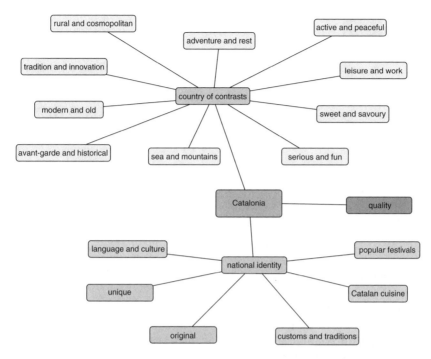

rural and cosmopolitan

active and peaceful

adventure and rest

tradition and innovation

leisure and work

country of contrasts

modern and old

sweet and savoury

avant-garde and historical

sea and mountains

serious and fun

Catalonia

quality

language and culture

popular festivals

national identity

unique

Catalan cuisine

original

customs and traditions

Source: Author's own.

Figure 7.2   Illustration of the Catalonia brand created using the Visone program

With these multiple aims, Catalonia seeks to demonstrate that it is a country of diversity and therefore suitable for everyone. But, in addition to these contrasts, it also seeks to identify itself with quality and the capacity of its people to engage with the rest of the world.

Wales, on the other hand, focuses on the single idea of differentiation from the rest of the UK, although it also seeks to be identified as a country of natural beauty (Figure 7.3), as is apparent in a video featuring its spectacular scenery. Various authors recommend focusing the brand on a single 'destination proposition'. For example, Pride (2004:162) argues that brands which opt for a single idea, are risking a lot but they are also the ones most likely to become powerful brands. Certainly, if the two main purposes of a brand are differentiation and identification (American Marketing Association), then these purposes will be achieved if the brands are based on single values rather than being shared by other brands. Attempts to represent many values or characteristics only lead

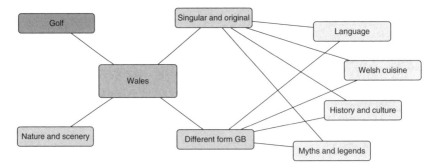

Source: Author's own.

Figure 7.3 Illustration of the Wales brand created using the Visone program

to dispersion and confusion and make it more difficult for consumers to assimilate the brand.

We now move on to compare Wales with its umbrella brand, the UK, and with its most recognisable internal brand, its capital city of Cardiff. We analyse the relationship between the three brands from the perspective of the values they convey, aspects of their identity and the effect that the umbrella brands have on internal brands. First, it is important to note that the VisitBritain website, which is responsible for UK destination marketing, has the Britain logotype at the top of the page and the Visit Britain logotype. In fact, it mixes them both so that they appear to be only one brand even though it is really only that of the institution. This is not the case with the official Wales website. Thus the UK brand appears in the top left-hand corner above a series of changing photographs representing the country and which show monuments, towns, scenery, cultural events, people and football.

It is apparent from the analysis of the website (Figure 7.4) that the UK brand is more comprehensive than that of Wales, which focuses exclusively on differentiating Wales from the rest of the UK. In contrast, VisitBritain is communicating values which are: unique, traditional, modern, refreshing, imaginative, multicultural and tolerant. In addition, the website presents the country as one of contrasts and diversity, which comprises nations with their own customs, cultures, scenery and traditions. The website analysed also provides more detailed information about the internal brands that, as an umbrella brand, it incorporates: i.e. London, England, Wales and Scotland (as we mentioned above tourism has long been devolved to Northern Ireland). We should also note,

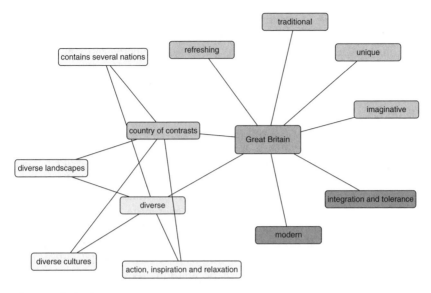

Source: Author's own.

Figure 7.4   Illustration of the Great Britain brand using the Visone program

however, the existence of a separate section of the website which is not directed at potential tourists but at stakeholders in the tourism industry. Here, information is provided about the organisation itself and there is a brief explanation of the UK brand, its objectives and the values it aims to convey. To access this information, registration is required. What is interesting is that the values described in this section are very different from those of the website analysed. Three terms sum up the essence of the brand: depth, heart and vitality.

Therefore, there is a discrepancy between the values that Visit Britain professes for the UK brand and those which appear on the official website for tourism. Despite this, if we examine the values conveyed through the website, we see that the UK brand has two features in common with the Wales brand. First, the UK is considered 'unique', in the same way that Wales is 'different'. Secondly, the UK is projected as a country of contrasts which includes countries with different customs, cultures and traditions. This corresponds perfectly with the sense of differentiation transmitted by Wales as one of these different countries. Thus, the UK does, in fact, act as a true umbrella brand for Wales. It embraces the Wales brand on its own website, highlights the theme of identity and refers to Wales as one of its internal brands. We may conclude, therefore, that the Wales and the UK brands complement each other perfectly and, although they do not choose to transmit the same values, there is full coherence between them.

The Cardiff brand also promotes a single value – that of a city transformed. This idea combines the past and tradition, based on the language, culture and historical figures, with the city's transformation into the modern, cosmopolitan centre it is today. Cardiff is now the locus of culture, commerce, power and political discourse in the newly devolved Wales and lies at the heart of the 'new' mythic geography of Wales being created as part of Wales' nation-building project (see Pritchard and Morgan, 2003). Cardiff is a new capital (created in 1955) and its status is subject to conflicting interpretations. Whereas London's and Edinburgh's claims to be capitals have never been disputed, Cardiff's claim chiefly rested on being the largest settlement in the country (Hague and Thomas, 1997). It played no significant role in the political history of Wales before the nineteenth century and has no special cultural or religious significance to the Welsh population. Its economic sphere of influence is also small by comparison with other capitals and it was never previously a financial or administration centre as historically Wales was never a coherent political entity. Cardiff's designation as capital was very much a political project, as have the subsequent actions taken to bolster this status (Thomas, 1992). Remaining a capital city for any length of time is always dependent on more than simply being designated such – it requires popular acknowledgment and acceptance. More often than not, a capital city will be expected to provide an appropriate symbol of the country of which it is capital. It need not be typical of that country but it must be worthy of its special designation (Thomas, 1992) and in Wales Cardiff has been significantly regenerated and redeveloped, especially in the area of Cardiff Bay, which is now home to the National Assembly for Wales.

The Cardiff brand is thus based on this image of change which the city wishes to highlight (Figure 7.5). In the last ten years, Cardiff has gone from being a run-down, impoverished industrial centre to become a modern, cosmopolitan city with a high level of culture and design, much like several other UK cities such as Manchester and Birmingham. This is a result of efforts by the UK and Welsh governments to provide investment, renovate the Cardiff Bay area and transform the city into a cultural, financial and leisure centre. Thus, the Cardiff brand perfectly reflects a transformed city which embraces both its traditional and cultural heritage and its modern and cosmopolitan character. Furthermore, it differentiates the city from others since it is based on a distinctive, real territorial aspect of its own. Finally, the Cardiff and Wales brands have one thing in common.

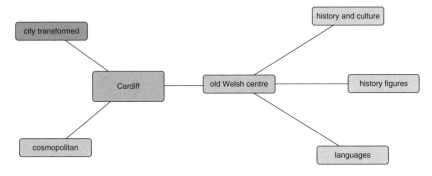

Source: Author's own.

Figure 7.5   Illustration of the Cardiff brand using the Visone program

They both share the predisposition to associate themselves with their own culture, language, history, legends and traditions.

Turning to Catalonia, we now proceed to analyse the Spain brand, through its website, and the Barcelona brand. We seek to explore the relationship between the values of these brands and establish the degree of fit between the umbrella brands and their internal brands. The '*Turismo de España*' website has a homepage which shows changing photographs at the top which depict different places of interest, such as *La Alhambra* in Granada and the city of Arts and Sciences in Valencia. However, in contrast to the other websites analysed in this chapter, it only contains the brand and the logotype of Spain, not those of the body responsible for promoting tourism. Nor does the name of that body appear, although it does contain the greeting '*Bienvenidos a España*' (Welcome to Spain). Therefore, the aim is to transmit the Spain brand and not to promote an institution of any kind.

Nevertheless, the website does not provide any explicit information about the brand, its symbols or its objectives. Neither is the Spain brand transmitted implicitly via text or images on the website. It is a very informative website which provides information about the different tourist destinations which come under the Spain brand and the most significant tourist facilities and attractions, namely: sun, cuisine, hospitality, heritage and nature. It is also an interactive website through which travel plans and reservations may be made. However, it does not, in any way, transmit the Spain brand nor its emotional values. The current logotype of the Spain brand, which dates from the 1980s, is an image of the sun painted by the artist Joan Miró. The logotype has traditionally been associated with the sun, the seaside, fun, *flamenco* and bullfighting. There has been a strong

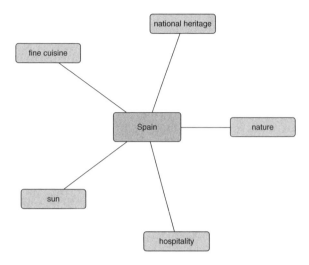

Source: Author's own.

Figure 7.6   Illustration of the Spain brand using the Visone program

link to the autonomous community of Andalusia, with its culture and traditions. However, as is often the case, the reality of Spain is different to the
stereotyped image that has been formed in the minds of many foreigners.
This may be why both public and private institutions have shown a keen
interest in changing this image in recent years. In fact, in 2003, '*Proyecto
Marca España*' (Project Spain Brand) was created precisely to build a new
brand and image for Spain. One which would transmit the modern-day
political, social and cultural reality of the country; a brand which would
not focus on only one of the many cultures that comprise Spain and that
together come under the umbrella brand.

So, the official tourism website of Spain contains the logotype and the
brand, but this brand is not associated with any symbolism, values or
culture (Figure 7.6). It is only associated with some minimal tourism facilities. This may be due to the fact that Spain is very culturally and socially
diverse and the Spain brand intends to act as an umbrella for all its territories without singling out a particular community, as it did before. It may
be that it prefers to focus on the functional and tangible elements which
are common to all of Spain's destinations: sun, cuisine, hospitality, heritage and nature. These are, however, very generic and do not distinguish
Spain from other countries or destinations.

Regardless of the reasons for the lack of a Spain brand which is comprehensive, embued with its own identity and differential characteristics, the

fact is that the new Spain brand is still in the early stages of development. This is recognised in the '*Plan de Turismo Español*' (Spanish Tourism Plan) 2008–12. One of the objectives of this plan is 'to strengthen the position of the Spain tourism brand in international markets by including among the brand's attributes the different Spanish products and destinations (. . .) It is considered necessary to continue working on the evaluation and enhancement of the tourism brand image. Therefore, certain creative elements must evolve, thus fomenting emotive aspects. . .' Below we describe the attributes that the Spain brand promotes through the website analysed.

Thus, there is a minimal relationship between the Catalonia and Spain brands regarding the focus on tangible resources since Catalonia also possesses these resources and therefore shares a common interest in them. In this sense, we might well say that the Spain brand really does perform the functions of an umbrella brand. On the other hand, the Spain brand does not identify with emotional, cultural or identity values. It, therefore, does not exploit the resources of emotional communication to popularise its brand and make it more attractive for consumers and potential consumers. Regarding the Barcelona internal brand, the analysis of the website shows that it is the most comprehensive brand as it explicitly associates numerous emotional values (Figure 7.7). These values are transmitted both in text form and through images and lend coherence to the whole website, including the typography, which is the same as that used for the logotype. Nevertheless, we should note that, as with the majority of the websites analysed, the logotype and the brand used are not those of Barcelona itself, but those of '*Barcelona Turisme*'. This is the institution that promotes tourism in the city and the logotype and brand appear at the top of the page above some changing photographs of Barcelona. In spite of this, the Barcelona brand intends to associate itself with many values of a functional, tangible and emotional nature, attaching more importance to some than others. These are the six values that appear in the photographs and the text in the upper half of the homepage and which may also be found in other parts of the website: The six values are:

- Mediterranean spirit. A city open to the sea. (Picture of beach scene.)
- Shopping Line. Stroll, shop and live. (Picture of a shopping street.)
- For all ages. A wide range of leisure activities and entertainment. (Picture of a family in a park.)
- Metropolis for meetings and incentives. Experience and prestige. (Picture of offices.)
- Capital of Modernism. Meeting point for art and culture. (Picture of the roof of Batlló House of Gaudí.)

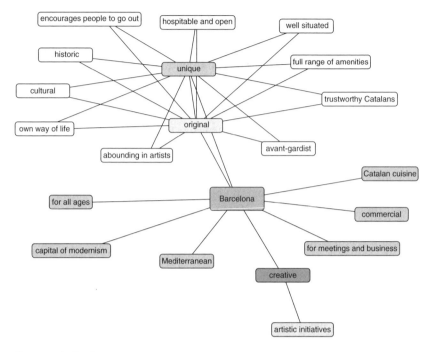

Source: Author's own.

Figure 7.7   Illustration of the Barcelona brand using the Visone program

- Capital of Catalan cuisine. Quality, tradition and state-of-the-art. (Picture of a food market.)

Thus, the emotional values with which the Barcelona brand is associated are transmitted not only via adjectives, as is the case with most destination websites, but also through enticing phrases and their corresponding photographs. This approach facilitates the transmission of the desired values. However, the city does not identify with these six values alone. Barcelona comprises many things that it wishes to convey. It is creative, original and unique, hospitable and open; a city which encourages people to go out, historical, cultural, avant-garde and abounding with artists, well situated and with its own way of life.

As may be seen, this is a very comprehensive brand and it is, therefore, difficult to identify the destination through any single idea or value. This in turn makes it difficult to create an image of the territory and to associate it with a particular concept, given that it transmits so many symbols and qualities. The website analysed does, however, transmit all these emotional values extremely well. There are significant links between the Barcelona brand and its umbrella brand 'Catalunya' despite the difficulty in integrating so many emotional values as is the case of Barcelona. Indeed, Barcelona and Catalonia share some of these values, which facilitates the dissemination of internal brands by the umbrella brand. Both Barcelona and Catalonia depict themselves as: unique, hospitable and open, avant-garde, historic and cultural and important gastronomic centres.

CONCLUSION

The first conclusion of the analysis of the websites is that there is considerable confusion between the destination brands and the brands of the tourism promotion institutions. The brand and the logotype are presented on the majority of the websites. However, the texts employed set out to associate values and symbols with destination brands. This causes confusion between brands and may lead to a destination marketing organisation's brand being confused with the territorial brand. In reality, if the tourism website does not display the territory or destination brand, but uses in its place the brand of the promotional agency, it may reflect the fact that the destination brand needs further development. A second conclusion is that the majority of the brands analysed are not single-focused, but attempt to associate themselves with a wide range of symbols and values. The attempt to reach the largest possible number of audiences using such a range of values only leads to ambiguity, dysfunctionality and difficulty in establishing a strong, single positioning and image for a brand. One of the limitations of destination brands lies in the complexity of combining a segmentation strategy with the creation of a single brand image. Brands target different audiences, whether they be citizens, investors or tourists. Since each audience has its own interests and needs, brands generally design differentiated marketing strategies for each one. It may, therefore, be a complicated, even contradictory, task to create different strategies and try to integrate them in a single brand position.

However, as Pride (2002) notes, 'the marketing strategies pursued must be imaginative, single minded and consistent. A challenger brand must be focused: challenger brands sacrifice activity in certain areas and are brave enough to overcommit in those areas where they believe they will make a real difference. Perhaps more than anything else challenger brands need to be idea centred, not consumer centred' (2002:161–2). With regard to the strategies used by the two main brands analysed in this study, Wales and Catalonia, it is to be noted that both of them are based on differentiation and cultural identity. The tourism strategies of the tourism agencies of Wales and Catalonia are closely aligned with political moves to promote Welsh and Catalan cultural identities in a climate where lifestyle and image are crucial determinants of inward investment. Indeed, it is interesting that recent research suggests that business decisions regarding investment and relocation are increasingly being made on 'soft factors' such as the culture and architecture of a place and less on the 'hard factors' of infrastructure and economy (Pride, 2008).

However, focus on the culture of a place in the context of a semi-autonomous region of a larger state may be problematic. Thus, the Wales brand conveys distinctiveness and an independent identity within the UK but this might offend non-Welsh people if they feel excluded from the Welsh identity and, therefore, prejudice the image that they form of the Wales brand. This in turn, may influence their decision-making as far as tourism and investment is concerned. This is what happened with the Catalonia brand in Spain during the period prior to the introduction of the Statute of Autonomy in 2006. The appeals for a separate identity and the attempts to make distinctions between Catalonia and the dominant culture led to a rejection by Spanish people of the Catalan culture and community. Thus, the image of Catalonia in the rest of the Spanish state suffered dramatically during this period and in fact, certain campaigns were initiated against Catalan products, such as the attempt to boycott *Cava* (sparkling wine).

We see then, that although the strategy for a brand based on a cultural identity should have a single focus, the brand must be transmitted in different ways and to different degrees depending on the target population, whether this be domestic or foreign. Similarly, those brands which communicate a specific cultural identity may discourage investment by companies from the country with which the brand seeks to distance itself. Factors such as cultural differences, different customs and traditions together with the use of a different language can influence an organisation's investment decisions. Wales and Catalonia are attempting to establish distinctions between themselves and their respective umbrella brands. How, then, can these umbrella brands incorporate their internal brands in a coherent way? The UK has an important role as an umbrella brand since it bases this brand on the diversity and the contrast of its various countries, their cultures and their landscapes. It presents itself as a country of integration and tolerance. Consequently, the claims to identity in Wales are acknowledged and integrated in the umbrella brand. What of the future for Wales the brand? There is clearly a greater drive for more distinctiveness since it achieved devolved governance in 1999. Moreover, in the last few years there has also been a significant increase in para-diplomacy as part of a nation-building project for Wales (Haf, 2008). In contrast, Spain does not associate itself with any emotional values and, therefore, does not share any such values with the Catalonia brand. It does share associations with a rich and varied cuisine but not any of the other attributes contained in the Catalonia brand. Although there is currently little integration with the umbrella brand of Spain and the relationship between both brands is uncomfortable at times, the future of the Catalonia brand will continue to be one of cultural distinction, communicating the territory through a nationalist view and basing on its differential features.

8. Branding Aalborg: building community or selling place?

Anette Therkelsen, Henrik Halkier and Ole B. Jensen

INTRODUCTION

This chapter explores the internal and external challenges to city branding in the case of the Danish mid-sized city of Aalborg. Like many other European cities, the city has faced a transition from industry and shipyard activities towards knowledge and service-oriented production. In the midst of such transition, policy makers, private stakeholders and local institutions are articulating new visions of the city's imagined future. Linked to such efforts is the municipality-led initiative of *Branding Aalborg*, a city branding campaign launched in 2004 and running to 2009.

The chapter investigates central actors and processes of the *Branding Aalborg* initiative to understand the possible tensions between branding the city internally to its inhabitants, business communities and institutions versus externally selling the city to foreign investors, employees and tourists. In parts of the place branding literature, these widely different markets are seen as mutually supporting, and both are the aims of place branding campaigns, as internal appreciation of the place is seen as a prerequisite for external attractiveness and external demand as reinforcing local pride and place satisfaction. Though it is clearly worthwhile studying the challenges involved in integrating the different needs and place perceptions of internal and external target groups into one brand, such effort would arguably gain from being preceded by a study of the strategic preferences and choices of place marketers including the priority given to internal and external target groups, as practitioners may obviously pursue different lines of reasoning than academics. Internal and external market orientation is closely related to the way in which practitioners understand place branding just as the priority given to various branding activities is a clear sign of their understanding of branding – whether branding is seen as primarily a communicative exercise focusing on developing an appealing communicative platform or a more holistic undertaking that views communication and product development as two mutually supporting processes. With inspiration from semiotics, these two choices are termed 'city of words' (symbolic representation) and 'city of stones' (physical place-making) respectively, and the extent to which a relationship is acknowledged between the two will form a central part of studying the strategic choices of selected place marketers in the city of Aalborg.

To bring forward the strategic challenges and issues facing city branding in the specific case of Aalborg, three central stakeholders are studied: the branding initiator and driver, the *Branding Aalborg* Secretariat, and two local stakeholders, the tourism organisation *VisitAalborg* and the regional investment organisation of *Invest in Denmark*. More specifically, the purpose of the chapter is to discuss the strategic approach to place branding of these three stakeholders in terms of market orientation and priority of branding activities, and on this basis establish whether consensus and ownership towards the branding initiative exist. This will be done by scrutinising the policy process surrounding the place branding initiative, as the different phases of and role distribution within the branding initiative will help establish whether the basis for a strong and viable place brand exists.

The chapter is structured in six parts. After the introduction follows a cross-disciplinary theoretical discussion, which scrutinises the strategic choices and processes behind place branding initiatives. Next the empirical material and methods employed in the study are outlined before the history, process and content of the *Branding Aalborg* initiative are presented. Next the analysis follows where explorations of the attitudes towards and interest in the branding efforts of three stakeholders are discussed by focusing in on two central strategic choices. In conclusion the chapter outlines the changing balance between external and internal orientations in the *Branding Aalborg* initiative as well as implications of different priority given to branding activities among the stakeholders studied.

THEORETICAL FRAMEWORK

A central assumption of this chapter is that in order to fully understand the phenomenon of place branding the three academic disciplines of marketing, urban studies and policy studies must be addressed, unlike the practice of much contemporary branding analysis which tends to focus on one or two of these disciplines. The analytical perspective that is brought forward holds that branding surely is about marketing and that marketing practices have to do with the articulation of policies within institutional networks. However, place branding strategies obviously also deals with real ways of organising space in order to bring forward particular ways of physically 'making place'. Hence the subsequent theoretical discussion draws on literature from these three theoretical disciplines in order to gain an understanding of two important strategic choices in place branding: market orientation and priority of branding activity on the one hand, and how these choices may be influenced by the policy-making processes involved in place branding initiatives on the other. Thus the present chapter seeks to contribute to a more interdisciplinary and critical approach to place branding that seems to be currently emerging (Morgan in Beràcs, 2006) and which works as a counterbalance to the mainly marketing oriented approach that has dominated for several years.

External and Internal Markets – a Strategic Choice in Place Branding

Along with Dinnie (2004), it seems fair to argue that place branding is very much a practitioner-led field and that academic research into this area is just starting to gain momentum. Inherent in this argument it is possible to find a central explanation as to why place branding literature to a high degree is characterised by a business approach that focuses on selling the place to external markets rather than building a community among internal stakeholders. The reasons given as to why it is important to enter into place branding activities revolves around global competition and the economic gains inherent in attracting a multitude of different place consumers (tourists, investors, companies and talented employees) as well as in using a place-tag in export marketing (e.g. Kotler et al., 1999; Morgan and Pritchard, 2001; Caldwell and Freire, 2004), and so an externally orientated explanatory framework dominates among the drivers behind place branding initiatives. An obvious limitation to such work on place branding rests with the fact that internal markets in the form of local residents, established companies and organisations are given limited attention, and hence the potential of place branding in (re)building a sense of belonging among existing place consumers and contributors is marginalised. And although questions of place identity are dealt with (e.g. Kotler et al., 1999), these are seen as a means of attracting external markets.

Within urban planning and urban sociology, the internal dimension of community building has traditionally been the central focus, but since the mid-1990s the attraction of capital, investments and tourists has also been on the agenda, mostly as an issue of enhancing urban competitiveness in the context of globalisation (Jessop, 1997; Krantz and Schaetzl, 1997; Hall and Hubbard, 1998; Rogerson, 1999; Greenberg, 2000; McCann, 2004). An obvious current example of this within the planning profession is the wide-spread attention to the 'creative class' (Florida, 2002): today most urban developers and mayors are much concerned with how to turn their cities into attractive arenas for capital-rich 'creatives', and, as will be evident, the case of Aalborg is no exception to this. Also like marketing, urban planning seems increasingly to have its attention turned towards selling places to attractive external markets.

Recently, contributions have, however, started to appear which seek to draw attention to both the internal and external challenges of place branding (Kavaratzis and Ashworth, 2005; Hankinson, 2007). In their alignment of place branding with corporate branding, Kavaratzis and Ashworth (2005) highlight that taking into consideration the diverse interests of various groups of locals, maintaining their continual consumption of the place and thereby facilitating identification with the place is a serious challenge to place branding initiatives, alongside the external market related challenges of attracting diverse markets to a given place. Also among consultancy firms, gaining local acceptance has been given more attention, leading for instance Olins to state that: 'Brands that involve whole populations need popular permission' (Olins, http://www.wolff-olins.com/oresund.htm). The basic tenet of a corporate place branding approach is that external and internal audiences are mutually supporting target groups in that place branding initiatives potentially can provide locals with a sense of belonging and local pride and this can be further strengthened by external demand for one's place. Conversely, being an integral part of the place product, satisfied local citizens are likely to function as ambassadors of the place to external target groups and thereby contribute to a differentiated profile. A salient question is, of course, how to combine the highly diverse interests of different groups of local citizens and simultaneously maintain a clear external message, as conventional marketing wisdom holds that in the global market place simple, uniform messages stand a better chance of grabbing the potential customer's attention than complex, disconnected ones (Therkelsen and Halkier, 2004). Combining local identity and external marketing related interests may hence prove a highly difficult strategy that practitioners may hesitate to engage in – in principle its benefits seem obvious, but in practice it may be difficult to persuade private sector representatives in the branding committee that time and money should be spent on long-term local place commitment instead of only on short-term monetary gains.

Symbolic Representation and Physical Place-making – Another Strategic Choice

Taking a further look at the place branding literature, it is obvious that a communication oriented understanding of place branding is widespread, which takes its lead from the often quoted brand definition of the American Marketing Association that characterises a brand as a name, sign, symbol or design that identifies and differentiates a product or service (Keller, 2003:3). Dealing with branding as a communicative exercise and marginal-ising its inherent physical dimensions is obviously also widespread among practitioners – numerous city brands consisting of a vision, 4–6 values and a communication toolbox testify to this.

Having realised the limited benefits of a purely communicative approach to branding, some marketing scholars argue in favour of a more holistic approach that considers branding a combination of customer-oriented communication strategies and leading-edge product quality (Morgan and Pritchard, 2001). Likewise Kotler et al.'s (1999) understanding of place marketing is based on a holistic approach in that their three-level figure of planning group, marketing factors and target markets shows that they consider various physical, product-related as well as communicative parameters as an integral whole of a place brand.

Whereas communication seems traditionally to have been given priority over product development in the marketing literature, a reverse priority of factors has been at stake within the field of urban planning that, quite nat-urally, has the urban built and social environment in focus. Increasingly urban planning seems, however, to be giving attention to discursive place-making. For instance Short (1999) takes his point of departure in the basic understanding of the difference between space and place and holds that: 'Space is turned into place through acts of discursive representation', (Short, 1999:38) which can be found in the naming and mapping of cities as well as in descriptions of cities emanating from place branding efforts. Likewise Shields' (1991) notion of 'social spatialisation' by means of which social agents appropriate spaces by inscribing them in a discursive order, points to an increasing interest in the communicative aspects of place branding. Such social spatialisation is rarely stable but rather expresses the contested nature of diverse urban representations, and urban brand-ing practices of contemporary cities must be understood as 'selective story telling' (Jensen, 2005) by which social agents appropriate space by inscrib-ing certain logic in space – both symbolically through logos, slogans and the like, but also materially through construction of buildings, infrastruc-tures and landmarks. Hence in an urban planning context, a separation of the symbolic and the material should only be understood as an abstrac-tion, as no place branding strategy can be made without a spatial referent and therefore the importance of understanding the relationship between the narrative and its place-bound context is of great importance (Eckstein and Throgmorton, 2003; Jensen, 2007).

It seems, however, that branding agencies and stakeholders as well as marketing scholars are generally less aware of the physical dimension of the branding exercise. On the one hand, physical changes are often as important as mental images showing that a city really is changing, and branding is often most powerful when it is linked into and coordinated with physical transformation processes and urban (re)development initiatives. Yet on the other hand, it is also stressed that although the link between physical urban transformation and branding needs to reflect local assets and characteristics, it is necessary to think beyond the city's borders because cities need to find their position within the wider regional/national/global context. Thus interventions into cities are always embedded within a particular representational logic, which originates from social agents who pursue certain normative ideas and rationales.

By acknowledging that an important relationship exists between symbolic representation and physical place-making, a central prerequisite for understanding the complexity of place branding is established, and also why place branding at times fails due to the absence of linkage between words and place. With inspiration from semiotics, the terms 'city of words' (sign) and 'city of stones' (object) are coined with the purpose of offering a framework for analysing their interrelationship as well as their dependence on the market. Hence in a Peircean sense (Peirce, 1978) 'city of words' is the sign that stands for its object 'city of stones' which necessitates a close relationship between the two. Simultaneously, the sign addresses a market that interprets that sign (interpretant) on the basis of various socio-cultural conventions as well as experiences with the object, and therefore, depending on whether external or internal target groups are addressed, the resultant interpretation will naturally differ. So as Figure 8.1 illustrates, strategic choices in relation to market focus and branding activities are closely intertwined and will be influenced by a number of forces among which are the policy process of the place branding initiative.

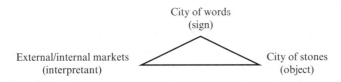

Source: Author's own.

Figure 8.1   The place branding triad

Strategic Choices and Policy Processes

Place branding has not been studied extensively from a policy analysis perspective, though a few scholars have contributed with theoretical and empirical studies that give attention to the politics of place branding (Ooi, 2004; Therkelsen and Halkier, 2008). Rather than accounting for existing literature, this section discusses how role distribution and different phases in a place branding process may influence strategic choices by applying an institutionalist approach to public policy (Halkier, 2006; Therkelsen and Halkier, 2008) and a traditional distinction between key phases in policy-making (Hogwood and Gunn, 1986). A place brand is inherently territorial and the legitimate representative of any territory is generally the corresponding level of government, in the case of city branding the role of local government and elected local politicians is likely to be prominent in the *agenda setting phase*. In the *design phase* the brand board will primarily be involved in liaising with a wide variety of stakeholders, many of which will not only be conveyers of their respective interpretation of the essence of the place but also have well-defined interests in making sure that their own interpretations are taken into account because they are seen as being beneficial in relation to their particular areas of activities. In the *implementation phase* the centre of gravity shifts towards the relationship between the board and its branding activities on the one hand, and the external and internal target groups on the other. Apart from the heterogeneous nature of both external and internal target groups, it is also worth noting that the internal audience is made up of the same local stakeholders that were more or less directly involved in the design process, and the likelihood of branding activities being adjusted to suit prominent local actors would seem to be a very real one indeed.

   Consequently, the case study of *Branding Aalborg* will take its point of departure in the place branding process model (Figure 8.2) which holds that in the agenda setting and design phases, the ideal-type process of place branding is characterised by a close interplay of branding stakeholders that represent public, private enterprise and private citizen interests. Moreover, in the design phase due attention is given to both the maintenance of internal markets and the attraction of new lucrative external markets. And in the implementation of the city brand, close links are ideally to exist between the communicative platform and physical place-making (including milestone events) so that the 'city of words' and the 'city of stones' stand out as an integrated whole.

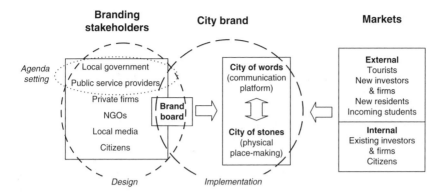

Source: Author's own.

Figure 8.2   Place branding actors and processes

EMPIRICAL MATERIAL AND METHODS

The empirical methodology applied is a combination of qualitative interviews, website analysis and document studies. The latter includes media coverage and debate of the city branding efforts in the local newspaper, *Nordjyske*, particularly in the period November to December 2004 when the campaign was launched.

Interviews were undertaken with the *Branding Aalborg* secretariat and *Invest in Denmark, Aalborg* in May 2007 to gain insight into the strategic choices made in the campaign and evaluation of these by both actors. The interviews were conducted according to the principles of the semi-structured qualitative interviews (Kvale, 1996) in which priority was given to letting the respondent speak freely on themes pre-defined by the researchers as well as making room for unforeseen themes to appear. Contact was also established with the third stakeholder, the local tourism organisation, *VisitAalborg*, to set up an interview, but this was declined with reference to lack of time and more competent informants at the branding secretariat. Nonetheless, some interesting information was conveyed via e-mail correspondence and in combination with a study of their web-based market communication and single internal trade documents, an impression of *VisitAalborg*'s relationship to the Aalborg brand manifests itself. Though no generalisations on stakeholder evaluations of the *Branding Aalborg* campaign can be made on the present empirical basis, the three stakeholders studied constitute central players in the city branding initiative and so a number of potentials and problems of the campaign are established which are also of a more general relevance for understanding place branding efforts.

BRANDING AALBORG: HISTORY, PROCESS AND CONTENT

The City of Aalborg owes its existence to historical developments of mobility and transport, situated by the Limfjord at the intersection of transport corridors between Norway to the north, Germany to the south, the North Sea to the west and Sweden and the capital of Copenhagen to the east. From the 1960s Aalborg and the surrounding region of North Jutland have been perceived as a peripheral part of Denmark, not only geographically far removed from Copenhagen but also with an increasingly outdated economic structure which combined a low level of industrialisation in outlying parts of the region with a predominance of traditional industries in Aalborg (shipyards, tobacco, hard spirits, concrete). With the growing problems experienced by traditional industries, high levels of unemployment became a chronic feature, and the city and region came to typify Danish-style industrial decline. From the late 1980s onwards this rather gloomy picture was, however, gradually modified, especially through the emergence of a cluster of new industries in telecommunications and related IT-areas, and the combined presence of innovative firms, a university with a strong engineering faculty and the availability of a large pool of highly trained graduates has attracted a good deal of major multinationals during the last decade (Teknologisk Institut, 2000). In short, Aalborg and North Jutland are not only facing challenges with regard to economic modernisation, but also in terms of image where the legacy of the industrial past is often perceived to overshadow more recent developments. Unsurprisingly, this has resulted in economic development initiatives, new forms of urban planning (Nordjyllands Amt, 2003; Aalborg Kommune, 2005a; 2005b; 2005c; Region Nordjylland Vækstforum, 2007) and attempts to resituate Aalborg on mental maps in Denmark and beyond, the latter of which place branding has formed a central part.

As shown in Table 8.1, the idea of *Branding Aalborg* was conceived in 1998 and it is possible to set up a timeline of events relating to the branding process (also Jensen, 2005) that is structured according to the dimensions of agenda setting, brand design and implementation, with the implementation phase divided into two rounds reflecting a change in strategy taking place in 2006 towards a more exclusive focus on communication efforts. The *Branding Aalborg* initiative is administered by the Branding Secretariat, which is placed directly under the Lord Mayor's Office. Thus,

Table 8.1 Time line for Branding Aalborg

Agenda setting	• *1998*: Genesis of the idea of *Branding Aalborg* (Lord Mayor)
	• *May 1999*: Delegation from Aalborg Municipality meets with Wally Olins
	• *August 1999*: Conference in Aalborg on 'Vision for the future'
Brand design	• *2000*: Preparatory meetings
	• *Primo 2001*: Working group starts planning
	• *Rest of 2001*: Steering committee established (broad variety of local stakeholders)
	• *2002*: Exploratory investigation by research institute and working group activity
	• *Spring 2003*: Steering committee's brand proposal drafted. Qualitative analysis of 'city product'
	• *November 2003*: City Council approves *Branding Aalborg*. The project put up for EU tender
	• *June 2004*: 15 proposals evaluated by an assessment committee
	• *August 2004*: A regionally based company, *Dafolo Marketing*, wins the bid
Implementation, first round	• *November 2004*: Winning campaign proposal presented for City Council and at press conference
	• *November 24 2004*: Official kick-off presentation of the *Branding Aalborg* campaign
	• *2004–9*: Municipality allocates 1 mill. DKR per year for the branding campaign. Brand board works on attracting local sponsors
	• *December 2004*: Action plan for 2005
	• *Spring 2005*: Search for two pilot firms to implement the branding campaign
	• *July–August 2005*: Scenario processes with 8 stakeholder groups
	• *August 2005*: Exhibition on Che Guevara's photography (*Che a life*) resulting in considerable domestic and foreign publicity
	• *November 2005*: The city website, Aalborg.dk, is send for public tender
	• *January 2006*: The local newspaper and tv-station, *Nordjyske Medier*, wins the bid
Implementation, second round	• *June 2006*: Journalist hired to create stories within the *Branding Aalborg* framework
	• *December 31 2006*: Launching of the Aalborg.dk website

Table 8.1   (continued)

	• *Primo 2007*: New communication strategy focused on exposing the brand in national media
	• *Primo 2007*: New website, www.aalborg.dk, and change of logo to contain aalborg.dk
	• *Medium 2007*: 3 working groups on marketing, event planning and logos/manual

Source: Author's own.

Figure 8.3   Branding Aalborg – *logo and merchandise*

there is a fair distance in both institutional as well as in professional terms from those in control of the city branding initiative and those city planners responsible for the 'city of stone'. The Technical Department which hosts the city planners has a number of initiatives in relation to the city's urban renovation schemes including the much debated harbour front development. However, they have not had much direct connection (or influence) on the *Branding Aalborg* initiatives which is seen as much more of a strategic exercise hosted in the Mayor's office.

'Aalborg – seize the world' has been chosen as the slogan for the campaign (Aalborg Kommune, 2005c) accompanied by a globe-shaped logo (see Figure 8.3), and both logo and slogan met a fair amount of critique in the public debate in relation to the abstractness of the graphic representation and generic nature of the slogan. This illustrates that parallel to several other cases, issues of local identification followed in the wake of the launching of the *Branding Aalborg* campaign.

Four values are identified that supposedly are quintessential to the identity of Aalborg: first of all, the notion of 'diversity' shows the city as one of opposites – small and yet globally connected, the rural countryside and the city core, peaceful enclaves and upbeat entertainment districts – which articulates an understanding of the local identity as being polychrome and diverse. Conversely it might also be read as an act of indecisiveness and might trigger the above-mentioned negative local reactions to generic and empty categories. Secondly, 'wide prospect' hints at not only open-mindedness and inclusiveness, but also the geographical region in which the city is located. Thus, there is a conflation in the discourse as it both refers to norms and place. For generations there has been a public notion of North Jutland as being special in terms of its blue sky and its wide horizons. Here the branding discourse taps into some of the folkways that could pave the way for a positive frame of identification. Thirdly, 'teamwork' draws on local self-perception of being strong and peripheral. Accordingly, since the region always has been on the margins, a particular culture of collaboration and cooperation has developed, though teamwork seems hard to understand as something uniquely belonging to Aalborg, and hence the discourse taps into more empty and generic concepts that void local specificity and identity. Finally, 'drive' again articulates the peripheral identity of the national underdog, however with a twist as references to the merchant history of the city depicts a place of high performance and activity. This is, furthermore, articulated against the capital city of Copenhagen, as Aalborg is said to be a 'counterpart to Copenhagen' (Aalborg Kommune, 2005c), which clearly goes to illustrate the underdog complex and self-perception in the region. The four values merge into a vision that reads:

> Aalborg wants to be a contrast to the traditional city: a bigger heart in a smaller space with wider prospects. We will cultivate the contrasts and create space for diversity. Seize the world and through knowledge, teamwork and drive, secure the framework for a life in development (Aalborg Kommune, 2005c).

Clearly, the vision highlights the underdog issue detectable in the values in that being a contrast to the traditional city is a rather negative branding practice that does not point forward in any particular direction. Knowing what one does not want to be, can obviously be an advantage, but in the context of branding a more positive attitude towards one's own assets and less of a critique of 'the other' might be a more subtle and effective tactic.

All in all, the values, the vision, and the logo do seem to expose some degree of coherence. In particular the elements articulating the global-local nexus and the importance of Aalborg as outward looking work especially well. What works less convincingly is the widespread use of generic terms and descriptions of what should have been the identity-building place-specifics of Aalborg. Moreover, the negative labelling of 'others' as a way of promoting oneself does not seem to be in accordance with the cultural climate favouring tolerance and inclusion.

ANALYSIS

On the basis of the case outline, the analysis will centre on the strategic choices inherent in the branding campaign and evaluations of these by the various stakeholders, just as the policy process characterising the branding initiative will be scrutinised to identify explanations of choices, evaluations and possibly diverting preferences.

Branding Aalborg Secretariat – Strategic Choices and Evaluation of Own Efforts

The head of the branding secretariat is, as might be expected, very positive towards the branding efforts and sees an increasingly acceptance of the initiative in the wider public:

> No matter if there is a speech made or if it is the launching of a big project, people seem to have gotten *Aalborg seize the world* into their everyday life and many use the values when they are marketing a product . . . we meet much more positive attitudes today . . . people start showing more and more ownership of *Aalborg Seize the world* (Head of *Branding Aalborg* secretariat, personal interview 14 May 2007).

According to the branding secretariat, the slow acceptance of the logo, the vision and the values resembles an 'incubation time' for the campaign, and so gradually the brand has sunk in and increasing ownership towards the brand is detectable among stakeholders. The secretariat, however, also acknowledges one major obstacle that has not been overcome and which seems to run counter to the positive evaluation of the broad brand ownership expressed above: the strategy of persuading two private companies to use the *Branding Aalborg* logos and merchandise in their own company specific marketing has not been accomplished, just as engaging the overall business community in general marketing activities has not been achieved. According to the branding secretariat there seems to be a duality in the perception of the business community in that they do appreciate the branding activities but only want to sponsor specific events and so matching funding from the business community has not been obtained. Hence brand ownership in the business community may not be as whole-hearted as initially expressed by the branding secretariat.

As mentioned in the theoretical framework, strategic choices on internal and/or external markets are salient but also hugely complex in place branding efforts, and the case of *Branding Aalborg* aptly illustrates this. Though the agenda of the branding initiative was set by the municipality, and not least the Lord Mayor (Table 8.1), the initial top-down approach was quite soon, in the design phase, supplemented by inputs from below as working groups, dialogue groups and not least the steering committee consisted of a broad cross-section of local stakeholders within politics, business, culture, education and public administration. Hence at the outset *Branding Aalborg* was meant both to sell place in the sense of capturing tourism, investment and profiling the local businesses as many of the stakeholders involved represented these interests, and to build community as the broad inclusion in articulating the brand vision and values bore witness to an aspiration to explore the identity of Aalborg from a variety of perspectives and ultimately to contribute to strengthening local belonging. Entering into the implementation phases, external markets seem, however, to have gained increasingly more attention at the expense of internal markets, which, in light of a limited budget, might be a consequence of a need to attract more funding from private companies that naturally are oriented towards profit-generating external markets. This is not, however, a strategy that the branding secretariat admits to be pursuing in that they see themselves as catering for both target groups.

Turning to the priority given to symbolic representation and physical place-making, it appears that main attention is allocated to formulating and later to refining an appealing communication platform, whereas far less attention seems to be given to integrating the branding campaign in the urban modernisation projects of the city, which other departments of the municipality are in charge of, creating new cultural attractions and setting up recurrent events. Asked directly about how they deal with 'the physical' in the *Branding Aalborg* initiative, the branding secretariat mostly think about it in relation to representation of space. Thus the specific locations for the photos used are all local places and as such they find that the physical Aalborg is well represented in the branding material. Moreover, the branding secretariat works strategically with the location of specific events in the city, for example in getting a number of different squares in the city into play when events are taking place. Nonetheless, 'city of words' takes priority over 'city of stones', thereby demonstrating a one-sided rather than holistic approach to place branding that may be problematic in terms of both internal and external market appeal as physical evidence of glorifying discourse is central to maintain attractive markets.

All in all, the branding secretariat seems content with the progress made so far by the branding campaign, but two major challenges also appear to have emerged: on the one hand, a shift from an inclusive place branding strategy where internal and external target groups are seen as mutually supporting and equally important, towards a externally oriented place marketing strategy which is less concerned with local support and more with immediate economic gains; and on the other hand, the fact that awareness of the importance of place does not seem to be very well articulated within the *Branding Aalborg* initiative. It is, however, necessary to look beyond the evaluation of the branding secretariat for a more comprehensive understanding of the branding initiative, as legitimisation of own actions, and with that its very existence, will naturally inflict upon their evaluation. Subsequently, the perceptions and evaluations of two potential stakeholders in the branding process will be accounted for.

Branding Aalborg in View of Tourism Interests

The local tourism organisation, *VisitAalborg*, has been part of the design phase and particularly the implementation phases of the *Branding Aalborg* initiative. In the design phase the tourism organisation was represented in one of the eight selected stakeholder groups that gave input to the preliminary branding platform, and later when the brand board was constituted, the director of *VisitAalborg* became one of the ten members of the board. Hence in relation to the continual revision of strategies as well as concrete initiatives, this organisation has ostensibly been a key player and a driving force behind the branding initiative.

In an e-mail correspondence, the director of *VisitAalborg* expressed a very positive attitude towards the *Branding Aalborg* initiative, which he terms a constructive process that has resulted in several good initiatives. 'In the tourism sector we have found great benefit in the branding initiative which encompasses a wide range of initiatives, which we have the possibility of using for tourism purposes' (Director of *VisitAalborg*, e-mail 30 May 2007).

Given its business area, *VisitAalborg* is likely to focus on attracting tourist markets, and there is nothing in the statements and actions on the part of *VisitAalborg* that suggests otherwise. One might, however, argue that a public tourism organisation should also be concerned with strengthening local identity and community building as this is part and parcel of the tourism product. Events and exhibitions that have been attracted to the city on the initiative of the brand board are subsequently highlighted and these are seen as a means to establish an identity of Aalborg as a place where things happen. Also efforts to coordinate and market cultural events via a common internet website are seen as useful for tourism purposes and with that for *VisitAalborg*.

Turning the attention towards *VisitAalborg*'s customer-directed website (www.visitaalborg.com), the absence of the Aalborg brand is, however, striking. Neither the colourful globe-shaped logo nor the slogan *Aalborg – seize the world* appears on their website, instead a different logo, that of the national tourism organisation, *VisitDenmark*, appears, which consists of a

Danish flag shaped like a heart and followed by the word 'Aalborg' – the latter of course identifying the local destination. Clearly brand affiliation with Danish tourism, more specifically the *Branding Denmark* strategy, materialises, which also manifests itself in the layout of the website in general as well as a similar naming of the organisations (*VisitAalborg* and *VisitDenmark* respectively). Hence in selling Aalborg as a place for tourism purposes, no usefulness is found in the communicative tools of *Branding Aalborg*, whereas mileage appears to be found in a national, purely tourism-oriented branding strategy. Whether the reason for this refusal to use the local communication platform should be found in the rather generic values and vision of the Aalborg brand is hard to determine, but given the equally general nature of the national tourism brand this is hardly the case. Judging from the quote above, *VisitAalborg*, however, finds the concrete events and exhibitions that emanate from the local branding strategy beneficial as they provide the tourism organisation with a richer portfolio of experience offers to market to potential and present guests, i.e. specific benefits relating to the functional core tasks of this tourism promotion body. Hence physical place-making (city of stones) is rated as a valuable part of the *Branding Aalborg* initiative. However simultaneously it appears as if lip service is being paid to the importance of the brand as the external communication practice of *VisitAalborg* does not correspond with their stated positive evaluation of *Branding Aalborg*.

Whereas the external, customer-oriented marketing of *VisitAalborg* bears no traces of the Aalborg brand, an internal trade manual and a presentation leaflet (VisitAalborg, 2005; VisitAalborg, 2006) flag the national tourism logo as well as the *Branding Aalborg* logo. This could indicate that the Aalborg brand is perceived as a brand for internal branding purposes, however, as the logo and slogan are relegated to a secondary position on the back cover and on the colophon, this does not really seem to be the case either. Furthermore, when consulting the presentation leaflet (VisitAalborg, 2006) on the paragraph concerning major partners of cooperation, no mention of the *Branding Aalborg* organisation is made, only regional and national tourism organisations are identified, and so it seems safe to conclude that neither for external nor for internal purposes is the Aalborg brand considered an important branding tool for *VisitAalborg*. In other words, the 'city of words' offered by *Branding Aalborg* seemingly has no usefulness to the tourism organisation.

The ownership towards the Aalborg brand displayed by this stakeholder may at best be termed ambiguous, and in view of the fact that *VisitAalborg* represents a stakeholder that has been an integral part of the branding process due to their long-term brand board membership, their communicative actions seem to endanger the credibility and viability of the city branding campaign both in relation to other real and potential stakeholders in the branding initiative as well as to external and internal markets for the campaign. This also constitutes a critical note to the branding literature at large in that early integration in the branding process does not automatically lead to stakeholders developing ownership for the brand.

Branding Aalborg for Inward Investment

Having analysed an organisation that at least on paper, is internal to the *Branding Aalborg* initiative, attention is now turned towards *Invest in Denmark, Aalborg*, which has stood outside the agenda setting, design as well as implementation of the branding initiative, but which potentially could be among future branding stakeholders. The inward investment organisation has recently developed from being a regionally sponsored body to being a regional office of the national promotional organisation, *Invest in Denmark*, and activities are now closely integrated both with regard to promotion – in effect a separate North Jutland website has ceased to exist – and for handling of individual investment cases (*Invest in Denmark, Aalborg*, personal interview, 14 May 2007).

The branding implications of this at the regional/local level are dual. The involvement of IDK in general forms of place branding at the subnational level remains limited: while the previous regional website did allow for some profiling of North Jutland as a whole, the previous regionally sponsored body could not engage closely with e.g. the *Branding Aalborg* initiative because it would be politically unacceptable to its regional government sponsors to be seen to focus too much on particular localities. And in the current situation, the importance of local promotional efforts would seem to be that IDK uses their materials as part of the information packages provided for prospective investors in connection with site visits (*Invest in Denmark, Aalborg*, personal interview, 14 May 2007). Not surprisingly, IDK is directing its attention towards external markets of prospective investors in relation to which a city branding initiative like *Branding Aalborg* can function as a source of local information. This, furthermore, indicates that the 'city of words' of the branding campaign is appreciated for the information it provides, regardless of the bias which is naturally inherent in such promotional discourses, though it is also clear that organisational structures restricts IDK from applying the city branding campaign in their own marketing efforts. In relation to 'city of stone' it, moreover, appears that a specific kind of place brand for North Jutland revolving around the presence of a strong ICT cluster in mobile communication clearly helps to raise the international profile of the region and city for investment purposes (*Invest in Denmark, Aalborg*, personal interview, 14 May 2007), and hence IDK see themselves as benefiting from physical place-making that supports the functional core tasks of their organisation.

CONCLUSION

The unfolding of events in the *Branding Aalborg* case is very much a story about a city wanting it all but in the course of events being forced to make strategic choices that only partly reflect the preferences of its stakeholders. At the outset *Branding Aalborg* was meant not only to sell place in the sense of capturing new attractive markets, because the initial phases of agenda setting and design clearly had the ambition of exploring the identity of the city and hence contributing to community building. Pressure from business stakeholders may be the reason for a change in strategy in the implementation phases, and clearly among the stakeholders studied in the present chapter there seems to be no contrasting views on the overall targeting of a place branding campaign, as selling place is clearly prioritised by all parties, and building community is relegated to a secondary position in the case of the branding secretariat and a non-existing position in the case of the tourism organisation and the inward investment body.

Differences in both evaluation of the concrete campaign and in the priority given to symbolic representation and physical place-making seem to be the reasons for disagreement. The branding secretariat is overwhelmingly positive towards the present state of the branding initiative, stating that increasing acceptance and usage of the brand is occurring among stakeholders. This stands in sharp contrast to the far more nationally oriented branding choices of two stakeholders studied here: the local tourism organisation has chosen to opt for a national tourism branding campaign, whereas the inward investment body being restricted by a centralised organisational structure has limited possibility for entering actively into a local branding campaign. Hence the 'city of words' is not seen as beneficial by the former and not possible by the latter to buy into actively. But interestingly, the 'city of stones' seems to be rated higher by the two stakeholders, albeit from quite different perspectives, in that the tourism organisation values the cultural events that *Branding Aalborg* initiates, and *Invest in Denmark, Aalborg* strongly supports any initiative to strengthen the ICT cluster, and so in both cases urban developments relating to the functional core tasks of the organisations are appreciated. The branding secretariat, however, has its prime attention directed at refining the communication platform at the expense of physical place-making, and so they seem to be poorly tuned into what can make at least these particular stakeholders actively join a branding initiative. It is worth considering whether any mileage would be gained by the local tourism organisation from combining the local and the national place branding initiative, as they, as opposed to the inwards investment organisation, have sole control of their marketing strategies. Apart from confusion in the visual communication (logo, layout and design), it is, however, likely that conveying a clear message about the place on the basis of two branding visions and value sets will be highly challenging just as the balancing act between a sector specific (the national brand) and a cross-sector brand (the local brand) may be difficult to master. This all in all leaves a combined national and local branding strategy a less obvious course of action for the local tourism organisation.

In more general terms, the present study would seem to indicate that sector-oriented organisations representing private interests are more oriented towards physical place-making (i.e. concrete offers for their potential customers) than towards symbolic representation aimed at enhancing the general image of the place, whereas public branding organisations seem more focused on symbolics. The viability of this contention would be interesting to study further in other empirical contexts.

In terms of cooperation within the local government, a lack of coordination between different local government branches, the Lord Mayor's Office that hosts the Branding Secretariat and the Technical Department responsible for urban renovation, might also be suspected to have led to a sub-optimal process and perhaps even a lack of synergy. This is, indeed, an illustrative feature of the general point made in this chapter: not only would academic branding analysis prosper from a linkage between the policy, communication and geographical analysis and theories, the actual branding practice also mirrors this lack of communication and understanding between the material city and the representations hereof. It is hence argued that the proposed 'bridging' between policy, communication and urban studies would be of value also in the way municipalities and cities approach city branding.

Furthermore, a central issue now for the *Branding Aalborg* initiative would be if the heavy leaning towards the selling-place dimension eventually makes it possible to re-address the building community theme or whether this is a lost opportunity. At least it seems clear that the shift in strategy has led to a new focus on the external branding and consequently refinement of the communication platform. Also the move towards the external challenges might suggest that initiating a public and inclusive process aiming at unfolding a wider discussion of locally embedded values and community identity might take more than what *Branding Aalborg* has been allocated. This seems like a call for realism, but it also suggests a branding process that has pointed less towards building community and thus ultimately missed some of the potentials articulated at the outset. There are two principally very different interpretations of this: on the one hand imagining community and articulating homogenous values may be much more difficult than the *Branding Aalborg* initiators had thought. This interpretation suggests that *Branding Aalborg* was too ambitious. On the other hand, one could stipulate that the building-community component was always just around to provide legitimacy, and that most of the agents and stakeholders involved, and certainly the ones studied here, primarily had the selling paradigm in mind. Such an interpretation would clearly be less acceptable to proponents of the original, ideal-type, holistic ambitions for *Branding Aalborg*, but the relatively limited time and money invested would seem to indicate that from the outset *Branding Aalborg* came closer to an conventional place marketing activity than to a process of community building. This is not to suggest that selling place is a problematic strategy on its own, but what seems less fortunate, however, is the attempt to imprint the public debate in the up-start with the impression that *Branding Aalborg* would function as a collaborative identity-building platform inclusive of citizens from all walks of life.

It might be that place branding initiatives on a broader scale are characterised by ambitions of building community as well as selling place, but in the face of economic reality, local community resistance or indifference and broad stakeholder involvement they end up being conventional place marketing initiatives. Also in this respect further studies will show whether the *Branding Aalborg* case is typical for place-branding initiatives in Europe and beyond.

INTERVIEWS

Jørn Bang Andersen, Marketing Manager, *Invest in Denmark* headquarters in Copenhagen (10.8.05)

Tine Hartmann Nielsen, Regional Project Manager with *Invest in Denmark, Aalborg* (14.5.07)

Maria Hilligsøe Stubberup, Regional Project Manager with *Invest in Denmark, Aalborg*, previously with *North Denmark* Invest (14.5.07)

Eva Beim Wind, Regional Cooperation Manager with *Invest in Denmark, Aalborg* (14.5.07)

Anni G. Walter, Head of *Branding Aalborg* Secretariat, personal interview (14.05.07)

9. Mind the gap: reputation, identity and regeneration in post-industrial cities

Myfanwy Trueman, Nelarine Cornelius, Mirza Mohammed Ali Baig and Joyce Liddle

INTRODUCTION

A multi-ethnic society in a post-industrial city, that has experienced society meltdown and riots, will face the stark reality of a damaged business community and poor image. Over a decade ago Porter (1995: 57) observed the need for inner cities to take advantage not only of their strategic location, local market demand and integration with regional clusters, but also, and most importantly their human resources; warning of the negative consequences if local communities were not involved in regeneration initiatives. More recently Amin (2006) notes that the challenge for city planners is to 'negotiate class, gender, and ethnic or racial differences placed in close proximity'. In other words managing the complexity of a city's human resources is far from easy, but is essential if real progress is to be made in a corporate social responsibility (CSR) context. However re-building reputation, quality of life and business confidence takes time, particularly if it is to address the needs and priorities of local communities (Cheshire, 2006; Price and Brodie, 2001). Moreover effective networks, partnerships and communications strategies may prove difficult to form within a hard-to-reach (HTR), multicultural business community (Gospodini, 2006: 312; Henderson et al., 2003).

Consequently this exploratory research examines public policy and the stakeholder environment that affects strategy formulation and partnership building in resurgent cities. It takes a marketing communications perspective because a failure to engage proprietors of small businesses in cities appears to be a major stumbling block for city planners in their attempts to regenerate inner cities (Buurma, 2001). The work is grounded on an HTR, largely South Asian business community, in the post-industrial city of Bradford UK. The Manningham district of this city has been chosen as a case study since it illustrates how South Asian Muslims, with strong allegiance to their country of origin (COO), find it more difficult than other émigrés to adjust to and expand their small family businesses in Western societies. Here a failure to address the predominantly young population, where 60 per cent are less than 30 years old, or engage the women in these communities with career aspirations, has had an adverse effect on regeneration, and may have contributed to triggering the riots in 2001 (Ouseley, 2001; Carling, 2008). Recent landscape improvements to the street environment may restore some business confidence, but if projects do not have the understanding and support from HTR groups, their non-compliance will undermine confidence, and detract from the visual appearance and reputation of inner cities (BMDC, 2004). Conversely if issues of ethnicity, public policy and identity are addressed indicating a CSR approach, there are opportunities for local communities to improve their quality of life and take ownership of the street environment, thereby encouraging civic pride as well as economic prowess (Harsman, 2006).

The research aims to explore first, ways in which the HTR business community can be reached, by examining influences such as key stakeholders, opinion formers and their networks and linkages; secondly to discover which communications channels are currently used by these groups with reference to different media, icons and visual evidence in the street environment; and thirdly to record priorities and beliefs that can enhance trust in relationship building, business confidence and quality of life for local communities.

Background Literature

A number of academics have stressed the significance of understanding ethnic minorities and the associated cultural dimensions for effective city marketing (Burton, 2000; Penaloza and Gilly, 1999; Bouchet, 1995; Costa and Bamossy, 1995). They embrace ethnicity and incorporate community needs into market intelligence, stressing the importance of culture to retain identity for these groups, even though strong ethnic networks that reflect COO values may present communications barriers to understanding public messages. On the other hand Pires and Stanton (2000) believe that there is no apparent reason why these networks should not be used as promotional vehicles. Nonetheless city planners, as well as companies who wish to do business with ethnic minority groups, will have to review marketing plans and take account of a 'growing market pluralism' as well as today's 'multi-ethnic reality' (Nwankwo and Lindridge, 1998). Furthermore, according to UK government research into communications and the ethnic minority population, commercial advertisers 'have largely missed the boat' and frequently portray these groups in a stereotypical or caricatured fashion (Anon, 2004), or how they imagine them to be (Carling, 2008), instead of recognising a need to address a complexity of cultures, values and beliefs to gain an understanding of the needs and aspirations of disparate communities in post-industrial city neighbourhoods. Here it is important to understand the characteristics of public sector marketing communications, since this affects the behaviour of citizens and is critical for successful regeneration (Buurma, 2001).

Cheshire (2006: 1243) observes that communications underpins 'agglomeration economies', and that poor communications, as much as poor communities, will exacerbate the inertia of change. Similarly Amin (2006) stresses the importance of 'relatedness', as well as 'rights', 'repair' and 're-enchantment', as a basis for engaging local communities, if resurgence is to take place. Both urge the need for a 'bottom up' inclusive, rather than 'top down' approach, based on an understanding of social and cultural needs as well as commerce, reminiscent of the work of Travino and Weaver (2003) into effective leadership in USA organisations. In the context of regeneration, leaders from within communities are more likely to be 'trusted', and engage local small businesses (Kavaratzis, 2004).

New urban leadership patterns fit into an emerging institutional and political context. Urban leadership, individual or collegial, only makes sense in a European environment that favours stronger local institutions and horizontal networks that reflect some aspects of CSR. There has always been a tension between fragmentation and coordination in urban areas, as various forms of economic, social, and cultural practices co-exist in densely occupied spaces. Different economic, family and cultural units want solutions to their problems, and compete with others to seek relative autonomous status in urban areas through segregation and migration. Local government has to manage these tensions and complexities by forging unified strategies so that all groups may benefit within the city space (Borraz and John, 2004).

Across Europe there are three essential ingredients for achieving successful civic renewal. (1) Citizens must have more opportunities and support to become more actively involved in defining and tackling community problems and improving their quality of life, (2) public agencies must work in partnership with communities to meet public needs, and (3) involving communities can help in the planning of services (CCPTE, 2007). Sustainable communities can only be achieved with the active support and engagement of the public, and the Office of Public Management has been helping agencies to match their service profiles with the needs and wishes of those affected by new policies to tackle crime and anti-social behaviour. In general local councils are being encouraged to listen and learn from their communities (ACEP, 2007).

In the UK the Department for Communities and Local Government (DCLG) has produced a White Paper 'Strong and prosperous Communities', and 'Together We Can', a set of action plans to enable people to engage with public bodies and influence decisions that affect their communities (DCLG, 2005). There is a new Academy for Sustainable Communities (ASC) that has ambitions to create sustainable communities that balance social, economic and environmental issues, leading to thriving and socially cohesive localities that are well designed and have well-planned public serves (ASC, 2006). Moreover Ruth Kelly, then UK Minister for DCLG outlined two underpinning principles, first to reduce crime and create economic prosperity by narrowing the gap between poor and affluent communities and secondly, to build social cohesion and civic pride by confronting discrimination and re-engaging local communities (Kelly, 2006).

That leadership as a key to regenerating such local communities is confirmed by a growing number of government and official publications (ODPM, 2004 and DCLG, 2005). In the UK context, the publication of the '10 Year Vision for Local Government', and the 'Exemplars of neighbourhood Governance' (DCLG, 2006), point to potential success indicators and factors hindering neighbourhood management. Local Strategic Partnerships must now decide what priorities should be enshrined in a Sustainable Community Strategy, and local government has been given a general competence for the economic, social and environmental well-being of each region and district. Local leadership is therefore a crucial factor in driving transformation (Liddle and Diamond, 2007). The failure of traditional decision-making forums had created a vacuum where more deliberative, consultative and participative forms of leadership are vital (Pratchett, 2002).

However, these initiatives, although laudable, do not make clear how to engage HTR communities or overcome the perceived policy gap at local government level. Nor does it address the tension between economics on the one hand and social needs as well as environmental issues on the other. One approach has been to focus on the need for strong leadership and a sound skills base for local authority members, officers and other collaborating agencies, but this alone cannot engage diverse communities that may be disenchanted with local services, security issues and perceived lack of dialogue. This research would argue that there is a need to overcome poor communications and lack of trust between city planners and local business groups before they are likely to enter into a dialogue or commit themselves to support regeneration initiatives. Such a scenario becomes more difficult to manage where there are long term, negative perceptions of a city and fragmented, multi-ethnic groups with different cultural, social and economic needs. In other words there is a need to engage with these communities if a common agenda is to be developed (Carling, 2008).

MATTERS OF CULTURE, RELIGION AND IDENTITY

In Bradford's Manningham district, the majority of South Asian business-men were either born in Pakistan, India or Bangladesh or are first and second generation British Asians, who arrived to meet labour shortages in the post-war textile industry. Although many have assimilated into a British lifestyle, and those born in the UK have the advantage of an education to assist acculturation, Webster (1992) observes that recent immigrants tend to rely on ethnic networks for their business and social needs. Berry (1980) describes acculturation as, 'Phenomena which result when groups of individuals having different cultures come into continuous first hand contact, with subsequent changes in the original culture patterns of either or both groups'. Not surprisingly many second and third generation immigrants have achieved a higher level of acculturation and become more integrated into the host society, thus being more receptive to standard marketing communications practice (Pires and Stanton, 2000). The challenge for Manningham is that second generation immigrant proprietors can perpetuate the beliefs and values of their country of origin, making it more difficult to adapt to the business culture of their adopted country, with further implications for public policy marketing (Carling, 2008).

Much of the regeneration literature does not deal with acculturation in terms of regeneration and reputation, although some reference is made to the notion of culture and identity. Research conducted by Jamal (2003) found that people (both ethnic and mainstream) co-exist, interact and adapt to each other while still retaining unique and distinct cultural identities. Thus there are certain cultural and religious characteristics that are retained within ethnic minority communities over a considerable period of time, particularly for South Asian Muslims. At another level ethnicity implies many dimensions including 'a sense of common customs, language, religion, values, morality, and etiquette' as well as business protocol (Webster, 1994).

Many studies attempt to categorise groups and observe similarities based on country of origin to explain the relationship between culture and expected behaviour. Early work by Hofstede (1994) examines dimensions of value to explain differences among cultures. This showed that 'Asian' cultures, such as India and Pakistan, put a greater value on collectivism and the extended family than Western countries such as the UK and USA. In turn this influences their approach to business. Similarly a strong regard for power and paternalism reveals that the opinion formers (often elders), have a strong influence on these groups. They have a resistance to change thereby avoiding uncertainty, and are more likely to retain and preserve their values when they migrate to other countries.

Yet people always have the choice to change and adapt to new situations despite the fact that identity and tradition provide some security and certainty when faced with a difficult or even hostile environment in a new country. Similarly religion plays an important role. The Pakistani and Bangladeshi residents and businessmen are Sunni or Shiite Muslims and those of Indian decent are Muslim or Hindu. They regularly visit Mosques and temples, where religious leaders are very influential figures. These venues provide opportunities to exchange information and ideas as well as networking. But city planners often target only the community elders or opinion leaders, and may miss opportunities to reach women and the young generation who may be more receptive to new ideas and change.

Leadership within the complex policy arenas such as the BME communities in Bradford, consist of many individuals, agency representatives and coalitions, where capabilities need to be exercised in iteration to achieve a common agenda (Sotarranto, 2005). Any effective strategy and communications about new, regeneration initiatives require an in-depth knowledge and understanding of the substance of local community needs. However it also requires a grasp of the dynamics of this complex process, knowledge of key players and an understanding of how communication issues fit into the multiple chains of policy and decision-making. In addition it is important to know what small businesses think of policies for regenerating a city. What are the driving forces for each business? Who should be involved? How are specific networks created and strengthened and how can plans for the business community be linked into the wider social and economic regeneration of the city?

As far as the HTR South Asian communities of Bradford are concerned, many Muslim proprietors see their business as an extension of the family (Basu and Altinay, 2003). One of the few studies to examine differences between the diverse 'South Asian' small businesses in Britain found that Indians demonstrate a strong, entrepreneurial orientation, compared with Pakistanis who tend to perceive business on a small family scale (Metcalf et al., 1996). They attribute this to the different skill levels and financial resources of Indian immigrants. Moreover Basu (2004) observes that Pakistani firms are less likely to have a commercial background than Indians, but nonetheless the 'Asian' label is often used by city planners to address both communities as if they were a coherent whole (Carling, 2008).

From a positive viewpoint, some researchers advocate a culture and value-based approach for communication with ethnic groups, since regeneration programmes that reflect cultures and values appear to be more effective in generating a positive response (Cui and Choudhary, 2002). In fact there is a link between cultural cues and improved loyalty (Anon, 2000), and the diversity within these South Asian communities has led researchers to recommend more detailed segmentation of ethnic markets, even to the level of micro cultures (Svendsen, 1997). Message clarity is important and successful communications across cultures should use brief, clear sentences that are not stereotypical or condescending, and avoid colloquial expressions, slang or technical terminology (Nwankwo and Lindridge, 1998). This raises the importance of verbal communications on a one-to-one basis to enhance understanding and trust, particularly for a HTR group. Here Francesco and Gold (1998) suggest open questions, such as 'What is your view of the situation?' or 'How do you feel about?', rather than closed questions such as 'Do you understand?' Interviewers may be selected from the local community to match gender or ethnicity and improve understanding as well as the quality of response.

Examples of Successful Communications Strategies

The most successful communications that target ethnic communities, are usually those sent by other ethnic businesses rather than city planners. These are described by Jamal (2003) as 'ethnic marketers', who believes that they play an important role in establishing and reinforcing the cultural and religious identities of their target communities. They not only exploit the informal communications networks but also ethnic targeted media such as Sunrise Radio and Asian satellite television channels. Naturally many non-ethnic companies also attempt to communicate within these groups. AT&T, for instance, has marketing programmes that reach at least 30 different cultures in 20 languages (Cui and Choudhary, 2002), and Derrick (2004) notes that agencies need to take a long-term perspective when targeting ethnic audiences if real progress is to be made. But many mistakenly want to 'come in quickly, throw money around and see an immediate improvement'. He quotes one advertiser who comments, 'you have to build a rapport within the community. If you are seen to be more understanding by the community, then it is likely to be more receptive to your message.' This approach should have resonance for city planners who appear to have a different agenda from the local business community, which in turn may have a different agenda from local residents, particularly the predominantly young population, who may have an allegiance to neither (Ouseley, 2001). To be effective there is a need to transcend the communications gap between policy makers, business groups and local communities. To this end poor communications and a lack of engagement observed by Amin (2006), can be equated to poor governance. Consequently this research examines some of the difficulties in communicating and engaging with small companies that are hard-to-reach (HTR), in an inner city district.

Research Approach and Sample

In selecting a sample of local businesses for the research, it was important to ensure that they were representative of a HTR group from the largely South Asian community. To this end, twenty small businesses were identified that had *not* responded to a local planning initiative to improve the street environment along Manningham Lane. These people were least likely to engage with regeneration projects and so it was important to discover why this was so, particularly in the context of developing a two-way, rather than one-way communications strategy.

In terms of ethnicity, fourteen of the respondents were born overseas and there was only one non-Muslim. Seven were from Pakistan, five from Bangladesh, one from India and another from Iraq. Of those born in the UK, five were of Pakistani Muslim origin and one was an Indian Sikh. Only one third of this group (four from Bangladesh and three from Pakistan), actually live as well as work on the premises. In order to target these respondents a 'snowballing' technique was applied (Goodman, 1961; Patton, 2002). 'Snowballing' is a non-probability sampling method used for accessing hard-to-reach groups. In conducting these twenty face-to-face, semi-structured, key informant interviews a research protocol was adopted. Questions addressed first, the main areas that business owners felt would improve their immediate vicinity and make business activity a more positive proposition and secondly, what they believed was being communicated through the use of signs and logos used to communicate with various stakeholders for the city in general, and Manningham in particular. Each business proprietor was interviewed individually, using a semi-structured questionnaire to investigate their perceptions about local regeneration projects and to discover their preferred communication networks and support mechanisms. Respondents were encouraged to consider these matters from a business perspective.

Of these small businesses, five were food shops or convenience stores, five sold new or second-hand furniture and two sold textiles and saris. A demand for technology was met by two retail outlets for personal computers and the professions were represented by two firms of solicitors. Finally there was a Muslim bookshop, a dry cleaning shop, a hotel and a restaurant. In all, this HTR sample meets a wide range of local community needs and represents a number of different networks and opinions that can impact upon regeneration projects.

Following guidelines developed by Patton (2002) general topics for discussion were planned in advance but the exact wording and the order of these were decided interactively during each interview. Rather than counting instances, or generalising results, the analysis was focused on the similarities and differences between male and female respondents as they described their career experiences (Miles and Huberman, 2003). Participants were also asked to rank order a series of statements relating to factors that motivated them.

FINDINGS AND DISCUSSION

The results of this survey found that many businesses on Manningham Lane *do not* communicate with each other on a regular basis. This suggests that they operate independently and lends further credence to the notion that this 'community' is less than cohesive. Although most are of Muslim faith, they come from five different nations and it is clear that the 'non-white' business community is extremely diverse. Bangladeshi, Indian, Pakistani, Iraq and UK communities have as many differences as they do similarities. Language, religion and culture are dividing issues making it difficult to label the group as one. However many are united in the desire to run a profitable business, and many have had to endure similar hardships in coming to the UK and adapting to a foreign country. But their differences mean that they live and run their businesses independently, and have their own unique agendas (Basu, 2004; Metcalf et al., 1996).

In fact as immigrants arrive in their host country, the need to adapt is lessened where there are self-supporting communities. These groups usually meet at the mosque and often have family and business networks (Pires and Stanton, 2000; Anon, 2000). Those that support these communities often provide goods and services almost exclusively for Bangladeshis or Pakistanis and do not follow the 'rules' of Western businesses. Consequently anyone who wishes to communicate with this diverse group may need to target each proprietor separately (Svendsen, 1997). However messages can be reinforced with English and Urdu posters for the Pakistani mosques, and English and Bengali for the Bangladeshi mosques.

Yet in general those born in the host country have more in common with each other, than those born overseas. Those second generation émigrés have a higher level of acculturation (Berry, 1980) and are more likely to be in a position to respond to official host country communications or with professional organisations (Svendsen, 1997). For example the two solicitor practices in this group communicate with each other, as well as other businesses through professional contacts. In this way they may be considered more accessible to mainstream communications than their non-UK-born counterparts, although interestingly, neither had responded to the city planners circular. In turn, this 'acclimatised' group may not communicate with those proprietors newly arrived from Pakistan, India or Bangladesh.

Preferred Channel of Communications

The most popular, official channel amongst the group is the local newspaper, the *Telegraph & Argus*, which appears ideal for reaching many ethnic-minority homes within the city. Moreover the 'Asian Eye', a supplement for the Asian community, was read by only two respondents, but specialist national newspapers are popular, such as *Euro Bangla*, for Bengalis and *The Daily Jang*, for Pakistanis. Both papers present an opportunity to target households and businesses in the city, and may create a sense of meaning and identity for each targeted group to reach parts of the community whose first language is not English. Another opportunity is presented by a free newspaper, *The Muslim Times*, available in mosques throughout the UK, but not mentioned by the interviewed group. In other words although there are a range of papers for these HTR groups, it is not easy for anyone to reach this diverse, ethnic audience using conventional news media channels.

Interestingly, satellite television is increasingly popular within this sample that regularly use four out of five Urdu or Hindi language stations. Although these channels have not been used by city planners, many advertisers, both ethnic and non-ethnic, have taken advantage of these marketing opportunities. These stations offer cheap advertising space, and family viewing is often based around them (Cui and Choudhary, 2002). They are popular with all age ranges, including those born in the UK and Indian sub-continent (Fletcher, 2003). They also provide a natural conduit to reach the women and younger generation, as well as elders and opinion formers, presenting a further communications channel for city planners engaged in regeneration initiatives.

Similarly the predominant use of Asian radio within the interviewed group reflects the desire of large parts of this community to read, watch and listen to media that is in their mother tongue and caters to their specific needs. This can be seen in the popularity of Radio Ramadan that broadcasts religious programming during the holy month of fasting. For example Derrick (2004) describes its use in an anti-smoking campaign targeted at Muslims. In 2004 'Iqra FM' was granted a license to broadcast within the Bradford area, and is advertised on posters in the Muslim owned businesses along Manningham Lane. This shows that this group will support and promote projects that they perceive as important. Another radio station – Sunrise Radio – is used by seven of those interviewed. It broadcasts continuously throughout the year and has programmes that target all of these groups.

By contrast the internet was *not* used by most of the businesses in this survey, and only the younger, UK-born proprietors, such as the solicitors and two technology companies, use this form of communication. This means that although E-marketing is a powerful communication tool, it is unlikely to reach this HTR group now, but may be a key vehicle in the near future when young UK-born children are likely to use the internet, proving an important information bridge to their parents and other opinion formers. This scenario illustrates observations made by Cheshire (2006) about the time it takes for cultural change of direction in an urban context. On the other hand within this district of Bradford, 60 per cent of the population are less than 30 years old (Trueman et al., 2008), so that familiarisation with and use of new, internet technologies may occur sooner rather than later.

Priorities and Beliefs

All twenty respondents were asked about their priorities for improving Manningham district. Their responses show that they value visual attractiveness but were dissatisfied with parts of the street environment that were derelict, strewn with litter, overgrown gardens, crumbling walls (Table 9.1). In terms of perceptions, most did not see beyond their immediate environment or understand that more needs to be done to improve the area as a whole. In fact there appears to be a breakdown of communications between this HTR group and city planners who seem to have a different agenda, since they use a zoning policy that considers Manningham to be largely residential rather than a business district (BMDC, 2004).

Furthermore, more than half (11) respondents were not satisfied with the focus on the recently installed hanging baskets and park benches that were part of a recent improvement initiative, since they did not correlate flowers or seating with economic prosperity. One commented:

Table 9.1   'How would you improve Manningham Lane?'

Business issues		Street environment	
Reduce rates	13	*More restaurants*	1
Reduce insurance	9	*More shops*	1
More parking	7	*More cleaning*	1
Security issues		*Improve shop fronts*	1
More police, wardens to manage	8	*Paint windows*	1
prostitutes, drugs and vandalism			
More CCTV	1	*Tidy gardens*	1
Replace railings	1	*Better pavements*	1
total	39	total	7
Respondents could name more than one factor			

Source: Author's own.

> The old towns of Blackburn and Glasgow a hundred years back were not beautiful places. They were dirty but economically powerful. . . Silicon Valley is not worth billions because it is beautiful.

Despite this, hanging baskets were perceived positively by a few respondents, although they see them more as a 'finishing touch' to a vibrant economy rather than a catalyst to create one.

But there is a danger that these businesses will be left behind if they have differing needs and perceptions from the assumptions of city planners (Metcalf et al., 1996; Basu, 2004). From an ethical viewpoint, baskets of flowers might be seen as a symbol of gentrification and a move to convert all cultures to a norm that is stereotypical of Western countries. This notion has implications for shaping society and business regeneration, where the accepted norms of a HTR group may be very different, even though all may have the same long-term objectives of an attractive, secure and thriving city.

But most of this sample are concerned by security rather than appearance, and did not make a connection between these two concepts. Several are unsatisfied with the level of policing, and complaints about drug dealers and prostitutes were made, with reference to one area where the Muslim community was largely instrumental in turning a former 'red light' area of Bradford into a safer community, by adopting a zero tolerance approach. There is also some disagreement about new public policy for open spaces. Those interviewed perceived lack of parking to be a major problem for customers, and felt it inappropriate to sacrifice parking space for the proposed new recreation areas on or near a busy road, especially since there is a large public park with leisure facilities nearby.

Lack of Trust and Confidence in Regeneration Initiatives

It is apparent that there are many issues facing the Manningham District, but one of the biggest barriers to community engagement is the perception that the organisations that are set up to help the community are not to be trusted (Trueman et al., 2008). Although city planners have set up a business support centre for the 'Asian' community (Asian Trade Link), this has not inspired confidence in part because it is difficult for one organisation to represent such diverse cultural and business requirements. One observed that 'Big business people have created a means of supplementing their own incomes by deception saying it's going to help the local community.' This illustrates the resentment and lack of trust that some smaller businesses can feel. Perceptions may not reflect reality, but demonstrate that often misinformation is taken as fact, reinforcing a need to develop regeneration projects that involve and empower local communities and use effective communications channels to encourage trust and ownership of new projects (Pearce and Ensley, 2003).

To sum up when respondents asked 'How would you improve Manningham Lane?' they prioritised lower rates and insurance costs as well as a need to improve parking. It was felt that more police were required, particularly by those who lived on the premises, and all wanted to reduce or abolish drug dealers and prostitution. A few thought shop fronts could be improved, railings replaced and gardens tidied or that closed circuit television cameras could be introduced. Yet although all acknowledged that in the long term an improved street environment would lead to more customers, a safer environment, increased property prices with lower insurance costs as well as a better range of shops; at present they saw this as secondary to security issues. This phenomenon is illustrative of the Type 1 and Type 2 development policy of de Chernatony's (2006) adaptation of Maslow's (1943) hierarchy of needs. Those ethnic communities who live in areas of decline, have fundamental needs regarding their immediate security and survival, rather than landscaping. Consequently hanging baskets may be symbolic of improved quality of life in a Type 2 development that is higher up the hierarchy of needs and closer to self-actualisation. This perception shows how it is important to understand the values, beliefs and quality of life for each community when developing an effective communications strategy for urban regeneration.

BRAND COMMUNICATIONS AND RECOGNISING VISUAL CUES

In order to examine how six urban regeneration organisations relate to this HTR group, respondents were asked if they recognised the logos associated with each one as well as its function and purpose. From this we can see that most recognised the 'b' symbol used by Bradford for its European capital of culture bid, but few understood its purpose. Moreover few recognised, and only one understood the purpose of Bradford Vision, a forum set up to coordinate regeneration projects and coordinate a regeneration strategy for the city (Table 9.2). Similarly the role of Yorkshire Forward, the regional development agency, was poorly understood. On the other hand Urban Splash, the company currently refurbishing the enormous Lister Mill in the Manningham district, had been noticed as well as the 'Manningham Means Business', and 'My Manningham' projects, set up by local businesses to improve the street environment.

However for most of this HTR group, the precise role of all these different organisations was unclear. Although local business driven initiatives were recognised and respected more than those of city planners, there was some confusion about the number of different authorities involved. Nonetheless all but one of those interviewed *were* prepared to support regeneration in some way, once they had a clearer understanding about the opportunities for the district, as well as how their own business might benefit.

DISCUSSION AND CONCLUSION

In short the profile of the HTR ethnic group is diverse and may reveal some of the values, beliefs and priorities of a minority culture that can enhance or detract from rebuilding business and shaping society. It shows that a number of opportunities for engaging this HTR group may be missed by city planners. For example a simple Urdu poster on a notice board in a mosque, a feature on Sunrise Radio or satellite television may form part of a communications campaign alongside advertisements in *The Daily Jang* or *The Muslim Times*. This approach is likely to create a sense of credibility and break down some cross-cultural barriers within the Muslim community (Derrick, 2004). Similarly the internet is likely to become more important for the predominantly young population in this district, particularly for those who have received a UK education and may understand the rationale behind media and message.

On the other hand from a process viewpoint there are many barriers that can inhibit communications. Large community networks, that provide a cushioned environment for new arrivals, and operate in isolation from society at large. Here the material manifestations of the country of origin can be so strong that, according to Jamal (2003), the first generation of ethnic immigrants may feel that they are still living in their own country.

Towards effective place brand management

Table 9.2   Recognition of logos and symbols associated with different initiatives

Logo or Symbol	Have you seen it?		Do you know anything about it?		WHAT DO YOU KNOW ABOUT IT?
	Yes	No	Yes	No	
Symbol for failed city of culture bid, now adopted to represent Bradford's regeneration	4	16	6	14	'. . .it's related to the improvement of Bradford' '. . .something to do with the city of culture bid'
Council forum to coordinate regeneration in the city and communicate initiatives for change	4	16	1	19	'. . .it's an organisation taking people forward'
Regional development agency	7	13	3	17	'Yorkshire Forward helps businesses grow' '. . .they sponsor events' '. . .to do with regeneration'
Private company regenerating Manningham's Lister Mill complex	9	11	3	17	'. . .they are fixing Manningham Mills' '. . .Urban Splash are converting Lister Mills into apartments'
Manningham Means Business Local business group Phase I	11	9	3	17	'. . .they want to help Manningham' '. . .it's connected to improvements in this area'
myManningham Local business group Phase II	12	8	6	14	'They are campaigning for businesses with an action plan' 'Business improvement' '. . .updating Manningham'

Source: Author's own.

This is evident in shops that appear to cater exclusively for these communities in terms of the goods they sell and their appearance. As a result these businesses tend not to market themselves to a wider population, even though this may be detrimental to their economic longevity and effectiveness (Carling, 2008). For them the appearance of these shop fronts within their own community may more than match and possibly exceed their expectations. At the same time there may be a lack of long-term vision amongst some ethnic businesses, if limited opportunities have driven them into retailing or restaurants without mission or vision (Metcalf et al., 1996; Basu, 2004). Similarly, despite the trend for children to take over the family business, if the younger generation obtain a university education they may be unwilling to continue the work of their parents. This creates a limited lifespan for the business and contrary to practice in Western society, does not inspire a need for growth or improvement. If the current premises are adequate, there is no incentive to create a beautiful shop or grow the business if it is to be sold at retirement age, rather than passed on to the next generation.

Furthermore, most of the respondents appear to be 'reactive' rather than proactive in terms of the amount of effort they are prepared to put into a street improvement project. For example some of this HTR group explained that they would be unlikely to telephone a number on a leaflet about projects in response to a circular, illustrating a feeling of mistrust of city planners and a suspicion of change. However if key stakeholders are approached individually, they are more likely to take part in improvement schemes. In other words, to target HTR groups requires careful consideration and assessment of individual as well as collective needs, reflecting observations by Travino and Weaver (2003) about ethical leadership conditions. Here we need to consider the actual profile of the business community aspirations and priorities at each stage of development.

A consistent message from city planners would also help, since a proliferation of brand descriptors such as 'surprising place', 'city of film' and currently 'city of light', can alienate rather than unite the population. In the past they have been confused by a barrage of different planning proposals that have not materialised, leading to a negative perception and lack of trust in regeneration initiatives (Manzanti and Ploger, 2003). This mirrors the findings of Kavaratzis and Ashworth (2007: 6) in their study of Amsterdam, who conclude that you need to 'make respondents believe in the core values of the city, 'feel' the city's brand and be proud of their city'.

From the Manningham research we can see the importance of focusing on each individual, group and neighbourhood if changes are to be meaningful for residents and businesses, ensuring that branding and regeneration projects reflect real concerns about the local business and street environment. This reflects the notion of empowerment leadership discussed by Pearce and Ensley (2003) to enlist social capital for change. If people feel part of regeneration projects, they are more likely to embrace the values of the city as a whole.

Moreover this research has raised several issues about key stakeholders and opinion formers since there appears to be a mismatch between the agenda of city planners, the COO traditions of community elders, and the needs of a predominantly young, second generation ethnic population in this district (Carling, 2008). At the same time the HTR respondents in this study reinforce the importance of a 'bottom up' rather than 'top down' approach, using existing channels of communications and micro-segmentation, if progress is to be made. In fact city planners may learn as much from the literature about customer relationship management as marketing communications if they are to engage these communities (Manzanti and Ploger, 2003). Yet all these key-stakeholders are linked in one way or another with the future business potential of Manningham, and the city as a whole. Poor relationships and weak communications channels will exacerbate problems within these groups, that are already part of a fragmented society from different continents and cultures, many of whom retain their own language, values and priorities in business prac-tice. This raises moral and ethical issues about the purpose of cities, and points to a need for empowerment to inculcate good will, trust and brand ownership (Amin, 2006).

Of the initiatives currently in place there is a sense of distrust that must be overcome through mutual understanding, education and effective com-munications that may incorporate opportunities presented by new technol-ogy as well as new, diverse industries. This is particularly important for the 60 per cent of the population who are less than 30 years old, since they may form a crucial bridge between old and new business practice. As Cui and Choudhary (2002) point out, if they are to be successful, those involved in business regeneration and shaping society need to be more aware of the needs, desires and cultural issues of their target audiences and build long-term relationships based on recognised priorities such as safety and secu-rity as much as an attractive street environment. In this way city planners are more likely to gain the trust of local communities and elicit a change of behaviour to support, rather than ignore or hinder progress (Buurma, 2001). Although, as Cheshire (2006) observes, changing direction in a city takes a great deal of time, this may be time well spent if it leads to an improved quality of life, a vibrant business environment and enhanced city reputation rather than an impenetrable perceptual gap and riots.

10. The '*be* Berlin' campaign: old wine in new bottles or innovative form of participatory place branding?

Claire Colomb and Ares Kalandides

INTRODUCTION

> The branding campaign is a first step to present ourselves in a clearer, more visible and decisive way. '*be* Berlin' means that we want to show Berlin as a casual and relaxed, international and open metropolis, radiating joy and creativity and where it is a pleasure to live in. It is the people that make up Berlin – the Berliners. They are Berlin. They are the ambassadors of our city. . . Berlin has 3.4 million facets, as many as there are inhabitants. Thus Berlin has many stories to tell. Stories of a successful change – despite all the difficulties that also characterise Berlin; stories of a change for the best. For as long as this city has existed, it has blossomed, lived and survived, because people came here to live their dreams and realise their plans. (Speech of the Mayor of Berlin, Klaus Wowereit, for the launch of the '*be* Berlin' branding campaign on 11 March 2008)

On 11 March 2008 the Berlin Mayor Klaus Wowereit publicly launched a new campaign for Berlin under the slogan '*be* Berlin' (in English), following a call for ideas launched by the Mayor's office in search of a new 'brand' for Berlin. Why does it still matter for Berlin's political leaders to search for a new image, a new slogan, a new 'brand' twenty years after the fall of the Wall and the reunification of the city? This need for a new 'Berlin brand' seemed to ignore what happened during twenty years of an intensive politics of image production, slogan making, city marketing and place branding which took place in Berlin post-1989. Throughout the 1990s and early 2000s, a complex network of actors were involved in various practices of place marketing and branding for Berlin, producing images of, and a discourse on, the city, urban change and place identity. In the early 1990s, as the centre of reunified Berlin became a giant construction site – around *Potsdamer Platz*, around the new government quarter and the *Friedrichstrasse* – a chaotic landscape of cranes and construction sites began to dominate the urban landscape of a city undergoing major

173

transformations. The emerging landscape of the 'new' Berlin was not only being physically built, it was also *imaged, marketed, staged* and *branded* to the public eye (Colomb, 2008) through various means: a red '*Infobox*' on the *Potsdamer Platz* displaying three-dimensional visualisations of the future Berlin, programmes of guided tours of the construction sites, advertising campaigns for 'The New Berlin' posted on the city's facades. . . In brief, 'along with the production process of the real-material built environment, there [was] also a production process of the imaginary, a social construction of a particular image and meaning' (Lehrer, 2002: 61), the discursive and visual construction of a new place identity.

This contribution analyses the recent shift in place marketing and branding practices which has taken place in Berlin after 2001, with a particular focus on the '*be* Berlin' campaign launched in 2008. The first part of the chapter introduces definitions of place marketing and place branding and provides a succinct overview of the critical insights on place branding offered by human geographers and sociologists. In the second and third part of this contribution, a brief overview of place marketing practices in Berlin and their evolution throughout the 1990s and early 2000s is given, to provide a context within which to interpret the subsequent changes in orientation and methods witnessed after 2001. In the fourth and final part, a critical analysis of the '*be* Berlin' campaign launched in 2008 is proposed, focusing on the following question: is the '*be* Berlin' campaign an innovative form of participatory city branding 'by its inhabitants for its inhabitants' or just old wine in new bottles?

PLACE MARKETING AND PLACE BRANDING: DEFINITIONS AND CRITICAL INSIGHTS

Over the past thirty years cities around the world have invested in strategies of place marketing and branding aimed at attracting investment, economic activities, skilled workforce, talented creative workers, tourists and at strengthening local community pride and identity. Place marketing 'entails the various ways in which public and private agencies – local authorities and local entrepreneurs, often working collaboratively – strive to 'sell' the image of a particular geographically defined place, usually a town or city, so as to make it attractive to economic enterprises, to tourists and even to inhabitants of that place' (Philo and Kearns, 1993: 3). Berlin was no exception in this process: in the early part of the 1990s a number of public-private partnerships were set up to promote and market the city to various target audiences. 'Imaging' activities form a large part of place marketing activities: imaging is defined as 'the process of constructing narratives about the potential of places (. . .), a process of brokering the best metaphor, in ways that will shift or consolidate public sensibilities and invent the possibility for new kinds of place attachments' (Bass Warner and Vale, 2001: xv). Imaging activities are based on the assumption that people's attitudes towards a city – be they potential tourists, investors or residents – are conditioned by the visual representations, depictions and descriptions of that place conveyed through various media (Short and Kim, 1998). A large part of the activities of Berlin city marketers from the mid-1990s onwards focused on the production and dissemination of images of the 'new' Berlin under construction, as described in the second part of this chapter.

Place 'branding' forms a significant sub-part of wider place promotional activities. It is a process whereby the place is associated 'with wider desirable qualities in the perceptions held by relevant target audiences' (Kavaratzis and Ashworth, 2007: 16). In a context that considers competition as the principal relationship, if not the only interaction, between places, urban political leaders and marketers see branding as a way of gaining competitive advantage as well as securing internal 'identification' and inclusion. City branding is consequently understood as 'the means both for achieving competitive advantage in order to increase inward investment and tourism, and also for achieving community development, reinforcing local identity and identification of the citizens with their city and activating all social forces to avoid social exclusion and unrest' (Kavaratzis 2004: 70). The aim of 'place branding' is a dual one: to form a 'unique selling proposition' that will secure visibility to the outside and reinforce 'local identity' to the inside. Throughout the 1990s the concept of 'capital city marketing' (*Hauptstadtmarketing*) was predominant in the Berlin community of actors engaged in urban promotion. 'Branding', as a concept, has not entered the vocabulary and strategies of Berlin politicians and city marketers, although the term has often been used by practitioners with reference to traditional activities of place selling, not to proper 'place branding' as defined by Kavaratzis (2004) and Kavaratzis and Ashworth (2005).

Branding involves associating the place with 'stories' about it, through physical interventions, organisational change and communication measures (Kavaratzis and Ashworth, 2005). In those stories, the role of the 'genius loci', of invoked or constructed characteristics of local place identity is prominent. The creators of these 'stories' are often professionals in the sectors of public relations, communication, advertising and city marketing. The process of construction of stories and images is consequently 'a highly selective process that imposes single-stranded images onto urban diversity and reduces place identity to a constricted and easily packaged "urban product" (Broudehoux, 2004: 26). This argument forms the core of the critique of place marketing and branding activities offered by critical human geographers and sociologists. Their critical analyses have focused on three main issues. First, although the measures implemented are supposed to create distinctiveness, they actually do exactly the opposite: they create homogeneity to such a point that places become more and more interchangeable (Harvey, 1989). In the process, places lose their own *identity* and increasingly resemble one another – physically, through the serial replication of similar types of flagship projects (e.g. waterfront developments, iconic corporate buildings, convention centres etc.), and discursively, through the use of similar catchwords in marketing slogans.

Secondly, the very selective nature of the branding process is often stressed: in the process of re-imagining a city, some aspects of its identity are ignored, denied or marginalised or are transformed and instrumentalised through a process of 'commodification', whereby places, local identities and culture(s) are 'regarded as commodities to be consumed and as commodities that can be rendered attractive, advertised and marketed' (Philo and Kearns, 1993: 18) for economic gain or social control, or both. What is highlighted here are the power relations inherent behind apparently neutral managerial choices, which create dominant and obscured identities. Critical geographers have shown that the commodification of local history, cultures and identities is a conflictual process: there are tensions between the use of culture for marketing and branding purposes and the promotion of culture for its own sake, as an expression of identity and as a form of personal and social development. Which memories/cultures are to be represented and which are to be left out in the branding process? For the benefit of which audience is it done? The recent 'marketing of creativity', in particular, which has become so popular in many cities around the world, can be highly selective and reductionist (Kalandides and Lange, 2007: 123): it targets specific spaces, agents and neglects others – a process which has implications for local economic development policy choices. Additionally, gentrification researchers have since long shown the role played by images and branding in processes of neighbourhood change (Zukin, 1988; 1995). In the Berlin context, Bernt and Holm (2002) have argued that city marketing has partly influenced the gentrification of the East Berlin district of *Prenzlauer Berg*. These 'direct material and social side-effects (. . .) are easily overlooked by marketing' (Kalandides, 2007a: 2).

Thirdly, many critical authors highlight the ambiguity and tension between the outward and the inward orientation of place marketing and branding activities. In many definitions given in the literature, as illustrated above, place marketing and branding activities are credited with a dual orientation. The outward orientation aims at improving the competitive position of the city or region on the national or global stage to attract inward investment, visitors or new residents. At the same time, such activities are often directed towards the local population to stimulate the local acceptance of new developments in the city, create a sense of local 'pride', reinforce the 'identification of citizens with their city' (Krantz and Schaetzl, 1997: 477) or stimulate new forms of local mobilisation for endogenous economic development. Harvey, in *The Condition of Postmodernity*, analysed this inward function early on: 'the orchestrated production of an urban image can, if successful, create a sense of social solidarity, civic pride and loyalty to place and even allow the urban image to provide a mental refuge in a world that capital treats as more and more place-less' (Harvey, 1989: 14). If 'persuasion' and marketing campaigns are required, however, this may mean that the qualities of the place 'product' are not evident for the whole population, which led many critics to argue that urban marketing and branding are manipulative tools for urban conflict management. For critical researchers, this inward orientation is often seen as a device for social control, 'a subtle form of socialisation to convince local people, many of whom will be disadvantaged and potentially disaffected, that they are important cogs in a successful community and that all sorts of "good things" are really being done on their behalf' (Kearns and Philo, 1993: 3). The city 'image' or 'vision' can become a tool to redirect attention away from actual economic and social problems such as local unemployment, diminishing public expenditure on key services, weakening local democracy and increasing social inequalities. For those authors, place marketing and branding can thus be a means of exercising power by masking an increasing social polarisation as the restructuring of the city into a 'post-Fordist' economy unfolds. Various authors have consequently shown how place marketing and branding activities, and the associated urban policies aimed at re-shaping urban spaces, have been contested by local residents and critics in light of their perceived negative economic, ideological and cultural role in painful processes of urban restructuring and transition to a post-Fordist urban economy.

What is apparent in all of the above, in the definition of place branding as well as in its criticisms, is the central position that is given to the construction of a 'place identity' – whether re-imagined, manipulated, reinforced or contested – and to the question of who should be involved in the process of definition, construction and communication of this place identity. In the next section we shall briefly outline the evolution of practices of place marketing and the shift to place branding which took place in Berlin between 1989 and the early 2000s, with a particular focus on the actors behind such practices and the means through which a discourse on 'place identity' was created. This provides the context within which to make sense of the recent developments in Berlin place branding, in particular the '*be* Berlin' campaign, which has sought to give a voice to the Berliners themselves in the production of 'stories' about their city and its 'place identity'.

MARKETING THE 'NEW BERLIN' IN THE 1990S

The fall of the Wall in 1989 and the subsequent reunification of Germany opened an unprecedented era of institutional, physical, economic and social transformation in Berlin. In terms of place marketing, Berlin urban leaders and marketers sought to break from the negative images associated with the city's tormented past by constructing and transmitting a new image of the city and its identity to three main target groups: potential tourists, visitors and investors, in order to stimulate the urban economy; Germans throughout the Federal Republic, following the decision to move the Federal Capital from Bonn to Berlin; and finally, the Berliners themselves. This 'internal marketing' aimed at stimulating the social acceptance of urban change, creating a sense of local identity and civic pride and fostering 'the visual and emotional integration of two populations differently socialised' (Rabe and Süss, 1995: 20) in a city undergoing rapid transformations.

The arrival of a 'Grand Coalition' of Christian-Democrats and Social-Democrats in the Berlin government in December 1990 marked the beginning of a new orientation for urban policies (Strom, 2001), geared towards the promotion of the city as a 'service metropolis' and its re-positioning in the global inter-city competition. The perceived need to improve the image of the city and promote its 'locational factors' became an overarching goal translated into various policies to attract external stakeholders and capital into the city – for example through lobbying the Olympic Committee for the 2000 Olympic Games – and into public-private strategies of local economic development and place marketing. In 1993–94 a number of public-private organisations dedicated to economic promotion, tourism promotion and place marketing were set up. A new organisation was created to steer all generic place marketing activities for the city: *Partner für Berlin, Gesellschaft für Hauptstadtmarketing GmbH* ('company for capital city marketing', thereafter referred to as PFB), which worked in cooperation with the city's department of the economy and the Mayor's office. PFB is a private company funded by 'partner firms' from the private sector (150 in 2007). The city government commissions PFB for city-wide marketing campaigns and promotional activities directed at potential investors, visitors and local residents. In addition, a new public-private partnership responsible for tourism promotion was created, *Berlin Tourismus Marketing GmbH* (BTM). Under the impetus of PFB and BTM, place marketing activities in Berlin have actually acquired a degree of professionalisation, intensity and visibility rarely observed in other German cities. Their activities have been at the heart of the process of re-imaging and branding the 'New Berlin'.

The initial activities of PFB in the first two years of its existence were rather typical of a city marketing agency: the production of image campaigns and promotional brochures, advertisements in the international and national press, investor's guides, presentations, exhibitions and press statements. From 1996 onwards PFB developed more innovative activities aimed at 'staging the city' and its new urban landscape under construction through a series of cultural-architectural events organised in the summers of 1996 to 2005 under the title '*Schaustelle Berlin*' and '*Berlin: Offene Stadt*', which showcased the large construction sites and new urban projects through guided tours and open-air cultural and artistic events. Large-scale, flagship development projects such as the new *Potsdamer Platz* were intensively marketed to establish new urban images and new 'city myths' about Berlin (Häussermann and Colomb, 2003). Throughout the 1990s the marketing campaigns and events organised by PFB focused on three main sites, which were visually and discursively constructed into the symbols of the 'New Berlin' under construction: the new *Potsdamer Platz*, the government quarter and its representative buildings (in particular the *Reichstag*) and the regenerated area of *Mitte* around the *Friedrichstrasse*. In the place marketing discourse and images produced by PFB and the Berlin government, these sites were associated with a specific set of messages and values which were invoked by place marketers as desirable for the city as a whole: *Potsdamer Platz* as the icon of the new service metropolis of aspiring global status, the government quarter as the symbol of the transparent democracy of the new 'Berlin Republic' and its capital city, and the *Mitte/Friedrichstrasse* area as the expression of the 'European city' model with its retrieved 'urbanity' (Colomb, 2008).

Potsdamer Platz, one of the first construction sites of post-Wall Berlin, became the most widely used visual symbol of urban transformation in reunified Berlin, under the impetus of the private investors behind the development and of city marketing organisations. Through a mix of events staged on the construction site as well as massive communication and marketing campaigns, the large-scale building site was turned into a global spectacle attracting thousands of visitors and international media coverage, leading to what became referred to as 'construction site tourism' (*Baustellentourismus*) (Häussermann and Colomb, 2003; Till, 2003). The

'*Infobox*', a temporary building erected in 1995 to house various exhibitions and models showcasing the development, became an extremely popular destination (8.6 million visitors in five years). In the second half of the 1990s *Potsdamer Platz* dominated the imagery of official place marketing campaigns and documents. This omnipresence served two purposes. First, the marketing rhetoric surrounding *Potsdamer Platz* was characterised by an obsessive search for the restoration of a sense of geographical and historical continuity in post-Wall Berlin, between the Eastern and Western part of the city, and between the pre-1933 era and the present. In press articles, planning publications, in the *Infobox* exhibition and in city marketing publications, the metaphor of the 'retrieved' or 'new' heart of the city were recurrently used with reference to *Potsdamer Platz*. Secondly, the predominance of the high rise, corporate, iconic architecture of *Postdamer Platz* marked a clear attempt to reimage Berlin as a global (or at least European) capitalist metropolis with a dynamic service economy.

The second key site which dominated the imagery and discourse of place marketing in the second part of the 1990s was the urban district hosting the newly settled institutions of the German Federal government, in particular the *Reichstag* building (seat of the Federal parliament). A specific set of activities, named 'capital city marketing', made use of city marketing techniques to anchor the move of German federal institutions from Bonn to Berlin in the public consciousness of Germans and Berliners. The fact that a 'newly appointed' capital city had to promote its capital city status within its own national territory is a rather peculiar situation which can only be understood within the German historical context. Berlin suffered from decades of distrust by older generations of West Germans who tended to perceive the city as the capital of two authoritarian regimes in German history (the National-Socialist and the GDR regimes). The move of the federal institutions from Bonn to Berlin gave rise to an intense and passionate German 'capital city debate'. The Berlin authorities and the federal government decided that communication measures were necessary to win the hearts of unconvinced Germans for their new capital, by conveying a fresh and non-threatening image of the new capital city and dispelling bad historical memories and negative associations. This was done through the 'New Berlin' image campaigns of 1998–2000, which celebrated the move of federal institutions to the city and the birth of the 'Berlin Republic'. The imagery of the campaigns made heavy use of the visual transparency of the new *Reichstag* cupola designed by Norman Foster, which was associated with a discourse on the transparency of the new *Berliner Republik*, echoing the debates on the 'architecture of democracy' in reunified Germany (Wise, 1998; Welch-Guerra, 1999; Delanty and Jones, 2002; Barnstone, 2005).

Finally, a third area was present in the visual imagery of city marketing campaigns in 1990s Berlin, albeit to a lesser extent: the area around the *Friedrichstrasse* (the *Friedrichstadt*), rebuilt according to the principles of 'Critical Reconstruction' championed by Hans Stimmann, the city's building director between 1991 and 1996. 'Critical reconstruction' involved a 'return' to the urban form of the 'traditional European city' of pre-1933 times as a guiding framework for the reconstruction of the eastern inner city of Berlin (Burg, 1994; Burg and Stimmann, 1995). Representations of the area in the city marketing imagery served a discourse on the 'return to the European city' and on the restoration of a sense of historical continuity through the built environment. This was a recurring theme in the political, media and city marketing discourses on the urban identity of Berlin in the 1990s, anchored in references to the past era which preceded the Nationalist Socialist dictatorship and the GDR regime, i.e. the Weimar Republic (1919–33) or the eighteenth century Prussian Enlightenment period (Manale, 2003; Till, 2005; Süchting and Weiss, 2001). In Berlin, city planners and marketers have thus 'selectively borrowed urban forms and lifestyles of imagined past Berlins' (Till, 2005: 37), emphasising 'a common German past before troublesome difficulties in the 1930s' (Neill 2004: 74), and leaving out the remnants of unwanted histories (e.g. the GDR built heritage) from the imagery of place marketing.

BRANDING BERLIN AS 'CREATIVE CITY' IN THE NEW MILLENNIUM: FROM PLACE MARKETING TO PLACE BRANDING, FROM ICONIC SITES TO CREATIVE PEOPLE

Several factors contributed to changes in the marketing and branding of Berlin after 2000. First, the economic and demographic forecast made in the first years of the 1990s did not materialise to the extent wished for by local politicians. In 1989 Berlin had 3.4 million inhabitants. Early forecasts expected it to grow up to five million by the year 2010. By 1997 there were clear signs that there was instead a demographic decline, only partly offset by an influx of young people to the city (Häußermann and Kapphan, 2000: 95). The optimistic forecasts for economic growth faded away after 1992, when the speculative real estate boom came to an end. Investors were increasingly put off by the delays in the move of the federal government, the complexity of the planning system, complex questions of land ownership and restitution and general macro-economic conditions. The development industry had over-estimated the demand for office space; in 1998 vacant office space was estimated at 1.5 million square metres

(Krätke and Borst, 2000). It had become clear that the initial phase of Berlin's post-Wall reconstruction had been 'heavily dependent on virtual projections of globalization (rather) than on economic manifestations of the latter' (Ward, 2004: 242). The local policy elite started 'formally at least, (to buy into) a European model, rather than a "global" (or US) one – albeit more in recognition that the latter was unachievable than as a positive choice' (Cochrane, 2006: 372–3). This shift was later fuelled by the severe financial crisis, which came to public light in 2001 with the 'Berlin bank scandal' – a crisis that had been brewing since the mid-1990s.

By the late 1990s the grand visions of Berlin as 'global metropolis' foreseen a decade earlier by the city's economic and political elite had faded away. At the same time the capital city status of Berlin in the new Berliner Republic had been solidly established and was not questioned any longer. Paradoxically the need for intensive image production became even stronger as a result: the mismatch between the imagery produced at that time, and the reality of the disappointing economic trajectory of the city, explained the continuous search for new image campaigns, new slogans, a new 'Berlin brand', which has characterised the activities of the new ruling coalition elected in 2001. By the mid-2000s the 'New' Berlin was not so new anymore. The era of large-scale construction sites in the central areas was mostly over (even if there has been a lot of building work going on in various parts of the city); 'construction site tourism' was not what it used to be. The city has been on the edge of bankruptcy (Krätke, 2004a), and its financial capacity is not likely to improve for many years, which has forced the Berlin government to rely heavily on private funding and public-private partnerships in many fields. Economic growth remains sluggish, unemployment remains high, even if the creative industries have been doing well. Many holes and brownfield sites still punctuate the city's landscape. Yet a lot is brewing in the city, things which have been left out of the official promotional discourse for a long time, perceived as irrelevant or not economically useful in the dominant language of place marketing and inter-urban competition. It is precisely that 'ungraspable', dynamic diversity which marketing activities post-2000 and the new 2008 branding campaign have attempted to capture.

In 2001, following local elections, a new 'red-red' coalition of Social Democrats and the PDS (heir to the communist party of the former German Democratic Republic) came to power in the city. There was initially no significant shift in the overall rationale for urban policies in Berlin. This can be partly explained by the total lack of financial room for manoeuvre inherited by the new government. Yet in the early 2000s, the theme of the 'creative city' emerged in the local political and marketing discourse, marking an overall shift in emphasis between the early 1990s and the early 2000s from a focus on cultural consumption to a focus on cultural production and creative industries. In Berlin, cultural consumption (the richness and diversity of the cultural facilities and cultural life of the city) had been promoted since the early 1990s both in tourism promotion campaigns by BTM but also in the economic promotion campaigns designed by WFB and PFB. The theme of the 'creative city' only appeared in 2000 in an advertisement series by PFB, '*Das Neue Berlin – Die 5 Stärken*', which reflected the increasing importance assigned by Berlin policy-makers and marketers to the so-called creative industries, creative 'classes' and the spaces they inhabit.

The theme of 'creativity' has been adopted as a marketing slogan and focus of economic development policy by many cities across the world, sometimes with little empirical or economic basis. The analysis and policy recommendations made by Florida in *The Rise of the Creative Class* (2002), controversial and criticised as they may have been in academic circles, have been extremely influential on local policy-makers around the world, including in German cities (*Berlin-Institut für Bevölkerung und Entwicklung* 2007). In Berlin, looking at the economic data of the past ten years, there is, however, a solid basis to talk about a 'creative city'. In 2005 the *Senat* Department of the Economy carried out the first comprehensive survey of the 'creative economy' in Berlin. Creative industries were defined as the profit-oriented 'enterprises, entrepreneurs, and self-employed persons producing, marketing, distributing and trading profit-oriented cultural and symbolic goods' (Kalandides, 2007a: 7). In 2002 the 'creative economy' in Berlin represented 18 000 small and medium-sized enterprises, 90 000 employees (8 per cent of the workforce) and an annual turnover of eight billion euro (11 per cent of Berlin's GDP) (*Senatsverwaltung für Wirtschaft*, 2005). The 'creative industries' have been the fastest growing sector in the city's economy since the late 1990s, at rates higher than other German *Länder*. This stands in stark contrast to the sluggish economic and demographic growth of the city as a whole. The work done by the geographer Stefan Krätke (2002; 2003; 2004b) shows that Berlin has consequently developed a comparatively strong position in several sub-sectors of the knowledge-intensive industries, i.e. the media, software and life sciences sectors. Several factors have explained the successful growth of the 'creative' sectors in Berlin: cheap living and working spaces, tolerance, pre-existing artistic and cultural networks, and the relocation of influential global media corporations 'setting the trend' such as MTV Europe.

The Berlin government's approach to the growth of the 'creative industries' was initially reactive, but later turned to more proactive policy strategies (Kalandides, 2007b). As the Berlin *Senat* became increasingly aware of the reality, and potential, of the role played by 'creative industries' in the local economy, it started adapting its economic and urban development policies to support these sectors proactively. The *Senat* Department of the Economy set up a number of initiatives to support the cultural industries and the music and film sector. In 2007 the *Senat* Department of Urban Development commissioned a study to investigate how urban development policies could encourage the further growth of the creative industries (STADTart et al., 2007; Ebert and Kunzmann, 2007). In terms of place marketing, PFB intensified its promotional and support activities towards the cultural industries, in particular music, fashion, design and art. A 2001 advertisement specifically invited creative entrepreneurs to come and start up a firm in Berlin, using the nightlife and cultural scenes as key attraction factors. A year later, another advertisement, picturing the young, female CEO of MTV Central Europe, sold the constant change, experimentation, trend setting and creativity as hallmarks of Berlin.

One of the main characteristics of the content of the new campaigns promoting the idea of the creative city is that they have featured new urban spaces previously left out of the marketing imagery. Berlin's new geography of 'creativity' has been characterised by the concentration and clustering of creative industries in specific areas. The Eastern part of the city has been a particularly fertile ground. *Chausseestraße* in *Mitte* has attracted a strong presence of multimedia firms and has gained the epithet 'Silicon Alley' (Ward 2004: 252). The *Spree* river banks have become a major centre for music and media industries, with the relocation of the European headquarters of Universal Music in 2001 and of MTV Central Europe in 2004. Fashion designers have concentrated in *Prenzlauer Berg*, art galleries around the *Auguststrasse* in *Mitte*, product design in *Friedrichshain* and music labels in *Kreuzberg*. These new types of 'creative spaces' have gradually been making their way into the imagery of city marketing campaigns, into the publications of PFB and BTM and into the discourse of national and international media on Berlin as 'destination'. This includes spaces and sites not located in the cultural and political hotspots of central Berlin, e.g. the neighbourhood of *Friedrichshain*. As many of these 'creative spaces' are located in the Eastern part of the city, this means that buildings and sites from the former East, totally neglected in the promotional imagery of the 1990s, have made an appearance into promotional imagery – in particular some of the 'urban voids' domesticated by virtue of innovative 'temporary uses' (*Zwischennutzung*), such as Berlin's trendy 'urban beaches' (Barkham, 2007), which serve the image of the creative city. These spaces and sites are depicted by virtue of their new role as 'urban playgrounds' for artistic production, consumption, creativity, entertainment and leisure: the *MediaSpree* area, the *Badeschiff* (a boat turned into an outdoor swimming pool), temporary 'urban beaches'. . . International media have equally contributed to the promotion of the transformation of Berlin's Eastern districts into a new playground for artists, creatives, young travellers and tourists (Bernstein, 2005; Woodward, 2005; Barkham, 2007; The Independent, 2008), thus shifting the focus of media attention from the central iconic sites of urban redevelopment such as *Potsdamer Platz* to other areas (e.g. *Friedrichshain*).

Yet on the whole, in comparison to the 1990s, many advertisements produced by PFB post-2000 do not give a prominent visual place to the built environment. The focus tends to be on the young creatives or the 'culturpreneurs' themselves (Lange, 2007), whilst the city is sent to the background as a stage set for their activities. Acknowledging the importance attached to the architecture, the atmosphere, the 'look and feel' of particular neighbourhoods in the geographical clustering processes underpinning the growth of the creative industries, this relative absence is surprising. This may be explained by the fact that 'creative spaces' are much more diffuse, changing and more difficult to pin down than the sites of governmental power or those of global corporate power. Berlin continues to be the German capital of subcultures and alternative cultural experiments: this is something that official marketing campaigns cannot steer or capture very well, but can only try and capitalise on. City marketers are always 'running after', rather than setting the pace for, new urban creative trends: 'the goal of city marketing to isolate and tap distinctiveness seems per definition impossible, as it would mean taking a snapshot in space and time, of a material which, just a moment later, will have mutated again' (Kalandides, 2007: 4). The *'be* Berlin' campaign, launched in 2008, builds on this trend toward the depiction of individuals presented as 'creatives' at the expense of specific iconic or symbolic sites in the promotional imagery for the city. It epitomises the shift from 'sites to people' as the markers and symbols of a place, as the components and producers of its 'brand'.

FROM ICONIC SITES TO PEOPLE AS CREATORS OF A 'BRAND'. THE *'be* BERLIN' CAMPAIGN: INNOVATIVE FORM OF PARTICIPATORY PLACE BRANDING OR OLD WINE IN NEW BOTTLES?

After taking office the new Mayor of Berlin, Klaus Wowereit, began to take a proactive role in the promotion of the city, first by embarking on a large number of foreign promotional trips, 'indicative of an engaged desire to make Berlin's imagery work toward its economic promotion' (Ward, 2004: 251). In May 2007 the Mayor decided to set up an expert board and launch a call for proposals to search for a 'new branding strategy for Berlin', more specifically for a slogan, a graphic design and a 'basic communicative idea' which would underpin the future national and international promotion of the city (*Senatskanzlei Berlin*, 2007). Wowereit had famously described Berlin, in a newspaper interview of 2001, as 'poor but sexy' (*'Arm aber Sexy'*). This little phrase was quickly reported in the national and international media as one of the most accurate marketing labels ever given to the city (The Independent, 2008) and became an unofficial slogan for Berlin, both ironic and realistic. Yet the Mayor felt that a new, fresh image campaign for Berlin was necessary. Following the call for ideas, on 11 March 2008 Mayor Wowereit publicly launched a new campaign for Berlin under the slogan *'be* Berlin' (*sei Berlin*). The campaign is organised in two phases: the first one is directed towards the Berliners themselves, and aims at mobilising the active participation of the city's inhabitants, through collecting their narratives about Berlin, and encouraging the construction of strategic alliances among institutional players. The second phase, launched in March 2009 with an event in New York, was internationally oriented and used more conventional methods of city marketing such as events, advertising campaigns in the media.

The website of the campaign (www.sei-berlin.de) and the official speech and press statements which accompanied its release reveal that the campaign – its rationale, images, instruments, target groups and participants – seems to encompass a number of innovations in comparison to previous practices in Berlin – innovations in the process of designing the campaign, and innovations in the outcome. The campaign is not primarily targeted at investors or potential visitors, but (at least in its first phase) directed at the Berliners themselves – 'made by Berliners for Berlin'. It seeks to perform a 'new' kind of city branding, one which relies on the direct contributions of Berliners themselves, who are invited to *'be a storyteller, be an ambassador, be Berlin'* by sending their individual success stories and testimonies to the campaign's website. Collectively, these stories and the dozens of slogans created by Berliners make up the campaign. Instead of one message or slogan, it has encouraged a multiplicity of messages about Berlin, using the pattern 'be . . ., be . . ., be Berlin'.

Yet some degrees of continuity with past practices can also be outlined. The campaign confirms the trend identified above, i.e. a shifting focus away from the depiction of iconic sites and the built environment towards the portrayal of individual Berliners in the imagery. The theme of 'creativity' is expanded to encompass the normal, daily creativity of Berliners who make their city vibrant. It should be pointed out here that the use of the Berliners, of their personality and character, in promotional campaigns was pioneered in a West Berlin campaign of the 1970s (Schütz and Siebenhaar, 1996), as was the marketing of 'alternative culture'. In 1994 the first campaign designed by PFB, criticised at the time by the local media as a failure, was based on the testimonies of individual Berliners, such as a priest and a sportsman ('*Berliner werben für Berliner*', or 'Berliners advertise for Berliners'). In 2000 the Berlin magazine for city listings, *Zitty*, ran its own advertising campaign, with posters on the city's walls picturing 'normal' Berliners of various origin with the caption '*Die Stadt bin ich*' ('I am the city').

In the remainder of this section, some elements of analysis will be proposed in order to assess critically the first phase of the '*be* Berlin' campaign in relation to the three strands of 'critique' of place branding practices outlined in the first part of this chapter. With regard to the first argument, that of 'homogenisation' of place through similar discourses and replicated images, the campaign is clearly based on unique messages which are, in many ways, Berlin-specific. The campaign is a major innovation not only in Berlin but also worldwide, because it gives Berliners a voice in shaping the external representations of their city through new media such as the internet. The campaign seeks to shape a collective discourse on the city made of multiple fragments and voices, a patchwork of messages shifting away from simple meta-narratives and usual marketing jargon. Berliners themselves become 'storytellers' and it is their stories of the city that count. The guidelines given to Berliners on the campaign's website for the formulation of their 'personal story' are as follows: 'your story has to be authentic and original: what differentiates it from events in other cities, or makes it unique?' Your story should tell about change, and describe how Berlin has influenced you or has changed you in some way. Your story should be fun, engaging and encourage further actions or thoughts' (be Berlin, 2008a). Stories can be accompanied by photos or videos, and once posted online, can be commented upon and rated by viewers. They can also be updated. What is also striking about the campaign is that it appeals *to* civic pride and wants to be a stimulus *for* civic pride. It does not concentrate upon big iconic projects or the capital city status, but upon the less tangible complexity of the city which is understood as produced by its inhabitants. In the individual 'success stories' posted on the website, success is not only defined in economic terms, but in other ways too – scientific, cultural or 'non-profit' in particular.

With regard to the second argument voiced by critical authors on place branding – i.e. the selective nature of the process, the inclusion and exclusion of specific identities and groups – the '*be* Berlin' campaign is also rather innovative if compared to the previous campaigns of the 1990s. The image campaign features representatives of a type of Berliners that were previously completely left out of city marketing imagery, in particular

Berliners from an ethnic minority background. In the first set of posters which were designed for the launch of the campaign, teenagers of Turkish or Arab origin from a school of the *Neukölln* district (the *Rütli* school) are portrayed, presenting items of clothing which they successfully designed and marketed to change the image of their school. Later on in 2008, out of the hundreds of testimonies posted on the '*be* Berlin' website, eighteen characters were selected to be displayed in an image campaign on the city's walls: 'One is a fashion designer, another an Olympic champion, the third works as neighbourhood manager in *Neukölln* and seeks to help youngsters not to fall into violence and crime. Together these people are changing our city through their work and their commitment' (be Berlin, 2008b). One of the eighteen posters displays a youth worker from Arab origin, with the caption '*Fadi Saad is Berlin. The city lives from people like Fadi Saad. As neighbourhood manager in Neukölln he is changing Berlin*'. The integration of new social groups (ethnic minorities), new neighbour-hoods (e.g. *Neukölln*) and new types of activities (e.g. youth work) in the imagery representing the city can only be welcomed (Rada, 2008b), although it remains a modest step as there is still a dominance of 'white young creatives' in the remaining seventeen posters (be Berlin, 2008c). The short film that accompanied the campaign, however, does not feature any typical 'young creative' artist (be Berlin, 2008c). This was a conscious decision by the film director who wanted to show that that the kids from the *Rütli* School, and the clothing label they produced, are 'as creative as the fashion or web designers whom one can see in all Berlin beer adver-tisements' (Thalheim, in Apin, 2008). This still raises a question about the commodification of 'difference'. The vibrancy and diversity of the Berlin population is gradually being instrumentalised by the campaign now that it approaches its second phase, and can be interpreted as an extension of the promotional discourse on the 'creative city'. 'Tolerance' and 'diversity' are promoted because they are fertile grounds for the 'creative classes' à la Florida. It will be interesting to see how the portrayal of Berliners, includ-ing less 'conventional' characters such as the ones described above, evolves once the '*be* Berlin' campaign is internationalised and turned into an 'outward'-oriented place branding operation to attract tourists, investors, students, and 'young creatives'.

Finally, in relation to the third strand of critique summarised in the first section – that branding campaigns can be a form of 'urban conflict man-agement', manipulation or social engineering in cities increasingly divided as a result of economic restructuring and neoliberal urban governance – it is interesting to note that in the mind of its inceptors, the '*be* Berlin' campaign clearly seeks to address social divisions through an appeal to a collective identity feeling ('*Wir-Gefühl*') with a broad, inclusive scope. This has to be set within the context of a city increasingly divided along socio-economic and ethnic lines, in addition to the lingering 'east-west' division. The promoters of the campaign partly justify the need for the campaign using arguments which were already present in the discourse of economic-political elites in the early 1990s: that 'Berliners do not like their city' or are very negative about it, that they need to be encouraged to think, and talk, positively about it, both to improve the internal social cohesion of the city and its image toward outsiders. The campaign is, in that sense, in continuity with the various events and campaigns that throughout the 1990s, were designed to improve the 'mood' of Berliners in the city and stimulate their acceptance of the 'New Berlin'. Yet, as critical geographers have noted (Harvey, 1989), this form of collective mobilisation can also be used to divert attention away from material-structural inequalities and other forms of discrimination. Sceptical observers have asked whether the 'ten million euro for two words' spent on the campaign (Rada, 2008a) would not have been better used in conflict management or local economic development measures in deprived neighbourhoods 'so that the losers [of Berlin's transformation] don't wreck their neighbourhoods like the youth in the Paris *Banlieue*' (Rada, 2008b).

CONCLUSION

To return to our initial question – whether the '*be* Berlin' campaign is an innovative form of participatory city branding 'by its inhabitants for its inhabitants' or just old wine in new bottles, the answer seems to lie somewhere in between these two interpretations. The process of designing the campaign and its outcome to date are innovative and original, and clearly challenge the first two sets of critical arguments on place branding commonly found in the critical human geographical and sociological literature. This is less so when assessing the campaign against the third element of critique mentioned in the first section of this contribution, i.e. the role of place branding in 'social engineering' in cities in transformation. There is evidence that in the Berlin context, the campaign conforms to several trends which had started a few years earlier, in particular attempts to engage the Berliners with urban change and raise their 'mood' about the city, in a difficult economic context made worse by the deep-seated financial crisis of the city's government. City marketing and place branding practices have performed a number of roles in Berlin: they have underpinned a project of urban change, helped to communicate planning decisions, which had often already been made, legitimised political choices on urban design, tried to encourage the social and cultural integration between East and West Berliners by fostering 'pride' in the 'New Berlin' (Colomb, 2008). Critics have described such practices as legitimising devices and public relation exercises designed by the political and economic elite. In the 1990s some of the heavy-handed marketing surrounding, in particular, the *Potsdamer Platz* development, did mask the lack of transparency and of genuine public participation in decision-making. It is certainly the case that the focus on 'architectural spectacle' has deflected attention away from crucial political, economic and distributional issues underpinning many new urban developments in reunified Berlin.

Branding strategies are confronted with the impossible challenge of summarising and simplifying a complex, ambiguous, ever-changing cultural and social reality and urban landscape into neat brands. Recent developments in Berlin branding practices since the mid-2000s have broadened the range of spaces, people, messages and images displayed in the Berlin promotional imagery. This process is positive in the sense that it widens the range of facets communicated to the world about the city and involves the Berliners in the process of shaping the external representations of their city, but it may carry with it some risks for the very spaces and people it depicts: commodification of previously non-commercial activities, symbolic gentrification leading to real physical changes, instrumentalisation of social groups in a symbolic strategy of urban social management not addressing the real causes of inequality or discrimination.

This is why conflicts over the material restructuring of the city have been accompanied by less visible, more subtle, conflicts over images, discourses and representations of the city to its inhabitants and to the outside world. The Berlin place marketing organisations were the focus of debates and opposition within the Berlin Parliament, in particular with regard to the lack of accountability and transparency in their use of public funding. The glossy representations of image campaigns and promotional materials have been disrupted by the activities of citizens' movements which have uncovered and publicly promoted new 'layers of memory' and identity not represented in mainstream marketing (Till, 2005), by artistic interventions which subverted the marketing messages (Colomb, 2008), by subversive slogans and graffitis and by the work of alternative media which have thrown light on the sites of a different Berlin not fitting into the vision of the promoters of 'The New Berlin'. The '*be* Berlin' campaign was no exception to this: its slogan was ironically subverted by critics into 'be unemployed' or 'Be *Harz IV*' – but subversion is the fate of such slogans and campaigns: 'so it is with image campaigns. They are platforms that become used by everyone. Which is actually good' (Rada, 2008b).

11. Place satisfaction of city residents: findings and implications for city branding

Andrea Insch and Magdalena Florek

INTRODUCTION AND BACKGROUND

Cities increasingly compete for the attention and investment of prospective investors, tourists and residents, in order to achieve their developmental goals. As well as appealing to 'outsiders', cities must also appeal to residents – their loyal supporters. Despite increasing recognition of the important role of residents as city brand ambassadors, little is known of the factors that contribute to their perceived satisfaction with the city where they work, live and play. The notion of place satisfaction in the case of city residents is largely untouched within the emerging place management and marketing field. The importance of the ambitious goals of achieving satisfied and loyal citizens are difficult to dispute. For some, they are the ultimate indicators of place management success (Guhathakurta and Stimson, 2007; Kotler et al., 1999). City councils and other government authorities regularly monitor and track the level of satisfaction of ratepayers regarding the services they provide. Often this extends to satisfaction with different aspects of city life. Positive feedback from current residents confirms that they are performing well by meeting their expectations regarding the services they offer. These results can be used to promote the benefits of living in the city to potential residents to attract and motivate them to move. Where particular skills gaps exist in the workforce, certain features of the city (e.g. pace of life, natural environment) that might be appealing can be highlighted in addition to the common, basic requirements of living, working and playing in urban communities (Williams et al., 2008). Ensuring a consistently high level of satisfaction over time is vital, since this might influence residents' decisions to remain or search for other places to live. Understanding how different factors influence city residents' place satisfaction is an issue of vital importance to place management practitioners and researchers.

191

RESIDENT PLACE SATISFACTION – A REVIEW OF KNOWLEDGE

Satisfaction and related concepts have been the focus of research in many disciplines. Three main disciplines in particular have dealt with satisfaction in a way that is useful for understanding the concept of resident place satisfaction, namely, psychology, sociology and human ecology, and marketing.

First, the concept of life satisfaction from psychology is helpful in defining the place satisfaction of residents and the process by which individuals evaluate their satisfaction. Some consider life satisfaction as an outcome, while others consider it as a process of evaluation. For example, Özer (2004) views life satisfaction as a situation or a consequence obtained through comparing someone's expectations with possessions. On the other hand, Shin and Johnson (1978, cited in Pavot and Diener, 1993) describe life satisfaction as a judgmental process in which individuals assess the quality of their lives on the basis of their own unique set of criteria. Therefore, as Pavot and Diener (1993) conclude 'life satisfaction is a conscious cognitive judgment of one's life in which the criteria for judgment are up to the person' (p.164).

Secondly, those conditions or aspects that shape one's quality of life are discussed by scholars of environmental psychology. According to Wahl and Weisman (2003), the environment plays a meaningful role in creating a good life. Based on findings of Fernandez-Ballesteros (2001), those who are satisfied with their environment tend to be more satisfied with their lives. What increases people's well-being is the harmony between personal preferences and environmental features (Kilinç, 2006). People, and more specifically residents, perceive environmental features according to the importance of their needs (Kahana et al., 2003). Thus, perception of one's life determines its assessment and as such evaluation of quality of life alone is not sufficient to measure life satisfaction. The same assumption might apply when evaluating the satisfaction with the place that people live every day.

This field of psychology also provides the theoretical basis for conceptualising place in terms of its relationship to satisfaction and quality of life. Specifically, physical space is called 'place' when personal, group, or cultural processes have been given meaning through it (Low and Altman, 1992). If the social and physical resources within residential environment are convenient to satisfy the needs and preferences of residents, the attachment (which might be understood as loyalty in marketing terminology) to the place occurs (Shumaker and Taylor, 1983). In the same way that individuals can develop emotional ties to other people and objects, emotional and close bonds with places can develop (Low and Altman, 1992).

According to many studies, development of emotional bonds with places is a prerequisite of psychological balance, good adjustment, sense of stability and involvement in local activities (e.g. Rowles, 1990; Hay, 1998). In this context place attachment has been defined as 'the affective link that people establish with specific settings, where they tend to remain and where they feel comfortable and safe' (Hernandez et al., 2007).

As Rubinstein and Parmelee (1992) suggest, the personal experience and social interaction are crucial aspects of attaching people to particular places and, what is more, making a place part of one's identity. This suggests that experience is necessary to evaluate an individual's satisfaction, as a consequence of a clash of expectations with a place's reality. Similarly, Rubinstein and Parmelee (1992) understand sense of place to be a result of people's life experiences, specific circumstances and personal interpretations. Consequently, personal satisfaction can differ significantly from the objective indicators of a quality of life assessment. Previous research has demonstrated that a person's age and generation both influence their level of neighbourhood satisfaction. Infirm elderly people may report a higher level of satisfaction as they have stronger community attachment due to the perceived difficulties in finding a new place to live (La Gory et al., 1985). Furthermore, residents with different levels of environmental competence respond differently to the same set of local conditions. The main insight from this field is that residents occupying the same physical spaces do not necessarily perceive these environments in the same way. Length of residence, as Kasarda and Janowitz (1974: 336) argue, 'plays a far more important role in assimilation into the social fabric of local communities than does population size, density, social class, or stage in life-cycle'. Studies have demonstrated that length of an individual's residence affects community behaviour and positively influences community attachment through the social bonds between residents. Furthermore, an individual's age can interact to influence affective measures of attachment to the community (Theodori, 2004).

Mainstream marketing has dealt with the idea of life satisfaction through the concept of consumer well-being. Not surprisingly, the way marketers measure satisfaction emphasises an individual's satisfaction with their material possessions over a product's life-cycle – acquisition, preparation, consumption, possession, maintenance and disposal (Lee et al., 2002). According to Lee and Sirgy (2004), consumer well-being also involves assessment by experts of society's costs and benefits from consumption over the life-cycle of products. Researchers have examined a variety of product categories and service providers and have linked consumer satisfaction with a mix of retail establishments in an individual's community to life satisfaction (i.e. the subjective quality of life) (Meadow,

1983) and between possession satisfaction and life satisfaction. These links are stronger for older people and low income individuals (Leelakulthanit et al., 1991). Further, Lee et al. (2002), argue that satisfaction with all stages of the product life-cycle affects other areas of life that influence overall life satisfaction. Following this logic, it could be argued that a city resident's life can be split into different stages of their residency, which, in turn, can influence other aspects of their life satisfaction.

Most indicators of life satisfaction tend to focus on the notion of consumption satisfaction as defined in the marketing literature. This phase in the life-cycle is more important for services and has been defined as the 'satisfaction resulting from the use of goods and services in the particular community' (Lee and Sirgy, 2004: 51). Place satisfaction can be considered in a similar way to service experiences, since cities can be considered to be bundles of services that are experienced by residents. Like consumer services generally, residents' consumption of a city's community assets 'cannot be possessed or inventoried' (Lee and Sirgy, 2004: 51). Thus, to improve city residents' perceived well-being and in turn their satisfaction, providers and managers of city services must direct their efforts to maximise the quality and perceived satisfaction with the bundle of services residents consume during their residency.

The concept of post-purchase dissonance has been applied to the context of places by Kotler et al. (1993). They state that 'choosing a place almost always involves some post-purchase dissonance' (p.58). According to Kotler et al. (1993), a buyer's satisfaction is based on the closeness between their expectations and the place's perceived performance. In the case of residents, they are exposed to the place performance all the time since by living there they experience the city continuously, including many aspects that are usually not accessible for temporary visitors. This means that residents' expectations and evaluations are not 'one-off' as it is, for example in the case of tourists. Thus, resident place satisfaction is dynamic and must be continuously monitored. The question still remains as to how this should be measured most effectively.

How to Measure Place Satisfaction?

Place satisfaction is a subjective state, evaluated from the place user's perspective – the way he or she sees it. Various research institutes have developed different measures and indices related to life satisfaction, quality of life and well-being that are used to gauge and monitor these outcomes in cities, regions and countries (e.g. the Economist Intelligence Unit's Quality of Life Index, the Quality of Life Index of International Living or the Australian Unity Wellbeing Index). From the perspective of marketing and consumption, the Customer Satisfaction Index (CSI), derived from the cumulative satisfaction concept (Olsen and Johnson, 2003), is widely used across countries to evaluate the satisfaction of customers (O'Loughlin and Coenders, 2002).

Rather than focusing on one-off transactions, this measure is based on the overall satisfaction with a product or service provider (Olsen and Johnson, 2003). It evaluates the consumers' entire set of experiences with a product or service to date (Fornell et al., 1996). Consequently, cumulative satisfaction is a suitable basis for measuring place satisfaction in the case of residents as they develop their satisfaction based on everyday experience over a period of time.

The general CSI tool has been modified to take country-specific factors into account (e.g. American ACSI, European ECSI, Swedish SCSB, Norwegian NCSB, Swiss SWICS, Korean KCSI). The American Customer Satisfaction Index (ACSI) served as a basis for evaluating factors influencing the level of residents' satisfaction with a city in the study developed by Insch and Florek (see further Insch and Florek, 2008). Overall, this tool combines indices for drivers of satisfaction (customer expectations, perceived quality, and perceived value), satisfaction (ACSI), and consequences of satisfaction (customer complaints and customer loyalty) (see Figure 11.1). An analysis of particular indices and impacts can determine which drivers of satisfaction, if improved, would have the

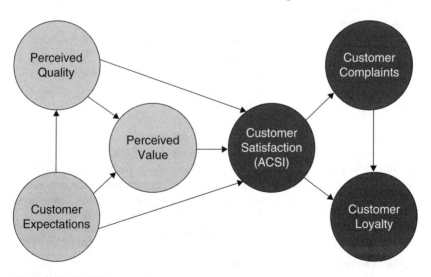

Source: ACSI, 2008.

Figure 11.1 The American Customer Satisfaction Index (ACSI, 2008)

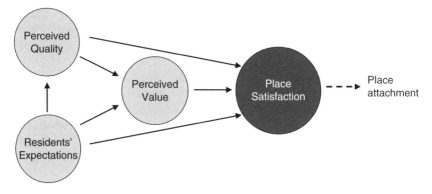

Source: Author's own.

Figure 11.2   Working model of resident place satisfaction

most effect on customer loyalty. Loyalty, in turn, should be understood as being two dimensional, namely behavioural and attitudinal.

Several elements of the ACSI framework are adopted and adjusted to form the basis for measuring city residents' place satisfaction (for details see Insch and Florek, 2008). In this way, it is possible to identify several linkages between particular elements that build residents' satisfaction and their attachment, which is an individual's emotional link to a place that leads to relevant attitudes and behaviours.

Each of these elements was investigated in a survey of residents of Dunedin, New Zealand. Dunedin is New Zealand's fifth largest city in population, located on the east coast of the country's South Island. A survey of residents enables their expectations about various social and physical assets in their city to be compared to their evaluation of the quality of these aspects of the city. Any gaps between their expectations and evaluations of quality can then be identified. Residents' perception of the value of living in the city is an assessment of the ratio of perceived quality relative to price (O'Loughlin and Coenders, 2002). Overall, residents' general level of place satisfaction is expected to be correlated with their expectations, perceptions of quality and value for money. As with customer loyalty, the level of attachment of residents is seen as a consequence of their overall satisfaction with the city.

Survey Design and Administration

A telephone survey was designed to obtain information on place satisfaction among city residents of Dunedin. A structured survey was first tested

Table 11.1 Effects of socio-demographic variables on residents' perceptions of overall value and satisfaction

Perceptions ⟍ Demographic Variables	Perceived Value for Money	Place Satisfaction (3 Items)
Age		1 p = 0.000***
Annual Income	p = 0.015**	
Years Living in Dunedin	p = 0.048**	1 p = 0.000***
		2 p = 0.040**
		3 p = 0.019**

Notes: ***=Difference is significant at 0.01 level; **=Difference is significant at 0.05 level.

Source: Author's own.

on a small group of local residents and their feedback was used to refine the wording of the questions and to shorten it to an acceptable length. The final survey consisted of four sections, with questions to measure each of the items discussed previously.

Potential residents were screened to ensure that they met the minimum age of 18 years or older. Respondents' age and gender were recorded and they were then asked the length of time they had been living in Dunedin, as well as the amount of choice they had when they moved to Dunedin. These questions helped to determine whether length of residence or amount of choice affected their perceived value for money or cumulative place satisfaction.

Next, respondents were asked about their expectations in relation to 10 different aspects of city life, a range of physical, social, environmental and personal considerations about living in the city. These items are listed above in Table 11.1. To generate this list, previous studies of environmental psychology were reviewed, as well as public documents about Dunedin, such as the city council website, promotional materials and quality of life surveys. For each aspect, respondents rated the level of importance they placed on it. Respondents were then asked to evaluate their level of satisfaction with each of the aspects of living in the city. In the same section, participants were asked about the perceived value for money that living in Dunedin provided them.

Respondents were then asked to evaluate their level of satisfaction with each of the aspects of living in the city. Then, three items to measure overall place satisfaction were presented. A cumulative measure of place satisfaction, adapted from Olsen and Johnson (2003) comprised of three items – 'ideal place to live', 'overall expectations' and 'overall satisfaction'. The final section of the questionnaire gathered demographic information from respondents, such as level of education, annual income, birthplace, length of residence in New Zealand and suburb of residence.

Sample Description

A stratified random sampling technique was chosen in order to maximise the representativeness of the data. A total of 649 people were contacted as eligible to participate, and 291 agreed to participate.

The sample comprised 37 per cent male and 63 per cent female respondents. Respondents aged 66 years and over made up the largest group, followed by 46–55 years of age (20 per cent) and 36–45 years of age (18 per cent). Most respondents (69 per cent) had lived in Dunedin 20 years or more, with 32 per cent having lived in the city since birth. At the other extreme, 5 per cent had lived in Dunedin for less than two years. The majority of respondents were born in New Zealand (80 per cent). Respondents born in Europe made up the next largest group (14 per cent). 93 per cent of the sample had been living in New Zealand for 20 years or more. Almost one third of respondents had lived there since birth, so they did not make this decision directly. Half this number thought they had no choice in deciding to move to Dunedin from their former place of residence. Most of the respondents thought that they had exercised either a fair or a great deal of choice (41 per cent). Just under half of the respondents (47 per cent) reported their gross income as $NZ30000 or less (equivalent to €12400 or less). Most respondents had achieved a qualification after leaving secondary school (60 per cent), among these 10 per cent had a postgraduate qualification. Respondents lived in a variety of suburbs in Dunedin, covering a broad, diverse range of neighbourhoods both geographically and socio-demographically. In total 78 different suburbs across the six wards of Dunedin city were represented in the sample.

SURVEY FINDINGS

The results of the study are in two sections. The first looks at the different aspects of city life that contribute to resident place satisfaction. The second discusses the socio-demographic characteristics that are linked to resident place satisfaction. To enhance the readability of the results, only the significant outcomes are discussed in detail.

Expectations and Satisfaction with City Life

Resident's ratings of their expectations and satisfaction with aspects of city life were calculated. The mean for each of the 10 aspects or features of city life are shown in Table 11.2. As can be seen, work/life balance was considered highly important and residents also placed importance on personal and public safety. Residents evaluated satisfaction with three aspects of city life slightly higher than their importance, namely, the natural environment; cultural, arts and the creative scene; and location relative to other destinations and accessibility to other cities. Of all the features that residents evaluated, efficient public transport was perceived as being the least important. This difference, as well as differences in residents' expectations and satisfaction with personal and public safety, city's community assets, work/life balance and city vibrancy/energy were statistically significant. The results also indicated that for each aspect of city life, residents' expectations were moderately positively related to their perceived satisfaction with that aspect. Overall, these outcomes suggest that there is a margin for targeted improvement for most aspects of living in Dunedin, even if these margins are modest.

The relationships between residents' expectations and perceived value for money, as well as their satisfaction and perceived value were also examined. Exploring the relations between these items does not assume a one-way influence. Overall, residents' expectations and satisfaction with aspects of life in Dunedin are positively related to their perceived value for money of living in Dunedin. All but two of the ten expectation items are related to their perceived value for money, and all but three of their satisfaction items are related. More specifically, the findings indicated that neither residents' expectations nor satisfaction with efficient public transport was significantly related to their perceptions of value for money. Also worth noting is the significant relationship between residents' expectations of 'location relative to other destinations and accessibility to other cities' and value for money. This suggests that residents expect that these features will positively contribute to their value for money. However, their evaluations of these aspects do not meet their expectations. These outcomes suggest that these aspects of city life need to be investigated by city authorities in order to bring perceived satisfaction into alignment with value for money, so as to ensure that they do positively contribute to residents' perceived value for money.

Three measures of place satisfaction of city residents were used in this study – ideal place to live, overall expectations of living in Dunedin and overall satisfaction of living in Dunedin. Analysis of the different aspects of city life indicated that they are positively related to overall

Table 11.2   Gaps between residents' expectations and perceptions towards aspects of city life

Aspect	Expectations Mean (em)	Perceptions Mean (pm)	Paired Differences	
			Mean	SD
Work/life balance (a good job/career and leisure/family time)	4.31	3.85	0.46	0.97***
Personal and public safety	4.27	3.81	0.46	1.03***
The natural environment (landscapes, views, harbour, presence of wildlife)	4.21	4.23	0.02	1.03
The city's community assets (parks and gardens, historic buildings, museum, university)	4.18	3.92	0.26	0.99***
Cultural, arts and creative scene (galleries, live bands, festivals, theatre)	3.79	3.83	0.03	1.12
City's vibrancy and energy (thriving city)	3.71	3.58	0.13	0.98**
Openness of residents to new people, ideas and diversity	3.71	3.63	0.08	1.16
Sports grounds and facilities (Edgar centre, Moana Pool)	3.64	3.62	0.02	1.30
Location relative to other destinations and accessibility to other cities (ie. connections to other cities)	3.48	3.55	0.07	1.10
Efficient public transport	3.09	2.76	0.33	1.49***

Notes: ***=Difference is significant at 0.01 level ; **=Difference is significant at 0.05 level.

Source: Author's own.

place satisfaction, both in terms of residents' expectations and their perceived satisfaction with these specific aspects. Specifically, the majority of individual aspects of city life (both expectations and satisfaction) are positively related to each measure of cumulative place satisfaction. It is worth noting that the item 'efficient public transport' is not significantly related to the first measure of cumulative place satisfaction, 'ideal place to live' either for residents' expectations or perceived satisfaction. This suggests that residents' expectations and perceived satisfaction with public transport does not contribute to their overall level of satisfaction with life in Dunedin. The reasons why it is not rated highly in terms of satisfaction and of key importance to local residents should be investigated.

Finally, the relations between perceived value for money and each measure of place satisfaction were measured. The results demonstrated that value for money was significantly positively related to each independent measure of overall place satisfaction – 'ideal place to live', 'overall expectations', and 'overall satisfaction'. These results indicate that there is a positive significant relationship between residents' perceptions of value for money and their overall level of place satisfaction. To maintain favourable evaluations of value for money and thus resident satisfaction, local authorities must ensure that residents' satisfaction with each important aspect of city life is positively evaluated. If gaps between residents' expectations and their satisfaction with each aspect of city life develop, this may threaten their perceived value for money and in turn their overall satisfaction with living in the city. Over time, residents may decide to move away and destroy the bonds that they have formed with the place. Further, they may complain to others about their dissatisfaction and persuade them not to settle there.

Socio-demographic Influences on Value for Money and Place Satisfaction

Possible socio-demographic influences on perceptions of value for money and evaluation of satisfaction with living in Dunedin were explored. The results indicated a significant effect overall for resident's annual income and the number of years they had lived in Dunedin on their perceived value for money.

Finer analysis also revealed specific differences between groups based on the number of years they had been living in Dunedin. There were significant differences in perceived value for money for residents living in Dunedin less than one year and those one year to just under two years. Significant differences were also found for those living less than a year and since birth, and between those residents living in Dunedin between 10 and 20 years and those living in the city since birth.

As supported by previous research, residents' age was influential in determining their overall level of reported satisfaction. In particular, significant differences were found for age on one of the measures of place satisfaction 'ideal place to live'. Overall the mean score of place satisfaction for each of these measures increased with age. The number of years living in Dunedin also had a significant effect on each of the place satisfaction items – 'ideal place to live', 'overall expectations living in Dunedin', 'overall satisfaction living in Dunedin'. Further analysis showed that place satisfaction tended to increase with time, or the length of time residents had lived in the city and with age.

These results suggests that the place satisfaction of residents is related to length of time living in the city and that evaluations are higher for those who do not have any means of comparison (since birth) or those migrating at an early age (20 years or more) or with only a distant memory of another city for comparison. Some of the significant differences for the second indicator ('overall expectations living in Dunedin') do not follow the overall pattern and might suggest that there might be a certain period (5–10 years) at which residents consider other residential options and their evaluation might not be as favourable as those residents who have recently moved to a new city and are settling in.

SUMMARY AND IMPLICATIONS FOR PRACTICE

This chapter is motivated by the goal of developing useful indicators to evaluate and monitor city resident place satisfaction, and represents the first step through a study of key determinants. As well as meeting the needs of practitioners, this approach addresses the lack of conceptual development of resident place satisfaction in place management theory. Exploration of the principal relations between elements and socio-demographic influences of resident place satisfaction presented in this chapter creates a number of implications for city authorities and place management practitioners.

Application of the model in at least one city, in this case Dunedin, New Zealand, suggests that the individual and cumulative measures of satisfaction are relevant and potentially useful for identifying gaps in satisfaction and monitoring changes in residents' perceptions over time. Even though these different aspects were developed with a particular city in mind, they are broad enough to be applied to other cities of comparable size.

Repeated surveys, conducted at regular intervals, would permit the detection of gaps between expectations and performance (in this situation residents' satisfaction) and allow appropriate action to be taken to fill them. Such detection of likely bases of dissatisfaction and frustration is a precursor to stemming a possible out-flow of residents. In particular, the measure, value for money, may serve as a sensitive indicator for benchmarking purposes, both internally and externally. In this regard, the results of this study suggest that residents may 'shop around' at various stages in their city residential life-cycle, as their perceptions of value for money appears to shift over the term of their residency. Most notably, there are significant differences in the levels of satisfaction of newcomers, compared to long term residents. The results suggest that residents are more critical or dissatisfied during their first year, thus local authorities should ensure that efforts are made to make their transition to living in the new city as uncomplicated as possible and they should provide new residents with sufficient information to ensure that they find the neighbourhood and city amenities and services that most closely fits their lifestyle needs. Above all, those charged with city promotion must ensure that new residents' expectations are not raised to a level which cannot be adequately fulfilled, in other words, the city must be able to deliver on its promises in all areas, including social interaction, community spirit, outdoors and recreation, culture, access and transportation to and around the city.

The results of the survey also suggest that resident place satisfaction increases with age and length of residency (and/or possibly that residents remain in the city as they are content and satisfied living there). In this respect, familiarity does not necessarily breed contempt but greater appreciation. This result accords with previous research, which suggests that satisfaction and place attachment are positively related to length of residence. It might be the case that there are more barriers to leaving a particular place over time, such as the complex network of social relationships, financial investments and other commitments. On the other hand, individuals who have lived in their neighbourhood and city since birth do not have a frame of reference or basis for comparison. Therefore, their assessments may be positively skewed. This local positive bias may not be adequate to stem a major outflow of residents if economic conditions change and residents perceive that their financial situation may deteriorate rapidly if they choose to stay. Furthermore, this sense of pride and goodwill may also not be enough to attract outsiders.

IMPLICATIONS FOR RESEARCH

The initial testing of relations between different elements and determinants of resident place satisfaction presented in this chapter requires replication and additional testing to confirm or refine the relationships between the constructs. Ideally, additional testing should occur in the same city at a regular interval and in a different city of similar size to provide appropriate bases for comparison. Internal benchmarking for a city will assist in determining the adequacy and stability of the measures. Resources permitting, a larger scale survey could also be conducted within a single city or region to maximise the representativeness of the sample. This would also permit additional statistical analyses to be performed including cluster analysis, comparisons between communities/neighbourhoods within a city and an examination of the drivers of satisfaction and the development of a scale of resident place satisfaction. Future research should also investigate the relations between satisfaction and loyalty in the place context and particularly place attachment. Even though these constructs have been the focus of research in environmental psychology, their link to satisfaction has not been thoroughly examined. These linkages should be the focus for place marketing management practitioners and researchers since they may provide the early warning signs of mounting dissatisfaction and over time could prevent an exodus of residents.

12. Semiotics and place branding: the influence of the built and natural environment in city logos

Gary Warnaby and Dominic Medway

INTRODUCTION

Over the last 30 years, place marketing – and latterly the more overt emphasis on place branding – has become an increasingly common strategy for entrepreneurial cities, regions and countries seeking to gain some form of advantage in an ever more competitive environment. This has had significant implications for how the attractions and facilities located within such places – and indeed the places themselves as holistic entities – are communicated to potential target markets and audiences. As such, places, according to Hubbard and Hall, may be 'constituted through a plethora of images and representations' (1998: 7). This chapter considers place representation and branding, with particular reference to the incorporation within logos of elements of the built and natural environment associated with particular locales. Utilising concepts relating to semiotics, the chapter identifies a number of ways in which representations of particular attributes of the built and natural environment (such as buildings, bridges, coastlines, rivers etc.) are used by places seeking to create a sense of differentiation and uniqueness in their branding activities.

RESEARCH CONTEXT: SEMIOTICS AND PLACE MARKETING

Semiotics has been defined as, 'the study of signs in society' (Bignell, 1997: 5), incorporating their production, functioning and interpretation (Boklund-Lagopoulou et al., 2003). Semiotics emerged as an area of study in the early twentieth century as a response to concerns as to 'the problematic of meaning and representation' (Boklund-Lagopoulou et al., 2003: vii). Characterised by significant interdisciplinarity, semiotics arises primarily from the separate but related work of Ferdinand de Saussure (1974) and Charles Peirce (1965 – see Bignell, 1997; Boklund-Lagopoulou et al., 2003; Crow, 2003 for overviews). De Saussure's work focused on linguistics, postulating that language is made up of signs (i.e. words) that communicate meanings, and that other things which communicate meanings could potentially be studied in the same way as linguistic signs (Bignell, 1997). Peirce was also concerned with structural models of the sign, which concentrated on relationships between the sign's components (Crow, 2003), but his work focused on visual and non-verbal, rather than linguistic sign systems.

Whether linguistic or visual, from a semiotic perspective, signs have two components – signifier and signified. The signifier is the vehicle which expresses the sign – namely, a pattern of sound which makes up a word or the marks on paper which are read as words, or the pattern of shapes and colours used in pictures to represent an object or person (Bignell, 1997). The signified is, 'the concept which the signifier calls forth when we perceive it', and the sign comprises, 'the inseparable unity of the signifier with the signified, since in fact we never have one without the other' (Bignell, 1997: 12). Barthes (1972: 113) refers to the sign as the 'associative total' of the signifier and signified. A third key element of sign systems is the referent, which relates to the actual things that signs refer to. As mentioned above, the signifier is a concept, which may or may not refer to actual things. Thus, when we talk about place marketing/branding as the signified, we may be referring to a particular sub-discipline of marketing which comprises a distinct set of marketing/branding activities (i.e. signifiers). However the specific marketing communications signs for an individual town, city, region or country could be regarded as referents.

There are different 'modes of relationship' (Hawkes, 1977) between signifier and signified, as proposed by Peirce – symbol, icon and index. Chandler (2007: 36–7) describes these three terms, which are not mutually exclusive (Bignell, 1997), as follows:

- Symbol – a relationship between the signifier and signified which is fundamentally arbitrary or purely conventional and which must be agreed upon and learned (e.g. language in general, numbers, national flags etc.);
- Icon – where the signifier is perceived as resembling or imitating the signified (i.e. recognisably looking, sounding, feeling, tasting or smelling like it);
- Index – where the signifier is not arbitrary but is directly connected in some way (physically or causally) to the signified, with this link being either observed or inferred.

Bignell (1997) states that because signs are used to describe and interpret the world, their function seems simply to label phenomena, or to denote them. However, in addition to this denotative function of signs in communicating a fact, they may create extra associations, which are termed connotations. The 'bringing together of signs and their connotations to shape a particular message' (Bignell, 1997: 16) is termed the making of myth by Barthes (1972). In this context, myth refers to, 'ways of thinking about people, products, places or ideas which are structured to send particular messages to the reader or viewer of the text' (Bignell, 1997: 17). For Barthes (1972: 130), myth 'essentially aims at causing an immediate impression', and Barthes goes on to state that 'it does not matter if one is later allowed to see through the myth, its action is assumed to be stronger than the rational explanations that may later belie it'. Barthes terms myth as distortion and as an 'inflexion' (1972: 129). Indeed, Bignell states that, 'myth is not an innocent language, but one that picks up existing signs and their connotations, and orders them purposefully to play a particular social role' (1997: 16–17).

While Barthes (1972) discussed such issues in terms of *political* ideology, much of the above is analogous to the representation of towns, cities, regions and nations in place marketing activities. The marketing of places has been regarded as 'a special type of marketing' (Ashworth, 1993: 648) in comparison to more stereotypical marketing activities. This is a consequence of various factors which define the particular context of the marketing of places, including the complexity not only of the place 'product' to be marketed (see for example, Ashworth and Voogd, 1990a; 1990b; Kotler et al., 1999; Paddison, 1993; van den Berg and Braun, 1999; Ward and Gold, 1994), but also of the organisational structures and mechanisms by which this activity occurs (see for example, Ave, 1993; Boyle, 1997; Camagni, 1993; Kotler et al., 1993; 1999; Short and Kim, 1999; Warnaby et al., 2002; 2004).

With regard to organisational structures and mechanisms for place marketing, Short and Kim (1999) articulate a 'political economy' perspective, which recognises the collaboration of – and potential conflict between – place stakeholders from public, private and voluntary sectors in designing and implementing place marketing activities. The potential conflict between the different ideologies of individuals and groups within the 'strategic network' (van den Berg and Braun, 1999) existing within a location may, in turn, have significant implications for how the place is represented to target audiences. The place image communicated is likely to be highly selective (Barke and Harrop, 1994; Griffiths, 1998; Hall, 1998; Holcomb, 1994; Short, 1999), and as Hall (1998) argues, the process of image creation may not be objective and disinterested – the interests and contributions of some groups may be marginalised, and place marketing activities may serve specific political goals and help to create and maintain the hegemony of specific groups (Sadler, 1993). As Griffiths states:

> Place marketing works by creating a selective relationship between (projected) image and (real) identity: in the process of reimaging a city, some aspects of its identity are ignored, denied or marginalised. For example, attention may be drawn to a city's industrial or mercantile heritage, while the practices of class exploitation or slavery that may have made this possible remain under a veil of silence. Strong local loyalties and civic pride may be highlighted, but not the traditions of trade union militancy or revolutionary politics. Great play may be made of a city's cultural diversity but not the systematic racial discrimination that in all probability accompanied it (1998: 53).

Thus, marketing and branding activity may weave a number of what Barthes would term place myths. Hubbard and Hall (1998: 7) state that, given the pervasive nature of place marketing, 'it might be argued that it no longer makes much sense to distinguish between the "myths" and "realities" of the city, as images of the city incorporated in promotional brochures, adverts, guidebooks and videos come to define the essence of the city as much as the city itself'. These images, promulgated via marketing and branding activities, attempt to ensure that a place identity is perceived in an appropriate manner – in other words, a suitable place image is created. However, such images – like many myths and their relationship with reality – may not bear too close a scrutiny.

PLACE IMAGE AND IDENTITY

In the corporate communications context, image is the perception that audiences have of the organisation, resulting from their interpretation of the totality of cues presented by it (Dowling, 2001; Fill, 2005). According to Melewar (2003: 214), it is 'the net result of the interaction of all the experiences, beliefs, feelings, knowledge, and impressions that each stakeholder has about an organisation'. By contrast, identity refers to the formation of cues, which can include symbols and nomenclature, incorporating corporate name, logo, advertising slogans, livery etc. (Dowling, 2001), by which stakeholders can recognise and identify an organisation (Fill, 2005; see also Dowling, 2001; Olins, 1989). Van Riel (1995) suggests that the personality of an organisation is projected via a corporate identity mix, incorporating behaviour, communication and symbolism. Corporate identity is essentially a means by which an organisation can be differentiated (Dowling, 2001; Fill, 2005), and as such, needs to be planned. Melewar distinguishes between images and identity in that: 'corporate identity resides in the organisation, whereas corporate image resides in the heads of the stakeholders' (2003: 214). In a specific place context, Barke and Harrop highlight this distinction:

> Places also have identities. The 'identity' may be regarded as an objective thing; it is what the place is actually like. Identity though is not the same as 'image', which defines how an organisation or a place is perceived externally. Naturally, image may be strongly influenced by 'objective' identity and image makers will seek to structure the perceptions of others but cannot finally control them. Images may exist independently of the apparent facts of objective reality (1994: 95).

The creation of an appropriate identity and image is an important aspect of place marketing (see Ashworth and Voogd, 1990a; 1994; Barke and Harrop, 1994; Holcomb, 1994; 1999; Hubbard and Hall, 1998; Kotler et al., 1993; 1999; Millington et al., 1997; Short and Kim, 1998; 1999). This imperative has, in turn, contributed to the increased use of marketing and promotional activities by places. Hospers (2006: 1017) states that any place marketing activities must, 'find a balance between identity, image and the desired reputation' (this latter aspect referring to the branding of the place in question). Thus, the place must be marketed in a 'realistic' way, and that, 'the selected brand must suit the identity of the locality in question'.

Indeed, places are being increasingly thought of and conceptualised as brands (see Anholt, 2002; Hankinson, 2004a; Kavaratzis, 2005). A key task of branding is differentiation from competitors (see definitions by de Chernatony and McDonald, 2003; Doyle, 1994; Hankinson, 2000; Jobber, 2007; Kotler and Keller, 2006; O'Shaughnessy, 1995), although in a place context the inherent difficulties in achieving this are widely acknowledged (see for example, Barke and Harrop, 1994; Burgess, 1982; Fitzsimons, 1995; Harvey, 1987; Holcomb, 1994; Short and Kim, 1998; Young and Lever, 1997). According to Kotler et al. (1999: 151), one 'pathway to place distinction is to add or preserve interesting local buildings monuments and sculptures', and they identify numerous places, 'where efforts have been made to use building attractions for placemarketing'.

Branding is regarded as a multidimensional construct (Aaker, 1996; Doyle, 1994; Hankinson, 2000), and de Chernatony and McDonald (2003) propose an eight-category typology of branding. Thus, a brand can act as a sign of ownership; a differentiating device; a functional device; a symbolic device; a risk reducer; a shorthand device; a legal device; and as a strategic device. If aspects of the built environment such as buildings, bridges, monuments and statues/sculptures etc. are thought of as 'contributory elements' (Sleipen, 1988) to a holistic place 'product', then many of de Chernatony and McDonald's (2003) branding functions may be, at least partially, realised. For example, such structures could be considered as functional attributes of the place product, which may then be promoted to various target audiences, perhaps as tourist attractions. Moreover, such structures may also – in isolation, or in combination with other 'contributory elements' – provide a degree of distinctiveness for the place, particularly if, for some reason, they are strongly associated with that individual place – what this chapter will term the associative property of a particular structure or natural phenomenon.

This associative property of a structure/phenomenon may arise from its uniqueness to a specific place and/or its role as a 'flagship' development. Bianchini et al. (1992: 245) define flagships as, 'significant, high-profile and prestigious land and property developments which play an influential and catalytic role in urban regeneration'. Smyth (1994) states that a flagship comprises: (1) a development in its own right, which may or may not be self-sustaining; (2) a marshalling point for further investment; and (3) a marketing tool for an area or city. The catalytic role of flagship developments is crucial – Bianchini et al. (1992: 249–51) argue that they provide a tangible asset that may act as both symbol and magnet to further development, and as such, are central to promotional strategies seeking to re-image urban areas – often providing advertisers 'with the substance to back their images'. As a consequence, they are often referred to by the layperson as 'iconic'.

The Oxford English Dictionary lists one of the meanings of the word 'icon' as, 'a person or thing seen as a symbol of something' (Soanes, 2002: 412). However, as outlined above, in the study of semiotics, terms are used in a more technical sense. Thus, the iconic mode of representation is one 'in which the signifier is perceived as *resembling* or imitating the signified' (Chandler, 2007: 36. Original emphasis). It is this, semiotic-oriented meaning of the term icon/iconic that will be used in the rest of this chapter.

Kotler et al. state that the use of 'visual symbols' has, 'figured prominently in place marketing' (1999: 171), and an obvious aspect of this are well-known 'landmark sites of places', such as Big Ben in London, the Golden Gate bridge in San Francisco, the Little Mermaid statue in Copenhagen and the Brandenburg Gate in Berlin, among many others. They state that, 'when used in a systematic way, these visual symbols appear on official stationery, brochures, billboards, videos, pins, and dozens of other places' (1999: 171), thereby facilitating an association between the symbol and the place by virtue of the resemblance between signifier and signified. In other words, they have associative property. One manifestation of this would be the tendency in movies to use 'location shots' of structures such as the Eiffel Tower, the White House or the Houses of Parliament to identify and represent Paris, Washington DC and London respectively.

Semioticians generally maintain that there are no 'pure' icons in the sense that these would necessarily take the form of a perfect copy of the signified. In reality an icon can resemble what it represents only in some respects as a result of stylistic conventions, artistic licence and other more practical considerations such as reproduction capabilities. An obvious example of such limitations in the icon would be in logo design, where the signified may be typically represented by a much simplified, or indeed, more abstract image.

In the corporate communications context, Balmer (1995) states that the use of graphic design can encapsulate the organisation's cultural values and underpin communications efforts. In this latter purpose, Dowling argues that identity symbols such as logos can (1) create awareness; (2) trigger recognition; and (3) activate an already stored image in people's minds. Logos are recognised as one of the '*basic components*' of visual identity (Dowling, 2001: 166; see also Melewar and Saunders, 2000). Melewar defines the visual identity as, 'an assembly of visual cues by which an audience can recognise the company and distinguish it from others' (2003: 201), and the extensive use of logos in place promotion (Barke and Harrop, 1994; Burgess, 1982; Warnaby and Bennison, 2006) suggests that this fact is not lost on those responsible for marketing in this context. Here, the use of logos in the representation of places is considered, with particular reference to the built environment, and also the natural environment, in that topographic features such as rivers, mountains, coastlines etc. may also be used in the creation of place images.

LOGOS AND VISUAL IDENTIFICATION SYSTEMS

Blythe (2003: 117–18) defines a logo as, 'the symbol the organisation uses on all its points of public contact'. In more detail, Henderson and Cote (1998: 14) state that the term 'logo' can refer to various graphic and typeface elements, which can be incorporated into 'the graphic design that a company uses, with or without its name, to identify itself or its products'. Taking a semiotic perspective, Zakia and Nadin (1987) regard logos as part of the sign system a company uses to communicate itself to internal and external audiences.

In their discussion of the characteristics of logos, De Pelsmacker et al. (2004) state that a logo: (1) should be the long-term visualisation of a company's strategy; (2) should be distinctive (in that it is a means of differentiating the company from its competitors); (3) should be relevant for the consumer (otherwise it would not be able to contribute to the development of distinctive image); (4) should be timeless, but modifiable; and (5) should be useable in all circumstances and in all communications instruments and tools. In their consideration of what constitutes a 'good' logo, Henderson and Cote (1998: 15–18) state that logos, 'should speed recognition of a company or brand'. This recognition, they argue, occurs at two levels: (1) consumers must remember seeing the logo (i.e. correct recognition); and (2) logos must remind consumers of the brand or company name (i.e. recall). A second characteristic of a 'good' logo should be positive affective reactions, as these can transfer from the logo to the product or company. The logo should also evoke the same intended meaning across people in order to, 'communicate one clear message that is difficult to misinterpret' (1998: 17). Finally, a good logo will create a sense of familiarity. In the specific context of this chapter, many of Henderson and Cote's characteristics could be regarded as relating to the concept of associative property, in that the content of the logo should seek to invoke knowledge and feelings in the consumer so that the place concerned is perceived to be distinctive in some way.

USING BUILT AND NATURAL ENVIRONMENT PHENOMENA IN PLACE MARKETING LOGOS

This chapter argues that place marketing logos can be initially classified in various ways: (1) their function (i.e. the purpose for which the organisation whom the logo symbolises exists); (2) the nature of the referent or referents (i.e. the actual built and natural environment phenomena that are incorporated into the logo) that the logo uses in its depiction of a place; and (3) their semiotic mode of relationship (i.e. whether the logo is more of a symbol, icon or index in terms of its representation of a place). Each of these classification categories will be considered, before looking at the key factors of audience characteristics and knowledge (on which association between referent and place is dependent) that necessarily influence interpretation and understanding of place logos. A more detailed consideration of such factors sheds light on the factors that may determine place logo effectiveness.

Decisions relating to logo design will occur in the context of the wider activities and organisational mechanisms that characterise place marketing practice. As noted previously, the complexity of the place product can result in place marketing taking a multifaceted focus (Ward and Gold, 1994; Ward, 1998), with the same physical space, and many of the attributes of that space, being simultaneously multi-sold to different groups of customers for different purposes (Ashworth 1993; Ashworth and Voogd, 1990b). Indeed, there are many different potential markets and these may or may not conflict. As highlighted above, the complexity of the place product may be matched by the organisational mechanisms for its marketing, and each of these potential target markets may be the specific focus of the activities of separate agencies, each with its own particular remit (see Warnaby et al., 2002; 2004 for examples of this relating to the marketing of towns and cities as shopping destinations). Thus, logos could be classified according to whether the function of the agency/organisation/administration creating it was focused on inward investment, tourism promotion, the promotion of a particular event (e.g. Olympic Games), or more general in its scope (e.g. local authority or other public administration entity). Of course there is potentially a significant tension between the ideal of a clearly targeted logo designed to serve a single market by effectively communicating the essence of a place for this market, and a more complex reality that often requires the same logo to serve multiple markets, and consequently runs the risk of appealing only to the lowest common denominator, if at all.

This organisational heterogeneity is reflected in the specific content of marketing and branding activities as each agency attempts to create its own identity for a place in order to appeal to the specific needs of their chosen target audience by promoting different combinations of individual urban goods/services and/or clusters thereof (Ashworth and Voogd, 1990b). This has obvious implications for how the identity of the place is portrayed. Such discourses have been termed marketing 'campaign regimes' by Short and Kim (1999), who identify a number of different place representation strategies that may be applicable depending on context. Thus, World Cities and 'Wannabe' World Cities are concerned with creating the most attractive international image. Old industrial cities will seek to promote themselves as places of consumption rather than production – 'Look, No More Factories' – describing the campaign regime in Short and Kim's terminology. For many cities promoting the place as an attractive site for businesses – being 'The City for Business' – is a crucial activity. Finally identifying, mobilising and commodifying the cultural assets of a city – *Capitalizing Culture* – may be the chosen path, or perhaps indeed, a combination of all of the above with obvious implications for the clarity of a place's market positioning.

In addition, Kotler et al. (1999) identify a number of strategies for place improvement, which have consequent implications for branding and marketing communications activities: creating the place as character (i.e. trying to create a unique *genius loci* or 'sense of place' through aesthetic urban design, historic architecture etc.); infrastructure improvement; the place as service provider, through the creation of quality public services; and finally the place as entertainment and recreation, via a focus on the creation of a range of facilities and attractions for both residents and visitors. Indeed, it may be these facilities and attractions (such as, according to Kotler et al., natural beauty and places, history, cultural attractions, sports arenas, festivals and occasions, museums, building monuments and sculptures etc.) – especially if uniquely associated with an individual place (i.e. a strong associative property) – which may be prominent elements of place logos and other communications activities. Thus, logos could be classified according to the primary visual symbolism incorporated within – e.g. river, coastline, mountain(s), bridge, historic building (i.e. tower, church/cathedral), statue, or other cultural symbol. The use of such phenomena of the built and natural environment in logos seeks to emphasise their associative property, in order to link phenomenon with place in order to create effective place differentiation via the chosen place identity system.

THE SEMIOTIC MODE OF RELATIONSHIP BETWEEN PLACE PHENOMENA AND PLACE LOGOS

As mentioned above, in Peirceian semiotics, three modes of representation are identified between signifier and signified – symbol, icon and index. All three modes of representation are evident in place logos. The symbolic mode – where the relationship between the signifier and signified is fundamentally arbitrary or conventional and must be agreed upon and learned – is manifest in numerous place logos, such as for example, where the logo incorporates a municipal coat of arms, or other emblematic representation of the place. However, in terms of the use of built and natural environment phenomena in place logos, the other modes of representation – iconic and indexical – are arguably more important in that they lend themselves more readily to attempts to develop associative property between such phenomena and the places within which they are located.

The iconic mode of representation is characterised by some degree of resemblance between signifier and signified (although this resemblance may not be exact), and the indexical mode occurs where there is some direct connection (physical or causal) between signifier and signified which can be observed or inferred. Bignell (1997) states that these modes of representation are not mutually exclusive, and in the specific context of place logos it may be useful to consider the relationship between iconic and indexical modes of representation as being extremes of a continuum, depending on the extent to which the representations of the built and natural environment phenomena are figurative or more abstract. In the context of art, the Oxford English Dictionary defines the term 'figurative' as, 'representing people or things as they appear in real life' (Soanes, 2002: 304), and the closer the representation of a phenomenon in a logo to actual reality, the more figurative (or iconic) it will be.

In contrast, the term 'abstract' is defined in the Oxford English Dictionary as, 'using colour and shapes to create an effect rather than attempting to represent real life accurately' (Soanes, 2002: 40). Thus the representations of built and natural place phenomena in logos will be less lifelike. For example, the logo of Greenwich Council in London represents the bend in the River Thames at the Greenwich peninsula (the site of the Millennium Dome, or O2 Arena as it is currently known) in a very abstract way, using straight lines (see Figure 12.1). Other natural phenomena that are represented in a more abstract way include mountain ranges, where the silhouette of local mountains can be used in an attempt to create some form of associative property between phenomenon and place. Thus, the logo of Innsbruck Tourismus (the town's tourism promotion organisation) comprises a jagged line representing a mountain range (see Figure 12.2). This silhouette represents part of the Nordkette Mountains that surround Innsbruck.

A similar device is used in the logo of Südtirol (South Tyrol) in Austria (See Figure 12.3), representing a panorama of the Dolomite Mountains, based on a sketch by the Chief Design officer and Managing Director of the MetaDesign agency. The colour palette of the logo 'captures the nuances of light and colour in the region' (Metadesign, N/D: 9). The 'Südtirol' 'umbrella brand' in the logo is presented in a typeface (inspired by Schwabacher, whose roots go back to the fifteenth century), designed for exclusive use by South Tyrol – as the design consultants state: 'the lively handwritten style of Südtirol conveys energy and authenticity while consistently communicating the values of the new umbrella brand' (Metadesign, N/D: 8).

Structures in the built environment also serve this purpose. For example, the Leaning Tower of Pisa is incorporated into the logo of the Pisa Tourist Board (APTPISA – see www.pisaturismo.it) through the use of a coloured, italicised letter '*I*' in the name Pisa (i.e. APTP*I*SA). As noted above, the Brandenburg Gate is a 'landmark site' within Berlin (Kotler et al., 1999: 171), and this structure is an integral element of the city logo. Commissioned by King Frederick William II of Prussia and built

Figure 12.1   Greenwich Council logo

Figure 12.2   Innsbruck Tourismus logo

Figure 12.3   Südtirol logo

between 1788 and 1791, the Brandenburg Gate is the entry to Unter den Linden, the boulevard leading to the monarch's palace. In the cold war, the gate became a symbol for the divided Berlin, with the Berlin Wall running just west of the Gate, but since the end of communism in 1989,

Figure 12.4   be *Berlin logo*

Only in San Francisco

SAN FRANCISCO

CONVENTION &

VISITORS BUREAU

Figure 12.5   San Francisco Convention and Visitors Bureau logo

the Brandenburg Gate has become a symbol of the reunified Germany. Indeed, in such circumstances the symbolism of a gate was very potent – the Brandenburg Gate re-opened on 22 December 1989, when the West German Chancellor walked through the gate and was greeted by the East German Prime Minister. The original Berlin logo depicting the Brandenburg Gate was designed nearly 15 years ago and has since come to be used as a seal in official departments (although the official sign for Berlin comprises a standing bear in a coat of arms which remain on flags, uniforms, official cars etc.). In the most recent city marketing campaign for Berlin (see Chapter 10 by Colomb and Kalandides), the city name is prefixed by 'be', as shown in Figure 12.4.

If the representation of the built and natural phenomenon in the place logo is more realistic and life-like, then the logo will tend towards the iconic, figurative side of the continuum. For example, the logo for the San Francisco Convention and Visitors Bureau illustrates one pillar of the Golden Gate bridge in its distinctive colouration from a ground vantage point (see Figure 12.5), and the consumer marketing logo for the island of Tasmania, off the coast of Australia, depicts an accurate cartographic representation of its coastline (see Figure 12.6), with the strapline *Tasmania – Island of Inspiration* (although accompanying slogans have changed during

Figure 12.6   Discover Tasmania logo

the seven years in which the logo has been used). This logo was initiated for use in marketing activity aimed at the domestic, mainland Australia market and was soon incorporated into international marketing activities. It is used specifically for communication aimed at individual consumers as opposed to business-to-business and official government communication, for which the government logo is used. The rationale behind the use of the coastline was to reinforce Tasmania's island status. For the domestic Australian market, it was felt that this would connect positive island experiences and connotations to consumers' perceptions of what a holiday in Tasmania would mean. Emphasising the island nature of Tasmania in the logo, in conjunction with the strapline *Discover Australia's Natural State*, was felt to be important in the international market to make a cognitive connection between Tasmania's island-ness and the nature-based aspects of the destination proposition. Thus, the extent of the *associative property* in such logos is obviously very strong.

Logos are almost invariably produced when places host landmark sporting or cultural events, such as Olympic Games or Capital of Culture designations. The European Capital of Culture for 2008, the city of Liverpool has produced a logo for the capital of Culture festival which incorporates the famous skyline of the City, including what have become known as 'the three graces' of the Liverpool Waterfront – the Royal Liver Building (1908–11), the Cunard Building (1914–16), and the former offices of the Mersey Docks and Harbour Board (1903–07) – as well as the city's two cathedrals. With regard to the Olympic Games, the logos for the London Olympics of 1948 and the Helsinki Olympics of 1952 incorporate realistic representations of the Houses of Parliament (and Big Ben) in London, and the Helsinki stadium originally built to host the 1940 Games before they were cancelled because of war. More recently, the mixed reaction to the unveiling of the logo for the London 2012 Olympics in 2007, resulted in various media competitions for members of the public to design unofficial alternative logos, many of which incorporated well-known features of the city's built environment such as the Houses of Parliament and Big Ben, Tower Bridge and the London Eye (see http://news.bbc.co.uk/1/hi/ talking_point/6729823.stm). This last structure, the largest Ferris wheel in Europe, was originally a temporary structure (with planning permission for five years) that has subsequently become a major tourist attraction and could be regarded as having a high associative property. Indeed, the potency of big wheels as attractions of major cities – with an even larger structure built in Beijing in 2009 another due to be built in Berlin in 2010 – is highlighted by Jeffries (2009).

This raises some interesting issues relating to the temporal dimensions of logos, and the elements of the built and natural environments incorporated therein. The elements chosen for incorporation into logos could conceivably change over time. A structure such as the London Eye that was originally planned as a temporary structure for the new millennium seems set to assume significant associative property for the place (if indeed, it has not already done so). Indeed, a prime example of an originally temporary structure which has assumed huge associative property is the Eiffel Tower, originally completed in 1889 for the World's Fair marking the centennial celebration of the French Revolution, which originally only had permission to exist for 20 years. The potency of this structure is outlined by Anholt (2006: 25), who in describing the position of Paris in the Anholt-GMI City Brands Index, states:

> Paris has one brand asset, however, which is uniquely valuable: the Eiffel Tower. This originally temporary structure is one of the few truly global megabrands in the City Brands Index, a landmark of iconic status which is spontaneously associated with Paris by nearly 80 per cent of all respondents worldwide. The presence of such a prominent and distinctive symbol is certainly one reason why Paris does so well in the rankings.

Indeed, the Eiffel Tower is a significant element of many logos of Paris-based organisations; e.g. Chambre de Commerce et d'Industrie de Paris (see www.ccip.fr) and Office du Tourisme de Paris (see www. parisinfo.com). Of course, in the future there is always the possibility that the Tower might gradually be displaced by other structures with similar associative property (e.g. La Defense or the Louvre Pyramid) as the city seeks to change its image, or to target more specific market segments such as inward investors or a more culturally oriented segment, for which these other 'signature buildings' might have more specific resonance.

DISCUSSION

The examples given above are only a few of the manifestations of the ways in which built and natural environment phenomena are incorporated into place logos as a means of capitalising on associative property, in an attempt to create and communicate place differentiation in an increasingly competitive environment. Obviously, not all places would be able to incorporate such distinctive phenomena (with strong associative property) into their place logos. Indeed, the extent to which those responsible for the design of place logos may be constrained in terms of the built and natural environment phenomena that can be used, and how these phenomena are represented in logos, may be influenced by two key factors: (1) the intended primary audience for the logo; and (2) the extent of this audience's knowledge about the place and the facilities and attractions located therein.

Fill (2005) emphasises that the planning of any marketing communications activity should begin with, and be informed by, a clear understanding of the target audience(s). The nature of the target audience for a logo may be a function of the organisation responsible for designing the logo. Thus, a tourism promotion agency may be oriented towards national and international target audiences, whereas a local authority/public administration may be more focused on residents and other geographically proximate groups. This may have significant implications for the second influencing factor – level of knowledge.

In this specific context, if the target audiences' knowledge of the place and its attributes is limited (as may be the case with internationally oriented targeting), then the use of any built and natural environmental phenomena may have to be limited to very distinctive and or famous phenomena, and their representation may have to be oriented towards the figurative in order to create maximum associative property. If the audiences knowledge about the place and its built and natural environment phenomena is limited, a more abstract treatment in the logo may not create a strong enough association with the place – in other words, Henderson and Cote's (1998) characteristics of 'good' logos, in terms of intended meaning and possible affective reactions, may not be realised. The greater the knowledge the target audience has of a place and its phenomena, then, it could be argued, the greater is the scope for logo designers to develop a more overtly abstract representation, because the audiences will have an understanding as to the logo's meaning and the semiotic devices by which this meaning is created in the minds of the audience. Thus, with such a well-known phenomenon as the Leaning Tower of Pisa, the use of an italic 'T' in the city name is enough to create associative property. Other, less well-known phenomena may need to be represented in a much more figurative way in order to create the appropriate association with a particular place.

This chapter is an exploratory consideration of the place logo, which is an important branding device in this context (see Barke and Harrop, 1994; Burgess, 1982; Warnaby and Bennison, 2006) and one which is somewhat neglected, both in the context of place marketing and indeed, more generally – Shimp (2007: 196), for example, states that, 'research on logos is surprisingly absent' from the marketing canon. Hopefully this exploration of logos in this place marketing/branding context provides some initial ideas in relation to this, and will stimulate further, more substantial research into a neglected area.

13. Personality association as an instrument of place branding: possibilities and pitfalls

Gregory Ashworth

INSTRUMENTS OF PLACE BRANDING

There are many instruments available to place management authorities attempting to apply the concepts of place branding, as described earlier, as part of strategies devised to create brand value in pursuit of whatever local objectives have been determined by them. These may include fiscal, organisational, political and infrastructural measures as well as a whole gamut of marketing techniques, from public relations to media advertising.

The core idea within such policies is the deliberate shaping and projection of a selected sense of place, conveying associations that establish a brand in the mind of the consumer as place user (Elliot and Wattanasuwan, 1998; Hauben et al., 2002). Of the many instruments that can be employed in the furtherance of this strategy, three are particularly favoured by place managers, and generally loom large in most place branding policies. These are signature buildings, hallmark events and personality association. All three treat elements familiar in other contexts to spatial planners, urban managers and urban designers, thus it is understandable that they should feel comfortable with them even when the marketing is not well understood.

The first is considered in a design context in Chapter 12, the second has a substantial literature (e.g. Ritchie, 1984; Hall, 1989; Andranovich, 2001) and the third will be examined in this chapter, if only because little attention has so far been paid to it in comparison with the other two.

However as has been argued earlier, it is only very recently that place managers have consciously made use of marketing strategies, devised marketing policies and applied marketing techniques in response to a perceived intensification of competition within global arenas. Consequently, as has been pointed out already by many contributors to this book, there is a paucity of not only theoretical and conceptual studies but also of comparative descriptive studies of branding as a local place management strategy. Therefore it is not surprising that personality association has been applied in practice more on an individual trial and error basis than as part of well-known carefully tested and validated procedures. The instances described here are generally one-off cases that did not consciously refer to each other. It is also worth noting from the outset that this technique is rarely used in isolation where it would be highly unlikely to succeed. It is more usually used in some combination of other techniques often including signature buildings and hallmark events.

THE NATURE OF PERSONALITY ASSOCIATION

Places in competition with others need to discover and establish the uniqueness of their identity, from which their 'unique selling points' or 'unique product propositions' can be demonstrated and brought to the attention of the consumer, whether resident, tourist investor or other. In the search for a unique identity, places associate themselves with a named individual in the hope that the necessarily unique qualities of the individual will be transferred by association to the place. As people are unique then places will acquire this character of uniqueness through this association with a nominated individual. Furthermore the nature of these associative attributes, as well as their existence, are assumed to enhance the place in some way. It is in this sought for transference of associations from person to place, that the branding lies.

This technique could be called the 'Gaudi gambit' in recognition of the notably successful personality branding of Barcelona in the 1980s. An extremely distinctive, colourful and immediately recognisable architect and designer of some 60 years earlier, who was previously little known outside professional artistic circles, was adopted as representative of a city attempting to emerge from its industrial and political past. Success is demonstrated by the current image of the city being now inseparable from the creative work of the man and indeed of the artist with the place. It is now almost impossible to think of the city without the designer or the designer without bringing the city to mind, but it should be remembered that this was quite explicitly attempted at a time when the selected designer was little known outside the city in which he had worked and when the city had an image only as a port and manufacturing city. Three of his creations were designated World Heritage Sites in 1984 and two more were added in 2005. However this recognition by the global official agencies should be seen as a confirmation of a newfound fame, increasingly endorsed by the local population and by international tourism rather than its catalyst. Of course the overall and quite dramatic success of Barcelona in re-imaging itself and establishing itself as an effective competitor in European artistic, tourism and investment markets was not a result of personality association branding alone. The marketing policies were only a part of much wider urban regeneration and strategic planning policies which included physical and economic restructuring of the city and its staging of hallmark events (notably the summer Olympic Games of 1992). It is also worth noting that in this story of unremitting success there were some intrinsic potential problems, which have been successfully contained or have not yet arisen. Antoni Gaudi was a devout Catholic as well as Catalan nationalist. Both of these could detract from his brand value at least in some markets and he was both artistically unconventional if not weird, and personally eccentric. There was no Gaudi school of artists nor indeed have there been followers of his design ideas. It was a high risk but equally high profit strategy in which timing seems to have played a major role.

This was however, neither the first nor the final occasion when this technique has been used. Indeed the early and evident successes of this technique have prompted an almost universal application of it in the belief that it is a simple, sure and relatively easy route to successful branding. However, this may not be the case and the assumed simplicity and ease must both be reviewed.

TYPES OF PERSONALITY

There is a need to be able to claim a special link between the person and the place and indeed, if successful, fight off the competing claims of other places upon the person. Some types of personality prove more suitable for brand association than others. Artistic and historical figures are the most popular.

Visual artists are easier to treat in this way than those producing a non-visual product. The more distinctive the creative work or the more notable and memorable the person and life, the easier such branding will become. As Gaudi (1852–1926) in Barcelona, so also Mackintosh (1868–1928) in Glasgow, Dali (1904–89) in Figueres, Hundertwasser (1928–2000) in Vienna or Dudok (1884–1974) in Hilversum are instantly recognisable and strongly if not always exclusively linked to the particular place. Small identifiable groups of artists can also serve, often with one named individual serving as representative of the group such as the Norwich, UK (Crome), St Ives, UK (Hepworth), Taos, New Mexico (O'Keefe), Groningen, NL 'Ploeg' (Werkman) schools of artists.

The way artists can first seek out and use places and subsequently become associated with the place and therefore used by it is well illustrated in New

Mexico (USA). Pioneer artists settled in 1898 in New Mexico, especially in Taos and Santa Fe, attracted by the warm dry climate, low costs of living, perceived sympathetic local culture and increasingly the presence of other artists, would-be artists, and connoisseurs. The visitors, the artists and craftsmen they had come to experience and financially support, and the local promotion and tourism facilities were almost exclusively 'anglo', but many of the cultural components they were using were either Hispanic or Indian in origin. The important point is that a distinctive cultural style was created, ultimately labelled the 'Santa Fe style', which has become a highly successful culture product. This is in part an adaptation from vernacular architectural adobe styles, gastronomy, textiles, pottery and in part a perceived relaxed 'latin' way of life. What began as a retreat for 'anglo' artists, became within a generation a major tourism product sold initially to the market of the cities of the eastern US as part of the idyll of the 'west'. Once established the tourism industry in turn began widening the cultural product in its continuous search for differentiation and expansion of the product line as the numbers and sophistication of the tourists increased. Eventually the Santa Fe style and its numerous by-products originally created by 'anglo' artists and tourists was readopted by Hispanics and Indians as an expression of their ethnicity. Simultaneously it has become, more widely, an environmental amenity, which has proved attractive to residential and commercial activities. The experimental practising artists who initiated the process and their followers have long since moved on in search of new cheaper less commercialised locations but their contribution to the brand reputation remains.

Although visual artists (painters, sculptors, architects, designers) are probably more suitable for ease of recognition, transference across cultures and languages and simple reproduction, nevertheless musicians are also popular. The effectiveness depends upon linking the music in some way to the nature of the place and its people. Individual composers and performers as diverse as Mozart (Salzburg), Presley (Memphis), Wagner (Beyreuth) or Elgar (Hereford), or even groups of related musicians, such as 'The Mersey Beat' (Liverpool), 'Tamla Motown' (Detroit), 'Country' (Nashville) and traditional Jazz in general (Memphis/New Orleans) can also be effectively linked to particular places.

The use of writers or dramatists is also fairly common, especially if the writing is place bound so that the text and place context are clearly linked. Wordsworth's Lake District, Austen's Bath, Hardy's Wessex, Couperus' The Hague, Joyce's Dublin and the like are all well known as not merely literature reflecting senses of place but also contributing towards shaping them in the minds of residents and visitors alike.

A remarkably successful and seemingly straightforward case of creating an association between a town and a literary figure is that of Stratford, Ontario, Canada. An economic crisis caused by the closure of the Canadian National Railway locomotive repair facility in 1964 was resolved through the exploitation of a personality association with the Elizabethan drama- tist Shakespeare and thus the replacing of an economic dependence on railway engineering with one on cultural performances, the town develop- ing the second most important annual Shakespeare festival in the world and largest in North America (670 000 visitors in 2003). The non-existence of any historical connection between the town and the personality, who had been dead for 200 years before the town was even founded, has proved no disqualification. The successful element was not any existing expertise, facilities or locational comparative advantage but only the town's name which linguistically associated it with another town in another continent which was already renowned as the birth place of the playwright. However becoming the 'city of Shakespeare' and using this to establish a viable culture industry was neither automatic nor simple. The conditions for the success here and in other such cases can be listed as an economic impera- tive with a severely limited range of options; a surplus capacity especially of land, labour and supporting services; a fortunate location relative to the market and also probably in the timing of the initiative; all of which contributed to the success of the personality branding and the creation of a profitable place product.

Architects can both contribute notable structures, which become sig- nature buildings for a place (as described in Chapter 12) but equally with much modern architecture there can be a strong element of personality branding in which the architect is as important as the building. The pos- session in your place of a Gehry, Foster, Rodgers, Niemeyer, or Libeskind building endows the place not only with a recognisable physical signature but also with a cachet of artistic patronage and global significance. The place, its government and its population in so far as it is aware, is declar- ing its avant-garde credentials, hoping that these extend beyond the aes- thetic to a wider commitment to sensitivity, creativity and innovation in other fields. Even if these ambitious claims are not realised, a signature structure is a clear, often raucous, statement that the place managers are doing something even if the public's aesthetic reaction is critical. A reveal- ing indicator of this is the ascribing, whether media induced or not, of a deprecating, humorous popular nickname to such a building (London's 'gherkin', Rome's 'typewriter', Berlin's 'toothpick' and the like).

Historical figures are also popular candidates for such branding but have the potential disadvantage of being possibly more divisive, less globally appealing and more subject to reappraisal over time as history is revised. However perhaps the strongest personality place associations that exist and have existed with a global recognition for centuries are the historical characters of Jesus (Nazareth, Bethlehem, and Jerusalem) and Mohammed (Mecca, Medina and Jerusalem).

Philosophers and intellectuals in general have the disadvantage of the intangibility of their creative product, which does not easily associate with a physical location. Grotius may have thought and written in Delft, Socrates in Athens, Kant in Königsberg, Descartes in Franeker or Erasmus in Rotterdam (considered in detail below) but it is difficult to grasp not only which attributes of the person are to be utilised to add value to the place product but also how the ideas can be promoted as a quality of the place.

Nomenclature without Association

Places have long been deliberately named after individuals but this is not necessarily personality association. Cities like Washington or Kaliningrad, or the Nelson Mandela Urban Region, in The Eastern Cape or even airports from Charles de Gaulle, Paris, to Oliver Tambo, Johannesburg, do not automatically become personality associated place brands, because the perceived qualities of the individual being mentioned are not specifically being recruited to apply to the place. The place is being used to commemorate the individual: the individual is not being used to add brand value to the place through the transfer of such qualities. The only marketing gain may be some enhanced place recognition or in cases such as John Lennon Airport Liverpool, some expression of a popular regional identity. This is generally personality nomenclature with limited associative transfer.

Celebrity Endorsement

Celebrity branding is where a currently well-known living individual from the field of sport, politics, or entertainment, enjoying a media induced fame, endorses the place, sometimes in the form of claiming birthright. This is of course a tautology as all personality branding involves a famous individual. However in celebrity endorsement it is not so much the qualities of the celebrity that are being transferred to the places: the celebrity may indeed possess, in other respects highly irrelevant or even undesirable characteristics. A sport or entertainment celebrity's judgement about the quality of urban amenity may have little substance. It is merely the idea that if someone we know and recognise, if not respect, for achievement in some field, endorses the place then we are likely to feel encouraged to do likewise.

A major problem with celebrity endorsement is the inherent ephemeral nature of media induced celebrity status in the modern world. There is a strong likelihood therefore that the renown of the personality fades while the campaign is still committed to the strategy. Morgan et al. (2002: 24) envisage an inevitable, if not calibrated, progress through a 'brand fashion curve' with phases of fashionable, famous, familiar and faltering at which point presumably some new celebrities need to be recruited. It is the tempo of this evolution that has notably accelerated in recent years.

DIFFICULTIES OF PERSONALITY ASSOCIATION

There is a prevalent assumption that personality branding is a straight-forward and almost inevitably successful exercise in which local history is ransacked in search of a well-known personality who is then adopted and promoted as a form of patron saint or place mascot who confers at least recognition and at best a range of desirable brand attributes.

However, the lessons of the success stories, some of which have already been related, are that accomplishment often depends upon a single mind-edness, itself often born of desperation, a coordination of the branding with other financial and physical techniques, and above all a substantial element of fortunate timing. A major difficulty with using previous success elsewhere as a guide for the future is that the successes were invariably the first in a particular field: replication is unlikely to be successful.

It must also be remembered that the creation of place–personality associations is not a monopoly of official place marketing agencies but is also implemented by non-official organisations or may just emerge from the local popular imagination, whether or not such associations contribute to the official branding objectives. It can be asked if these place brand associations always contribute much to place marketing beyond the definition and recognition of the place and some background atmosphere except of course for the niche markets of historical, literary and cultural tourism.

Negative or Undesirable Associations

There is also of course the necessity to be aware that some personality associations can be inappropriate or indeed completely undesirable. That the Hitler family came from Braunau, Austria, that Al Capone's criminal activities took place in Chicago or that Billy the Kid engaged in gun-fighting in Lincoln County, New Mexico, may not be viewed as advantages by the place management agencies concerned and place–personality disassociation is likely to prove very difficult for them to achieve.

Less obviously extreme negative associations are very common. It must also be remembered that cultural producers and performers were not in the service of place boosterism but of creative art. They may use the place characteristics for their own cultural purposes not as an adjunct to place management. Their artistic productivity is thus as likely to contribute undesirable as desirable attributes. McCourt's depiction of dismal, wet, drunken, apathetic Limerick ('Angela's Ashes' 1996) or the descriptions of living conditions in numerous nineteenth century industrial 'coketown' novels (Dickens, Gaskell, Zola and the like) would hardly be welcomed by the contemporary cities in which they were set (see Trueman, 2001 on Bradford). Indeed the branding problem for current managers has often been to escape from existing stereotypes and images that have been so effectively conveyed by past novelists and painters, as to lock the place into a set of highly undesirable connotations. Re-branding is always more difficult than branding. The Lancashire post-industrial city of Salford for instance was locked into an identity heavily influenced by Lowry's paintings of its drab industrial past. Ignoring or forgetting was made impossible by the increasing worldwide fame of the artist's work leaving as the only realistic strategy an acceptance and museumification of the artist and thus distancing the present from a contained past with the new and spectacular 'Lowry Art and Entertainment Centre' being the centrepiece of the signature redevelopment on Salford Quays completed in 2000. The message is clearly 'The place was dismal then but it is demonstrably better now – look around'.

Irrelevant Associations

There are associations which are not in themselves negative or undesirable but which contribute nothing particular to the brand the place managers are attempting to create and promote. As described above artistic personalities selected from the past are widely used as they have many marketing advantages of general acceptability, few negative reactions, ease of communication and reproduction and the like. However, despite this the question needs to be posed, what actually does such an association contribute to the place and is this association particularly beneficial? To become the place associated with a renowned artist, writer or musician certainly contributes place name recognition, historical continuity if the artist is from a more distant past, and some claim to cultural significance. It is saying, 'our place has been an important cultural centre for a long time'. Whether more than this can be utilised depends largely on the nature of the place and the objectives of the place managers. The most obvious use of the association would be to encourage cultural industries, somehow linked to the associated personality, and/or a cultural tourism industry based on the personality as tourism product. There are many cases of the latter:

fewer of the former. Although Stratford (UK) has effectively commodified Shakespeare into products saleable to tourists and cultural visitors such as to be a major economic activity of the place, this remains exceptional. Only a handful of places worldwide have so exploited their personality association as to base their economic and social *raison d'etre* upon it. For most places the association delivers little beyond some local pride of place and the claim to historicity and traditional culture, may be at best irrelevant and at worst a hindrance to a place endeavouring to project a brand typified by modernity, innovation, excitement, flexibility and adaptiveness.

Non-connotative Associations

There are also many associations of places with people that contribute a strong recognition but few connotations with any attribute of the person. This is especially the case with mythological characters.

The mythological existence of a personality is no disqualification in personality association although it does make competing claims easier to lodge as there is no historical record with which to defend a copyright claim. The dispute over the rightful ownership of Robin Hood, for instance, has been waged passionately between Nottingham/Sherwood Forest in Central England and Wakefield/Barnsdale in Yorkshire, for at least a generation, with questions raised in Parliament in 2002, not least because of the large tourism revenues involved. King Arthur's 'Camelot' is currently claimed by Winchester in Hampshire, Tintagel in Cornwall, Caerleon in Gwent, and Cadbury Castle in Somerset. Santa Claus has numerous post boxes and visitable addresses from Fairbanks, Alaska to Joulupukin near Rovaniemi, Finland. However apart from the global place recognition and, not to be underestimated, tourism revenues, it is difficult to see what qualities of the mythical characters concerned are being transferred to the places that are so fiercely competing to claim the personality. Which of Robin Hood's qualities (woodcraft, archery, redistributive theft) are valuable to the management objectives of the Nottingham City Council? Does the 'possession' of Santa Claus underpin the development of a local toy industry, children's welfare programme or international reindeer communications system in Rovaniemi? In all of these cases the only gain would seem to be historical continuity and global recognition.

Durability

A major problem with personality branding is the durability of the fame or the reputation of the personality selected. The market valuation of the associations is likely to change over time. A link once seen as effective and beneficial may become less effective over time, or just less relevant as the values of society or needs of the economy change.

There are many advantages in selecting a dead, preferably long dead, personality who is unlikely to change or to object. A living personality or one still inhabiting living memories may be uncomfortable with the branding, may present quite different and less valued associations with later work or the reputation may be subject to controversy and re-evaluation.

Art in particular is a fashion driven activity. The popularity of styles and thus their exemplars changes over time, often quite rapidly. The trick, as illustrated by Barcelona, is to select a personality whose fame is in the ascendant and ride it upwards, changing and discarding it as it wanes. Place–personality associations may long outlive their usefulness and yet prove difficult to alter or erase from consumer consciousness in the short term. For example the sixteenth century moralist churchman John Knox may have conveyed useful values of probity, diligence and sobriety to an Edinburgh in the industrial age but becomes a somewhat doubtful asset to a city currently transforming itself into a culture, entertainment and tourism centre. As stated above the more distinctive and recognisable the personality the better. However there may be a disadvantage in this distinctiveness as the more idiosyncratic the designs the less they are likely to be sustainable in the consumer imagination over the longer term as popular artistic tastes change. A Dali (Figueres) or a Hundertwasser (Vienna) have a shock appeal by their very eccentricity but such a shock is difficult to sustain as the unconventional becomes familiar.

Take the case of the West Yorkshire Pennines for long associated with the novels of the three Brontë sisters centred on the Haworth rectory where they lived and worked in the middle of the nineteenth century. Although 'Brontë country' with its Wuthering Heights and Jane Eyre associations is still a powerful attraction to many, it has been replaced in tourist promotion and the more popular imagination by 'Herriot country' after a television series (originally screened in 1978 with the final series yet to be scheduled). The substitution was made easier by both creative oeuvres having very similar place connotations, namely a wild and empty moorland landscape and harsh climate inhabited by a stubborn and tenacious moorland farming population.

Size and Complexity of Places

All branding may be easier to achieve in smaller cities than in larger ones. Large cities are often too multifaceted, multifunctional, and diverse to exist comfortably with a few simple brand associations. There are likely to be too many and too diverse goals and stakeholders in any such policy. Personality association becomes particularly difficult when there is an embarrassment of riches of possible contenders, many of which are already strongly established in popular imaginations. Large cities may be inappropriate subjects for associating with a single personality but this does not preclude districts or even streets within such a city pursuing such a policy. 'Jack the Ripper' (London's East End), Henri Toulouse-Lautrec (Paris' Montmartre) or even Sherlock Holmes (London's Baker Street), are all possibilities.

One case, typical of many, may serve to illustrate the problems of personality association in major cities. The city of Rotterdam in the Netherlands has a perceived identity problem, especially in competition with the other major Dutch cities. It quite successfully profiled itself in the period since the Second World War as a city of work, modernity and progress. Its self-identity and external image revolved around its harbour functions and associated industrial development ('the largest port in the world'), its practical blue-collar society and was reflected in its modern-ist functionalist post-war rebuilding. By the end of the twentieth century economic and social change had rendered this image unhelpful in compet-ing inside and outside the Netherlands for service activities with cities cultivating a post-modern, culture and heritage-rich, high environmental quality image. This long-term trend was exacerbated by the acquiring of a reputation after 2001 for working class xenophobic ethno-nationalism. The need for image change was evident and a new personality associa-tion was one instrument in this. The choice fell upon the internationally renowned sixteenth century humanist philosopher, Desiderius Erasmus, and the city is now being actively promoted as the 'city of Erasmus'. A number of problems are immediately evident. The man is not firmly attached to this particular city even in the imagination of its residents. He was only born there, and even that is disputed, and he lived for longer and produced more work in Cambridge, Venice, Freiburg im Breisgau and Paris, all of which could, if they wished, lodge a more convincing claim and Rotterdam does not feature in any way in his work. The inhabitants of Rotterdam are largely unaware of the life or work of Erasmus and more associate him with the local university or even an eponymous bridge built in 1996 than with his thoughts and writings. It is of course possible to attempt to remedy this ignorance and misconception through campaigns directed at locals and outsiders alike. More fundamentally philosophy is difficult to visualise or present in a visual way. It is uncertain how sixteenth century humanism can be expressed. The difficulty of commodifying such a philosopher reaches an apogee of absurdity in the production and marketing of a distinctive four-cornered black beret as a physical sou-venir. However, the central question is whether much is to be gained by associating what remains a modern port city and developing commercial office centre, notable for its experimental contemporary architecture and design with a sixteenth century philosopher.

CONCLUSIONS

The concluding lesson to be drawn from the brief analysis and cases related above is that personality association is a widely used instrument of place branding policies, which has on occasion been quite remarkably successful as a tool of place redevelopment and management. Success in achieving whatever management goals have been predetermined depends however upon the posing and answering of a series of questions prior to embarking on the branding programme;

- Can we find a person with whom to associate? Large and long inhabited places normally have a wide range of possibilities from which to select: smaller or more recently inhabited places may have a more restricted choice.
- Does this selected person have desirable associations or connotations or, if not, can these be shaped? Desirable in this context means associations that add value to the place brand or at the very least do not detract from it.
- Is this person already known and if so, to whom and related to the former question, for what? This personality recognition can be transformed into place recognition. In the event of little, or more often only local or specialist, knowledge, the question becomes can recognition of this personality be promoted more widely?
- Is this personality association durable, at least for the period that the policy is expected to operate? Conversely, will the recognition of the associations fade or even change in undesirable ways?
- Can this association be supported by other policy instruments, such as for example signature buildings, hallmark events, urban design or planning actions?

Personality association has the advantage of exploiting a widespread almost ubiquitous and freely available resource. It is relatively easy and cheap to perform and may well also accord well with other place policies for cultural development, civic consciousness or tourism (Kavaratzis and Ashworth, 2005). However only if the above questions are posed and satisfactorily answered by the place management agency conducting the branding exercise are there realistic prospects of success.

14. Conclusion: in search of effective place brand management

Gregory Ashworth and Mihalis Kavaratzis

INTRODUCTION

This book has explored several aspects of the theory and application of place branding. It has brought together, in a thorough and rigorous manner, contributions by scholars with a speciality in one or more of these aspects that have examined both theoretical suggestions stemming from the several disciplines that are involved in place branding and practical examples from many cities and regions across Europe. Perhaps the most obvious conclusion to be made is that there is still a lot of work needed before we can arrive at a comprehensive understanding and application of branding to places at all scales and in all continents. This embraces simultaneously discouraging and encouraging thoughts. The discouraging part has to do with the delay in developing a clear appreciation of what place branding is and what it can do for places. It also has to do with the recognised gap between theory and practice. As repeatedly noted in the book, practitioners are pressured by political circumstance to rush into a limited implementation and theoreticians have not yet managed to provide the foundations and framework that would widen this implementation and reach the desired results. The encouraging part has to do with the fact that some of the necessary work has already been done and the interest in problematic and, so far, neglected aspects of place branding is steadily growing. We feel that this book is testimony to the positive developments that are already apparent and will, hopefully, become mainstream practices in the near future. This brief chapter attempts to delineate the main conclusions that can be reached from the issues already handled in the chapters of this volume.

MAIN CONCLUSIONS

Four areas of discussion are identified here in order to summarise the main conclusions and to signify the areas upon which the future development of place branding could be based. These are the theoretical underpinnings of place branding, the place branding process, the significance of local communities and the role of communications. Arguably, all of the chapters included in this volume have raised significant issues surrounding all those areas and have made their contribution to each in varying degree.

In terms of the theoretical background of the place branding endeavour, it is clear that it uses approaches derived from several disciplines, including marketing, geography, planning, policy studies, psychology and many more. As discussed in the first part of this book and in the relevant parts of most other chapters, sub-areas, such as services marketing, corporate branding, tourism, identities studies, cultural geography, environmental psychology, the study of minorities and so on also have a significant role to play in the attempt to fully understand the complex and multifaceted phenomenon that place branding really is. The nature of the endeavour is such that the contribution and integration of all those and more areas of study is necessary in order to succeed in ultimately explaining the application of branding to places. As mentioned in the introductory chapter, with the increasing number of publications, special issues and international conferences on place branding comes a more intense interaction between those disciplines and the people involved in them; and with that, hopefully, a wider discussion and understanding. This book has explored the roots of place branding in general marketing and planning and several chapters have additionally highlighted the contribution of areas as diverse as, for instance, corporate branding (in the chapters by Hankinson and by Kavaratzis), policy studies (in the chapter by Therkelsen et al.) or environmental psychology (in the chapter by Insch and Florek), in this way heralding a more comprehensive theoretical foundation for place branding. Theories, however, are only as good as their scope for practical implementation. Therefore, there is a need to review any theoretical suggestion in the context of the practice of place branding. As most of the cases examined in this book exemplify, this is not an easy task within the contemporary framework of place branding where understanding is limited and expectations very high. The obvious desire of practitioners is to use branding as a fast cheap effective and highly visual panacea to all problems and their everyday challenges. Place branding, however, does not work automatically or at once as demonstrated in the many case studies presented here and it is this urgency for fast results that has misled many of the implementations of place branding, confining it to promotional activities, which is only a small part of the whole branding process.

Unsurprisingly all chapters included in this book argue for a long-term approach to place branding. This is because place branding involves a series of steps that acquire their meaning when followed sequentially and

comprehensively and not separately and partially. Furthermore, most of
these steps have very little to do with promotion and communications, in
contrast to the dominant practical implementation, which insists that it
is advertising campaigns that create satisfied guests and colourful logos
that cultivate civic pride. The rationale behind the place branding process
is that a place must first decide on what kind of brand the place wants to
become, how it can create the mental, psychological and emotional ties
that are necessary for the place to become this brand and what are the
functional, physical attributes that the place needs to create, improve,
emphasise or even avoid, in order to support this brand. Therefore, it
is vital that the place branding process is implemented as a whole and
not partially. Perhaps the best example of this notion is the process proposed for the cities of Pafos and Nea Ionia, Magnesia in the chapter by
Deffner and Metaxas. Similarly, the analysis of the marketing of Berlin
in the chapter by Colomb and Kalandides, shows the need for continuity
and consistency. The chapter by Huertas et al. has, among other issues,
touched upon another pitfall of the place branding process relating to the
fact that places exist at geographical scales and within specific cultural
and political contexts, which cannot be ignored when devising branding strategies or campaigns; a notion reinforced and taken further in the
chapter by Therkelsen et al. through the issue of the ownership of the place
brand. The several possibilities of effective tools that can be used in the
framework of the wider place branding process have been discussed in the
chapter by Mateo and Seisdedos, providing some more unconventional
ideas. The political nature of this process as demonstrated in the chapter
by Bellini et al. is also of great importance and a very useful addition to
thinking about this factor.

   In the place branding process, a central role is attributed to the creation
and manipulation of place images. This is a complex and multifaceted
matter. On the one hand, it is important because images play a major role
in the way people understand places and behave towards them and should,
therefore, play a prominent role in the way places are managed. On the
other hand, the process of the formation of images is unclear and the
opportunity and possibility that place management agencies have to influence this process is limited, partial and changeable. Unfortunately, in the
hasty attempt to project a positive image of the place, the choice of what
to showcase, and what not, is where the worst attribute of place branding
is exposed. Indeed, branding, in its contemporary form of application,
cannot steer clear of the accusations of excluding, ignoring, concealing,
camouflaging and ultimately destroying parts of the place's character,
history or even population. To make matters even worse, the interaction
between images and identities and their separate or common roles in place

branding are far from clear as discussed in the chapter by Deffner and Metaxas and as illustrated in the chapter by Colomb and Kalandides.

Perhaps the most intriguing aspect highlighted in this book is the role and significance of local communities in assuring the success of place branding. As shown in the chapter by Therkelsen et al., there is a chance to use place branding as a community building tool but this demands more effort and responsibility than contemporary local authorities seem to be willing to put into it. Trueman et al. have dealt with the very demanding topic of ethnic minorities and have managed through them to show the important discrepancies between official plans and policies and the ways in which local residents experience these policies. Perhaps a more optimistic note comes from the chapter by Insch and Florek who attempt to handle the issue of what makes residents satisfied with their place. The satisfaction framework they propose is certainly a very welcome addition to the literature and to the study of place branding as a whole. Another optimistic note comes from the first indications of a more participatory form of branding as outlined in the chapter by Colomb and Kalandides.

In terms of the communication tools that places use in their branding, all chapters of this book have in one way or another made the constantly stated but still under appreciated argument that place branding is much more than communication alone. Currently, most place branding efforts start and finish with the development of a catchy slogan and the design of a new logo, although there are more refined attempts that betray a wider understanding of branding. In general, as frequently applied in practice, place branding is centred on the creation of a favourable image or the change of a negative or indifferent image of the place. There are three main practical instruments for doing this. First, various promotional campaigns and *visual identity tactics*; secondly the creation of *landmarks* for the place or the invention of new ways to integrate existing landmarks in the promotion of the place, and finally, the staging of various types of *events* in the place. What is evidently missing so far is the link to the wider marketing and development goals set by the place and the understanding of the whole branding process as described in this book. Nevertheless, promotion is inevitable and therefore should be done in the most effective way. The chapters of this book that deal with communications have examined and clarified certain tools of such communication. The chapter by Warnaby and Medway has dealt with the significant issue of how natural and artificial landscapes can be (and are currently) integrated into place logos. Finally the chapter by Ashworth has discussed the possibilities of using personality association for place branding purposes, exposing the pitfalls as well as the promise of such attempts.

THE WAY FORWARD?

The several negative comments included in the above discussion might encourage a pessimistic and disappointed attitude to the future of place branding as a useful tool for the economic and social development of places. This is not our intention and this is not the conclusion of the individual chapters presented here. In fact, all chapters have discussed several negative aspects of the case under examination but their conclusions relate to ways in which these negative practices or misunderstandings can be mitigated or removed. In many cases, how they have already been reversed. As the title of this chapter already suggests, this discussion is a vital part of the search for effective place brand management. This concluding part of the book deals with the following key questions, 'is there a place for place branding in place development?' If so, 'what should place brand management be?'

As to the first question, the answer depends on the role that branding is called to play. If branding is understood as little more than promotion, there is very little that it can offer to the development of places. In this case, place branding will remain the task of advertising agencies able to provide creative ideas for the promotion of places and a few consultants ready to hastily suggest appropriate target groups and development projects. If branding is understood, as explained in this book, as a wide-ranging strategic choice that includes the place's vision, the involvement and motivation of all the place's internal and external customers and users and its economic, social and cultural consequences, then it could be very useful. If all aspects of branding are taken into account, as revealed in the cases presented in this book, then it can provide a much needed impetus for the reorganisation of a place's management and development. If branding is treated, again as exemplified by the chapters of this book, as the painstaking place brand management process it really is, then it can provide the common ground for responsible and sustainable policies to be developed. In this case, place branding becomes the task of responsible place authorities, devoted researchers and a few consultants ready to suggest appropriate ways in which public money can be put to effective solutions to development problems and challenges. However, what would such a place brand management process entail? This book has provided several initial ideas that might lead to pragmatic suggestions with chances to be widely accepted and adopted. Starting with the place's vision and broad strategy on what the place wants to become in the long term, going through the exhaustive discussion with everyone who has a right to be involved, passing through the allocation of funds for relevant projects of several types and concluding with the creative communication of all branding efforts to the appropriate recipients.

We hope that this book contributes to the development of a clearer theory, which in turn will contribute to an improved application of branding to places that need it to secure a better future for their residents. We also hope it will stimulate further discussion and will prove to be the first of many future publications that will adopt similar approaches towards the topic of place branding.

References

Aaker, D. (1991), *Managing Brand Equity: Capitalizing on the Value of a Brand*, New York: The Free Press.

Aaker, D. (1996), *Building Strong Brands*, New York: The Free Press.

Aalborg Kommune (2005a), *Forslag til Hovedstruktur 2005*, Aalborg, Aalborg Kommune.

Aalborg Kommune (2005b), *Forslag til Kommuneplanens Hovedstruktur 2005*, Aalborg, Aalborg Kommune.

Aalborg Kommune (2005c), *Aalborg. Values and Vision*, Aalborg, Aalborg Kommune.

ACEP (2007), 'Active Citizens for Europe Programmes, 2007–2013', Active Citizens Community Office of Public Management, http://www.gov.uk/justice/ac-justice.html (last accessed 24 May 2007).

Adams, J.W. (2008), James Adams' Speech at the World Cities Summit, Singapore, Embracing the Growth Potential of Cities, http://go.worldbank.org/9VDNZTVEU0 (last accessed August 2009).

Alsayyad, N. (ed.) (2001), *Consuming Tradition, Manufacturing Heritage*, London: Routledge.

Amin, A. (2006), 'The good city', *Urban Studies*, **43** (5/6), 1009–23.

Andranovich, G. (2001), 'Olympic cities: lessons learned from mega-event politics', *Journal of Urban Affairs*, **23** (2), 113–31.

Anholt, S. (2002), 'Foreword' to the Special Issue on place branding, *Journal of Brand Management*, **9** (4/5), 229–39.

Anholt, S. (2004), 'Nation-brands and the value of provenance', in N. Morgan, A. Pritchard and R. Pride (eds), *Destination Branding: Creating the Unique Destination Proposition*, Oxford UK: Butterworth-Heinemann.

Anholt, S. (2006), 'The Anholt-GMI City Brands Index: how the world sees the world's cities', *Place Branding and Public Diplomacy*, **2** (1), 18–31.

Anholt, S. (2007), *Competitive Identity: The New Brand Management for Nations, Cities and Regions*, Basingstoke, UK: Palgrave.

Anholt, S. (2008a), 'Place Branding: is it marketing or isn't it?', *Place Branding and Public Diplomacy*, **4** (1), 1–6.

Anholt, S. (2008b), 'Why nation branding does not exist', available at: www.cosmoworlds.com/downloads/orangecontest/SimonAnholt Nation Branding.pdf (last accessed July 2009).

Anon, B. (2000), 'The ins and outs of targeting minorities', *Bank Advertising News*, **24** (22).

Anon, B. (2004), 'Central Office of Information (COI) research reveals ethnic media habits', *Marketing Week*, London, p. 7, available at: http://www.coi.gov.uk (last accessed 12 September 2004).

Apin, N. (2008), 'be berlin ist ganz okay', die Tageszeitung, 13 March, (online), available at: http://www.taz.de/regional/berlin/aktuell/artikel/ 1/be-berlin-ist-ganz-okay/?src=SE&cHash=1fb0368307 (last accessed 15 January 2009).

ASC (2006), Academy for Sustainable Communities, http://www.asc.gov. org.

Ashworth, G.J. (1993), 'Marketing of places: what are we doing?', in G. Ave and F. Corsico (eds), *Urban Marketing in Europe*, Turin: Torino Incontra, 643–9.

Ashworth, G.J. (2004), 'The city of culture: can we create it through planning?', in H. Ernste and F. Boekema, *De cultuur van de locale economie, de economie van de locale cultuur*, Assen: Van Gorcum, 129–44.

Ashworth, G.J. (2006), 'Can we, do we, should we brand places?', paper presented at the CIRM 2006 Conference: Destinations and Locations, Manchester, 6–7 September.

Ashworth, G.J. and B. Graham (2005), 'Senses of place, senses of time and heritage', in G.J. Ashworth and B. Graham (eds), *Senses of Place: Senses of Time*, London: Ashgate.

Ashworth, G.J. and M. Kavaratzis (2009), 'Beyond the logo: brand management for cities', *Journal of Brand Management*, **16** (8), 520–31.

Ashworth, G.J. and P.J. Larkham (eds) (1994), *Building a New Heritage: Tourism, Culture and Identity in the New Europe*, London: Routledge.

Ashworth, G.J. and J.E. Tunbridge (1990), *The Tourist-Historic City*, London: Belhaven Press.

Ashworth, G.J. and H. Voogd (1990a), *Selling the City: Marketing Approaches in Public Sector Urban Planning*, London: Belhaven Press.

Ashworth, G.J. and H. Voogd (1990b), 'Can places be sold for tourism?', in G.J. Ashworth and B. Goodall (eds), *Marketing Tourism Places*, London: Routledge, 1–16.

Ashworth, G.J. and H. Voogd (1994), 'Marketing and place promotion', in J. Gold and S. Ward (eds), *Place Promotion, the Use of Publicity and Marketing to Sell Towns and Regions*, Chichester, UK: John Wiley.

Ave, G. (1993), 'Urban planning and strategic urban marketing in Europe', in G. Ave and F. Corsico (eds), *Urban Marketing in Europe*, Turin: Torino Incontra, 126–59.

Avraham, E. (2000), 'Cities and their news media images', *Cities*, **17** (5), 363–70.

Avraham, E. (2004), 'Media strategies for improving unfavorable city image', *Cities*, **21** (6), 471–9.

Baker, B. (2007), *Destination Branding for Small Cities*, Portland, Oregon: Creative Leap Books.

Balmer, J.M.T. (1995), 'Corporate branding and connoisseurship', *Journal of General Management*, **21**, 24–46.

Balmer, J.M.T. (2001), 'Corporate identity, corporate branding and corporate marketing: seeing through the fog', *European Journal of Marketing*, **35** (3/4), 248–91.

Balmer, J.M.T. (2002), 'Of identities lost and found', *International Studies of Management and Organisation*, **32** (3), 10–27.

Balmer, J.M.T. and E.R. Gray (2003), 'Corporate brands: what are they? What of them?', *European Journal of Marketing*, **37** (7/8), 972–97.

Balmer, J.M.T. and S.A. Greyser (eds) (2003), *Revealing the Corporation: Perspectives on Identity, Image, Reputation, Corporate Branding and Corporate-level Marketing*, London: Routledge.

Balmer, J.M.T. and S.A. Greyser (2006), 'Commentary: corporate marketing', *European Journal of Marketing*, **40** (7/8), 730–41.

Barke, M. (1999), 'City marketing as a planning tool', in M. Pacione (ed.), *Applied Geography: Principles and Practice*, London: Routledge, 486–96.

Barke, M. and K. Harrop (1994), 'Selling the industrial town: identity, image and illusion', in J.R. Gold and S.V. Ward (eds), *Place Promotion: The Use of Publicity and Marketing to Sell Towns and Regions*, Chichester, UK: John Wiley, 93–114.

Barkham, P. (2007), 'Ich bin ein sunbather', *The Guardian*, Travel Features section, 14 July, p. 2, (online), available at: http://www.guardian.co.uk/travel/2007/jul/14/saturday.berlin (last accessed 15 January 2009).

Barnstone, D.A. (2005), *The Transparent State: Architecture and Politics in Postwar Germany*, London: Routledge.

Barthes, R. (1972), *Mythologies*, (trans. A Lavers), London: Vintage.

Barucci, P. (ed.) (1969), *L'economia della provincia di Grosseto*, Milan: Giuffre.

Bass Warner Jr., S. and L.J. Vale, (2001), 'Introduction: cities, media, and imaging', in S. Bass Warner Jr. and L.J. Vale (eds), *Imaging the City: Continuing Struggles and New Directions*, New Brunswick, NJ: Rutgers University, Center for Urban Policy Research, xiii–xxiii.

Basu, A. (2004), 'Entrepreneurial aspirations among family business owners: an analysis of ethnic business owners in the UK', *International Journal of Entrepreneurial Behaviour and Research*, **10** (1/2), 12–33.

Basu, A. and E. Altinay (2003), *Family and Work in Minority Ethnic Businesses*, London: Policy Press.

Beaverstock, J.V., R.G. Smith and P.J. Taylor (1999), 'A Roster of World Cities', GaWC Research Bulletin 5.

be Berlin (2008a), '19 Fragen und 19 Antworten zu be Berlin', (online), available at: http://www.sei.berlin.de/fileadmin/media/3_kampagne/sei-botschafter/081126_faq.pdf (last accessed 15 January 2009).

be Berlin (2008b), 'Live dabei – Persönlichkeiten: Menschen, die Berlin verändern', (online), available at: http://www.sei.berlin.de/live-dabei/persoenlichkeiten/ (last accessed 15 January 2009).

be Berlin (2008c), 'Service – Downloads (to access the official posters and film of the be Berlin campaign)', (online), available at: http://www.sei.berlin.de/service/downloads/ (last accessed 15 January 2009).

Begg, I. (1999), 'Cities and competitiveness', *Urban Studies*, **36** (5–6), 971–86.

Bellini, N. (2004), 'Territorial governance and area image', *Symphonya*, 2004–1.

Bellini, N. and M. Landabaso (2007), 'Learning about innovation in Europe's regional policy', in R. Rutten and F. Boekema (eds), *The Learning Region: Foundations, State-of-the-art, Future*, Cheltenham, UK and Northampton, MA, USA: Edward Elgar.

Berács, J.C.R. (2006), 'Opinion pieces. How has place branding developed during the year that Place Branding has been in publication?', *Place Branding and Public Diplomacy*, **2** (1), 6–17.

Berg, L. van den and E. Braun (1999), 'Urban competitiveness, marketing and the need for organizing capacity', *Urban Studies*, **36** (5–6), 987–99.

Berg, L. van den, E. Braun and A.H.J. Otgaar (2002), *Sports and City Marketing In European Cities*, Aldershot, UK: Ashgate.

Berlin-Institut für Bevölkerung und Entwicklung (2007), 'Talente, Technologie und Toleranz – wo Deutschland Zukunft hat', Berlin: Berlin-Institut für Bevölkerung und Entwicklung, (online), available at: http://www.berlin-institut.org/studien/talente_technologie_und_toleranz.html (last accessed 15 January 2009).

Bernstein, R. (2005), 'Berlin: go West, young clubgoers', *New York Times*, Travel section, 30 October, (online), available at: http://travel2.nytimes.com/2005/10/30/travel/30surf.html (last accessed 15 January 2009).

Bernt, M. and A. Holm (2002), 'Gentrification in East Germany: the case of Prenzlauer Berg', Deutsche Zeitschrift für Kommunalwissenschaften 41(2), (online), available at: http://www.difu.de/publikationen/dfk/en/02_2/02_2_bernt.shtml (last accessed 15 January 2009).

Berry, W.J. (1980), 'Acculturation as varieties of adaptation', in A.M. Padilla (ed.), *Acculturation: Theory, Models and Some New Findings*, Boulder, CO: Westview Press.

Bianchi, G. (1996), 'Galileo used to live here. Tuscany hi-tech: the network and its poles', *R&D Management*, **26**.

Bianchini, F. (1993), 'Remaking European cities: the role of cultural policies', in F. Bianchini and M. Parkinson (eds), *Cultural Policy and Urban Regeneration: The West European Experience*, Manchester: Manchester University Press, 1–20.

Bianchini, F., J. Dawson and R. Evans (1992), 'Flagship projects in urban regeneration', in P. Healey, S. Davoudi, M. O'Toole, S. Tavsangolu and D. Usher (eds), *Rebuilding the City: Property-Led Urban Regeneration*, London: E. & F.N. Spon, 245–56.

Bianciardi, L. (1957), *Il lavoro culturale*, Milan: Feltrinelli.

Bignell, J. (1997), *Media Semiotics: An Introduction*, Manchester and New York: Manchester University Press.

Blythe, J. (2003), *Essentials of Marketing Communications* (2nd edition), Harlow: Financial Times Prentice Hall.

BMDC (2004), 'The Manningham Masterplan', Bradford Metropolitan District Council.

Boklund-Lagopoulou, K., M. Gottdeiner and A.Ph. Lagopoulos (2003), 'Editors' introduction', in M. Gottdeiner, K. Boklund-Lagopoulou and A. Ph. Lagopoulos (eds), *Semiotics*, London, Thousand Oaks and New Delhi: Sage Publications, vii–xxxviii.

Borja, J. and M. Castells (1997), *Local y global: La gestión de las ciudades en la era de la información*, Taurus.

Borraz, O. and P. John (2004), 'The transformation of urban political leadership in Western Europe, symposium', *International Journal of Urban and Regional Research*, **28** (1), 107–20.

Bouchet, D. (1995), 'Marketing and the redefinition of ethnicity', in J.A. Costa and G.J. Bamossy (eds), *Marketing in a Multicultural World*, London: Sage.

Boulding, K. (1956), *The Image*, Ann Arbor, MI: University of Michigan Press.

Boyle, M. (1997), 'Civic boosterism and the politics of local economic development – "institutional positions" and "strategic orientations" in the consumption of hallmark events', *Environment and Planning A*, **29**, 1975–97.

Bradley, A., T. Hall and M. Harrison (2002), 'Selling cities', *Cities*, **19** (1), 61–70.

Bramwell, B. (1998), 'User satisfaction and product development in urban tourism', *Tourism Management*, **19** (1), 35–47.

Brandes, U. and D. Wagner (2004), 'Visone: analysis and visualization of social networks', in M. Jünger and P. Mutzel (eds), *Graph Drawing Software*, Berlin: Springer-Verlag, 321–40.

Braun, E. (2008), 'City marketing: towards an integrated approach', PhD Thesis, Erasmus Research Institute of Management, Erasmus University Rotterdam.

Braun, G.O. (ed.) (1994), *Managing and Marketing of Urban Development and Urban Life*, Berlin: Dietrich Reimer Verlag.

Breakwell, G.M. (1992), 'Processes of self-evaluation: efficacy and estrangement', in G.M Breakwell (ed.), *Social Psychology of Identity and the Self-concept*, Surrey: Surrey University Press.

Breakwell, G.M (1993), 'Integrating paradigms: methodological implications', in G.M. Breakwell and D.V. Canter (eds), *Empirical Approaches to Social Representations*, Oxford: Clarendon Press.

Brent-Ritchie, J.R. and R.J.B. Ritchie (1998), 'The branding of tourism destinations: past achievements and future challenges', report in the annual congress of the International Association of Scientific Experts in Tourism, Marrakech, Morocco.

Broudehoux, A.M. (2004), *The Making and Selling of Post-Mao Beijing*, London: Routledge.

Buhalis, D. (2000), 'Marketing the competitive destination of the future', *Tourism Management*, **21** (1), 97–116.

Burg, A. (ed.) (1994), *Neue berlinische Architektur: eine Debatte*, Berlin: Birkhäuser.

Burg, A. and H. Stimmann (1995), *Downtown Berlin: Building the Metropolitan Mix*, San Francisco: Chronicle Books.

Burgess, J. (1982), 'Selling places: environmental images for the executive', *Regional Studies*, **16**, 1–17.

Burgess, J. (1990), 'The production and consumption of environmental meanings in the mass media – a research agenda for the 1990s', *Transactions of the Institute of British Geographers*, **15** (2), 139–61.

Burton, D. (2000), 'Ethnicity, identity and marketing: a critical review', *Journal of Marketing Management*, **16**, 853–77.

Buurma, H. (2001), 'Public policy marketing: marketing exchange in the public sector', *European Journal of Marketing*, **35** (11/12), 1287–302.

Caldwell, N. and J.R. Freire (2004), 'The difference between branding a country, a region and a city: applying the Brand Box Model', *Journal of Brand Management*, **12** (1), 50–61.

Camagni, R.P. (1993), 'Urban marketing as an instrument of competition between cities', in G. Ave and F. Corsico (eds), *Urban Marketing in Europe*, Turin: Torino Incontra, 310–19.

Carling, A. (2008), 'The curious case of the mis-claimed myth claims: ethnic segregation, polarization and the future of Bradford', *Urban Studies*, **45** (3), 553–89.

Cavalieri, A. (1999), *Toscana e Toscane. Percorsi locali e identità regionale nello sviluppo economico*, Milan: Franco Angeli.

Cavalieri, A. (2001), 'L'immagine della Toscana all'estero', in IRPET, *Dall'immagine della Toscana all'analisi degli investimenti esteri. Un contributo alla definizione del marketing territoriale della Toscana*, Firenze: IRPET.

CCPTE (2007), 'Citizenship-Connecting People through Europe 2007–2013', EU, available at: http://www.eacea.ec.europa.eu/citizenship/guide/index_eu.html (last accessed 24 May 2007).

Chandler, D. (2007), *Semiotics: The Basics* (2nd edition), London: Routledge.

Chaudhary, M. (2000), 'India's image as a tourist destination – a perspective of foreign tourists', *Tourism Management*, **21** (3), 293–7.

Chernatony, L. de (2006), *From Brand Vision to Brand Evaluation: the Strategic Process of Growing and Strengthening Brands* (2nd edition), Oxford: Butterworth-Heinemann.

Chernatony, L. de and F. Dall'Olmo Riley (1998), 'Defining a brand: beyond the literature with the views of experts', *Journal of Marketing Management*, **14** (5), 417–44.

Chernatony, L. de and M. McDonald (2003), *Creating Powerful Brands in Consumer, Service and Industrial Markets* (3rd edition), Oxford: Elsevier Butterworth Heinemann.

Chernatony, L. de and G. McWilliam (1989), 'The strategic implications of clarifying how marketers interpret brands', *Journal of Marketing Management*, **5** (2), 153–71.

Chernatony, L. de and S. Segal-Horn (2001), 'Building on services' characteristics to develop successful services brands', *Journal of Marketing Management*, **17** (7–8), 645–70.

Cheshire, P. (2006), 'Resurgent cities, urban myths and policy hubris: what we need to know', *Urban Studies*, **43** (8), 1231–46.

Cho, C. and H.J. Cheon (2005), 'Cross-cultural comparisons of interactivity on corporate web sites', *Journal of Advertising*, **43** (2), 99–115.

Choi, W.M., A. Chan and J. Wu (1999), 'A qualitative and quantitative assessment of Hong Kong's image as a tourist destination', *Tourism Management*, **20** (3), 361–5.

Clifton, R. and E. Maughan (2000), *The Future of Brands*, Basingstoke: Macmillan.

Cochrane, A. (2006), '(Anglo)phoning home from Berlin: a response to Alan Latham', *European Urban and Regional Studies*, **13** (4), 371–6.

Cochrane, A. and A. Jonas (1999), 'Reimagining Berlin: world city, national capital or ordinary place?', *European Urban and Regional Studies*, **6** (2), 145–64.

Colomb, C. (2008), 'Staging urban change, reimaging the city: the politics of place marketing in the "New Berlin" (1989–2004)', thesis submitted for the degree of Doctor of Philosophy (PhD) in Town Planning, University College London, The Bartlett School of Planning, London: University of London.

Costa, J.A. and G.J. Bamossy (1995), 'Perspectives on ethnicity, nationalism, and cultural identity', in J.A. Costa and G.J. Bamossy (eds), *Marketing in a Multicultural World*, London: Sage.

Crouch, D. and N. Lubbren (eds) (2003), *Visual Culture and Tourism*, Basingstoke: Macmillan.

Crow, D. (2003), *Visible Signs*, Lausanne: AVA Publishing.

Cui, G. and P. Choudhary (2002), 'Marketplace diversity and cost-effective marketing strategies', *Journal of Consumer Marketing*, **19** (1), 54–73.

CultMark Project (2005), Cultural Sector Report.

D'Agnelli, A.R. (2003), 'Dinamiche sociali ed economiche del grossetano (1951–81)', in S. Neri Serneri and L. Rocchi (eds), *Società locale e sviluppo locale*, Roma: Carocci.

DATAR (2005), 'Madrid en el concierto de las grandes ciudades europeas y mundiales', available at: http://www.antoniopulido.es/documentos/con051116.pdf (last accessed May 2009).

DCLG (2005), 'Strong and Prosperous Communities', Local Government White Paper, Department for Communities and Local Government, HMSO.

Deffner, A. (2000), 'Cultural industries in Athens: spatial transformations during the nineties', in Papers of the 6th World Leisure Congress Leisure and Human Development, Deusto University in Bilbao, Spain, 2000, 25 pages (CD-ROM).

Deffner, A. and T. Metaxas (2006a), 'Place marketing: preparing a place marketing pre-plan in the case of Nea Ionia, Magnesia, Greece', in the Proceedings of the 2nd International Meetings Industry Conference Marketing Destinations and their Venues, ACS Halandri, 8 pages (CD-ROM).

Deffner, A. and T. Metaxas (2006b), 'Is city marketing opposed to urban planning? The elaboration of a pilot city marketing plan for the case of Nea Ionia, Magnesia, Greece', 46th ERSA Conference Enlargement, Southern Europe and the Mediterranean, Department of Planning and Regional Development, University of Thessaly, Volos, Greece, 31 pages (CD-ROM).

Delanty, G. and P.R. Jones (2002), 'European identity and architecture', *European Journal of Social Theory*, **5** (4), 453–66.

Derrick, S. (2004), 'Marketers aim to fill cultural void', *Promotions & Incentives*, March, 11–14.

Didero, M., Gareis P. Marques and M. Ratzte (2008), 'Differences in innovation culture across Europe', a Discussion Paper, Bonn: TRANSFORM Consortium.

Dinnie, K. (2004), 'Literature review. Place branding: overview of an emerging literature', *Place Branding and Public Diplomacy*, **1** (1), 106–10.

Dowling, G. (2001), *Creating Corporate Reputations: Identity, Image and Performance*, Oxford: Oxford University Press.

Doyle, P. (1990), 'Building successful brands: the strategic options', *Journal of Marketing Management*, **5** (1), 77–95.

Doyle, P. (1994), 'Branding', in M.J. Baker (ed.), *The Marketing Book* (3rd edition), Oxford: Butterworth Heinemann, 470–83.

Duffy, H. (1995), *Competitive Cities: Succeeding in the Global Economy*, London: E. and F.N. Spon.

Ebert, R. and K. Kunzmann (2007), 'Kulturwirtschaft, kreative Räume und Stadtentwicklung in Berlin', *DISP*, **171**, 64–79.

Echtner, C. and J. Ritchie (1993), 'The measurement of destination image: an empirical assessment', *Journal of Travel Research*, **31** (Spring), 3–13.

Eckstein, B. and J.A. Throgmorton (eds) (2003), *Story and Sustainability. Planning, Practice and Possibility for American Cities*, Cambridge, MA: MIT Press.

Elia, G. (2003), 'Città malgrado. Profilo dello sviluppo urbano', in S. Neri Serneri and L. Rocchi (eds), *Società locale e sviluppo locale*, Roma: Carocci.

Elliot, R. and K. Wattanasuwan (1998), 'Brands as symbolic resources for the construction of identity', *International Journal of Advertising*, **17** (2), 131–44.

Endzina, I. and L. Luneva (2004), 'Development of a National Branding Strategy: the case of Latvia', *Place Branding and Public Diplomacy*, **1** (1), 94–105.

European Cities Monitor (2007), available at: www.cushmanwakefield.com.

Evans, G. (2001), *Cultural Planning: An Urban Renaissance?*, London: Routledge.

Evans, G. (2003), 'Hard branding the cultural city: from Prado to Prada', *International Journal of Urban and Regional Research*, **27** (2), 417–40.

Fairclough, N. (1995), *Critical Discourse Analysis*, Boston: Addison Wesley.

Fernandez-Ballesteros, R. (2001), 'Environmental conditions, health, and satisfaction among the elderly: some empirical results', *Psicothema*, **13** (1), 40–49.

Fill, C. (2005), *Marketing Communications: Engagement, Strategies and Practice* (4th edition), Harlow: Financial Times Prentice Hall.

Fitzsimons, D.S. (1995), 'Planning and promotion: city reimaging in the 1980s and 1990s', in W.J.V. Neill, D.S. Fitzsimons and B. Murtagh, *Reimaging the Pariah City: Urban Development in Belfast and Detroit*, Aldershot: Avebury, 1–49.

Fletcher, D. (2003), 'Reaching the ethnic consumer: a challenge for marketers', available at: http://www.redhotcurry.com/archive/news/2003/ipa_report2003.htm (last accessed 15 September 2004).

Florida, R. (2002), *The Rise of the Creative Class and how it's Transforming Work, Leisure, Community and Everyday Life*, New York: Basic Books.

Fornell, C., M.D. Johnson, E.W. Anderson, J. Cha and B.E. Bryant (1996), 'The American Customer Satisfaction Index: nature, purpose and findings', *Journal of Marketing*, **60**, 7–18.

Francesco, A.M. and B.A. Gold (1998), *International Organizational Behaviour: Text, Readings, Cases, and Skills*, Upper Saddle River, NJ: Prentice Hall.

Freire, J.R. (2005), 'Geo-branding, are we talking nonsense? A theoretical reflection on brands applied to places', *Place Branding and Public Diplomacy*, **1** (4), 347–62.

Gardner, B.B. and J.S. Levy (1955), 'The product and the brand', *Harvard Business Review*, **33** (2), 33–9.

Gartner, W.C. (1989), 'Tourism image: attribute measurement of state tourism products using multidimensional scaling techniques', *Journal of Travel Research*, **28** (2), 15–19.

Gilmore, F. (2001), 'A country – can it be repositioned? Spain – the success story of country branding', *Journal of Brand Management*, **9** (4/5), 281–93.

Gold, J.R. and S.V. Ward (eds) (1994), *Place Promotion: The use of Publicity and Marketing to sell Towns and Regions*, Chichester: John Wiley.

Goodman, L.A. (1961), 'Snowball sampling', *The Annals of Mathematical Statistics*, **32** (1), 148–70.

Goodrich, J. (1977), 'A new approach to image analysis through multidimensional scaling', *Journal of Travel Research*, **16** (1), 3–7.

Goodwin, M. (1993), 'The city as commodity: the contested spaces of urban development', in G. Kearns and C. Philo (eds), *Selling Places: The City as Cultural Capital, Past and Present*, Oxford: Pergamon Press, 145–62.

Gospodini, A. (2006), 'Portraying, classifying and understanding the emerging landscapes in the city', *Cities*, **25** (5), 311–30.

Graham, B. (2002), 'Heritage as knowledge: capital or culture?', *Urban Studies*, **39** (5/6), 1003–17.

Graham, B., G.J. Ashworth and J.E. Tunbridge (2000), *A Geography of Heritage*, London: Arnold.

Greenberg, M. (2000), 'Branding cities. A social history of the Urban Lifestyle Magazine', *Urban Affairs Review*, **36** (2), 228–63.

Greenberg, M. (2003), 'The limits of branding: the World Trade Center, fiscal crisis and the marketing of recovery', *International Journal of Urban and Regional Research*, **27** (2), 386–416.

Griffiths, R. (1998), 'Making sameness: place marketing and the new urban entrepreneurialism', in N. Oatley (ed.), *Cities, Economic Competition and Urban Policy*, London: Paul Chapman Publishing, 41–57.

Guhathakurta, S. and R.J. Stimson (2007), 'What is driving the growth of new "Sunbelt" metropolises? Quality of life and urban regimes in Greater Phoenix and Brisbane-South East Queensland region', *International Planning Studies*, **12** (2), 129–52.

Gunn, C. (1972), *Vacationscape: Designing Tourist Regions*, University of Austin Texas: Bureau of Business Research.

Haf, E. (2008), 'How can culture position Wales in the world?', Wales and the World Institute of Welsh Affairs Seminar, Cardiff, October.

Hague, C. and H. Thomas (1997), 'Planning capital cities: Edinburgh and Cardiff compared', in R. Macdonald and H. Thomas (eds), *Nationality and Planning in Scotland and Wales*, Cardiff: University of Wales Press.

Halkier, H. (2006), *Institutions, Discourse and Regional Development. The Scottish Development Agency and the Politics of Regional Policy*, Brussels: PIE Peter Lang.

Hall, C.M. (1989), 'The definition and analysis of hallmark tourist events', *Geojournal*, **19** (3), 263–8.

Hall, T. (1998/2001), *Urban Geography*, London and New York: Routledge.

Hall, T. and P. Hubbard (eds) (1998), *The Entrepreneurial City: Geographies of Politics, Regime and Representation*, Chichester: John Wiley.

Ham, P. van (2001), 'The rise of the brand state: the postmodern politics of image and reputation', *Foreign Affairs*, **80** (5), 2–6.

Ham, P. van (2008), 'Place branding: the state of the art', *The Annals of the American Academy of Political and Social Science*, **616**, 126–49.

Hammersley, R. and T. Westlake (1996), 'Planning in the Prague region: past, present and future', *Cities*, **13** (4), 247–56.

Hankinson, G. (2000), 'Brand management', in K. Blois (ed.), *The Oxford Textbook of Marketing*, Oxford: Oxford University Press, 481–99.

Hankinson, G. (2001), 'Location branding: a study of twelve English cities', *Journal of Brand Management*, **9** (2), 127–42.

Hankinson, G. (2004a), 'Relational network brands: towards a conceptual model of place brands', *Journal of Vacation Marketing*, **10** (2), 109–21.

Hankinson, G. (2004b), 'The brand images of tourism destinations: a study of the saliency of organic images', *Journal of Product and Brand Management*, **13** (1), 6–14.

Hankinson, G. (2005), 'Destination brand images: a business tourism perspective', *Journal of Services Marketing*, **19** (1), 24–32.

Hankinson, G. (2007), 'The management of destination brands: five guiding principles based on recent developments in corporate branding theory', *Journal of Brand Management*, **14** (3), 240–54.

Hankinson, G. (2009), 'Managing destination brands: establishing a theoretical foundation', *Journal of Marketing Management*, **25** (1/2), 97–115.

Hankinson, G. and P. Cowking (1993), *Branding in Action*, Maidenhead: McGraw-Hill.

Hannigan, J. (2003), 'Symposium on branding, the entertainment economy and urban place building: introduction', *International Journal of Urban and Regional Research*, **27** (2), 352–60.

Hannigan, J. (2004), 'Boom towns and cool cities: the perils and prospects of developing a distinctive urban brand in a global economy', paper presented at the Leverhulme International Symposium: The Resurgent City, April 2004, London School of Economics.

Harris, N. (1997), 'Cities in a global economy: structural change and policy reactions', *Urban Studies*, **34** (10), 1693–703.

Harsman, B. (2006), 'Ethnic diversity and spatial segregation in the Stockholm region', *Urban Studies*, **43** (8), 1341–64.

Harvey, D. (1987), 'Flexible accumulation through urbanisation: reflections on postmodernism in the American city', *Antipode*, **19**, 260–86.

Harvey, D. (1989), 'From managerialism to entrepreneurialism: the transformation in urban governance in late capitalism', *Geografiska Annaler*, **71** (1), 3–17.

Harvey, D. (1989), *The Condition of Postmodernity*, Oxford: Blackwell.

Hatch, M.J. and M. Schultz (2001), 'Are the strategic stars aligned for your corporate brand?', *Harvard Business Review*, **79** (2), 128–34.

Hatch, M.J. and M. Schultz (2003), 'Bringing the corporation into corporate branding', *European Journal of Marketing*, **37** (7/8), 1041–64.

Hauben,T., M. Vermeulen and V. Patteeuw (eds) (2002), *City Branding: Image Building and Building Images*, Rotterdam: NAI Uitgevers.

Häussermann, H. and C. Colomb (2003), 'The new Berlin: marketing the city of dreams', in L.M. Hoffmann, S.S. Fainstein and D.R. Judd (eds), *Cities and Visitors. Regulating People, Markets, and City Space*, Oxford: Blackwell, 200–18.

Häussermann, H. and A. Kapphan (2000), *Berlin: von der geteilten zur gespaltenen Stadt? Sozialräumlicher Wandel seit 1990*, Opladen: Leske + Budrich.

Hawkes, T. (1977), *Structuralism and Semiotics*, London: Routledge.

Hay, R. (1998), 'Sense of place in developmental context', *Journal of Environmental Psychology*, **18**, 5–29.

Helbrecht, I. (1994), 'Conflict, consent, cooperation: comprehensive planning in Germany beyond market and state', in G.O. Braun (ed.), *Managing and Marketing of Urban Development and Urban Life*, Berlin: Dietrich Reimer Verlag, 521–30.

Henderson, P.W. and J.A. Cote (1998), 'Guidelines for selecting or modifying logos', *Journal of Marketing*, **62** (April), 14–30.

Henderson, P.W., J.A. Cote, S.M. Leong and B. Schmitt (2003), 'Building strong brands in Asia: selecting the visual components of image to maximize brand strengths', *International Journal of Research in Marketing*, **20**, 297–313.

Hernandez, B., M.C. Hidalgo, M.E. Salazar-Laplace and S. Hess (2007), 'Place attachment and place identity in natives and non-natives', *Journal of Environmental Psychology*, **27**, 310–19.

Hofstede, G. (1994), *Cultures and Organisations Intercultural Cooperation and Its Importance for survival- Software of the Mind*, London: McGraw-Hill.

Hogwood, B.W. and L.A. Gunn (1986), *Policy Analysis for the Real World*, Oxford: Oxford University Press.

Holcomb, B. (1994), 'City make-overs: marketing the post-industrial city', in J.R. Gold and S.V. Ward (eds), *Place Promotion: The Use of Publicity and Marketing to Sell Towns and Regions*, Chichester: John Wiley, 115–32.

Holcomb, B. (1999), 'Marketing cities for tourism', in D.R. Judd and S.S. Fainstein (eds), *The Tourist City*, New Haven and London: Yale University Press, 54–70.

Hollis, N. (2005), 'Ten years of learning on how online advertising builds brands', *Journal of Advertising Research*, June, 255–68.

Hope, A.C. and S.M. Klemm (2001), 'Tourism in difficult areas revisited: the case of Bradford', *Tourism Management*, **22** (6), 629–35.

Hospers, G.J. (2004), 'Place marketing in Europe: the branding of the Oresund region', *Intereconomics: Review of European Economic Policy*, **39** (5), 271–9.

Hospers, G.J. (2006), 'Borders, bridges and branding: the transformation of the Øresund Region into an imagined space', *European Planning Studies*, **14** (8), 1023–41.

Hubbard, P. and T. Hall (1998), 'The entrepreneurial city and the new urban politics', in T. Hall and P. Hubbard (eds), *The Entrepreneurial City: Geographies of Politics, Regime and Representation*, Chichester: John Wiley & Sons, 1–30.

Hulberg, J. (2006), 'Integrating corporate branding and sociological paradigms: a literature study', *Journal of Brand Management*, **14** (1/2), 60–73.

Insch, A. and M. Florek (2008), 'A great place to live, work and play: conceptualising the quality of life of city residents', *Journal of Place Management and Development*, **1** (2), 138–49.

International Olympic Committee (2008), 'Games of the XXXI Olympiad 2016 Working Group Report', available at http://multimedia.olympic.org/pdf/en_report_1317.pdf (last accessed June 2009).

IRPET (2003), *La Provincia di Grosseto: l'altra Toscana?*, Firenze: IRPET.

Jaffe, E.D. and I.D. Nebenzahl (2006), *National image and competitive advantage: The theory and Practice of Place Branding,* Copenhagen: Copenhagen Business School Press.

Jamal, A. (2003), 'Marketing in a multicultural world: the interplay of marketing, ethnicity and consumption', *European Journal of Marketing*, **37** (11/12), 1599–620.

Jansen-Verbeke, M. and J. van Rekom (1996), 'Scanning museum visitors', *Annals of Tourism Research*, **23** (2), 364–75.

Jeffries, S. (2009), 'The age of the wheel', *The Guardian* G2, 18 February, 6–10.

Jenks, C. (ed.) (1995), *Visual Culture*, London: Routledge.

Jensen, O.B. (2005), 'Branding the contemporary city. Urban branding as regional growth agenda?', Regional Studies International Conference, Aalborg.

Jensen, O.B. (2007), 'Culture stories. Understanding cultural urban branding', *Planning Theory*, **6** (3), 211–36.

Jessop, B. (1997), 'The entrepreneurial city: re-imaging localities, redesigning economic governance or restructuring Capital', in N. Jewson and S.E. McGregor, *Transforming Cities: Contested Governance and New Spatial Divisions*, London: Routledge, 28–42.

Jobber, D. (2007), *Principles and Practice of Marketing* (5th edition), Maidenhead: McGraw Hill.

Kahana, E., L. Lovegreen, B. Kahana and M. Kahana (2003), 'Person, environment, and person-environment fit as influences on residential satisfaction of elders', *Environment and Behavior*, **35** (3), 434–53.

Kalandides, A. (2007a), 'Marketing the creative Berlin and the paradox of place identity', paper presented at the XXVIII conference of AISRe (http://www.aisre.it), Bolzano.

Kalandides, A. (2007b), 'In search of Berlin's competitive advantage – marketing the creative city', paper presented at the EUGEO 2007 First International Conference on the Geography of Europe 'Standort Europa at Risk', Amsterdam, 20–23 August.

Kalandides, A. and M. Kavaratzis (2009), 'Guest editorial: from place marketing to place branding and back: a need for re-evaluation', *Journal of Place Management and Development*, **2** (1), 5–7.

Kalandides, A. and B. Lange (2007), 'Creativity as a synecdoche of the city – marketing the creative Berlin', in H. Wan, E. Yueng and T. Yueng (eds), Hong Kong Institute of Planners & Urban Planning Society of China Conference 'When creative industries crossover with cities', Hong Kong, 2–3 April.

Kapferer, J.N. (1997), *Strategic Brand Management*, London: Kogan Page.

Kapferer, J.N. (2000), *Reinventing the Brand*, London: Kogan Page.

Kasarda, J.D. and M. Janowitz (1974), 'Community attachment in mass society', *American Sociological Review*, **39**, 328–39.

Kavaratzis, M. (2004), 'From city marketing to city branding: towards a theoretical framework for developing city brands', *Place Branding and Public Diplomacy*, **1** (1), 58–73.

Kavaratzis, M. (2005), 'Place branding: a review of trends and conceptual models', *The Marketing Review*, **5** (4), 329–42.

Kavaratzis, M. (2007), 'City marketing: the past, the present and some unresolved issues', *Geography Compass*, **1** (3), 695–712.

Kavaratzis, M. (2008), 'From city marketing to city branding: an interdisciplinary analysis with reference to Amsterdam, Budapest and Athens', PhD Thesis, University of Groningen, available at: http://dissertations.ub.rug.nl/faculties/rw/2008/m.kavaratzis/ (last accessed September 2009).

Kavaratzis, M. (2009), 'Cities and their brands: lessons from corporate branding', *Place Branding and Public Diplomacy*, **5** (1), 26–37.

Kavaratzis, M. and G.J. Ashworth (2005), 'City branding: an effective assertion of identity or a transitory marketing trick?', *Tijdschrift voor Economische en Sociale Geografie*, **96** (5), 506–14.

Kavaratzis, M. and G.J. Ashworth (2007), 'Partners in coffeeshops, canals and commerce: marketing the city of Amsterdam', *Cities*, **24** (1), 16–25.

Kavaratzis, M. and G.J. Ashworth (2008), 'Place marketing: how did we get here and where are we going?', *Journal of Place Management and Development*, **1** (2), 150–65.

Kearns, G. and C. Philo (eds) (1993), *Selling Places: The City as Cultural Capital, Past and Present*, Oxford: Pergamon.

Keller, K.L. (1993), 'Conceptualising, measuring and managing customer-based brand equity', *Journal of Marketing*, **57** (1), 1–22.

Keller, K.L. (1998), *Building, Measuring and Managing Brand Equity*, Upper Saddle River, NJ: Prentice Hall.

Keller, K.L. (2003), *Building, Measuring, and Managing Brand Equity* (2nd edition), Upper Saddle River, NJ: Prentice Hall – Pearson Education.

Kelly, R. (2006), House of Commons Speech, Hansard 9 May 2006.

Kickert, W., E.H. Klijn and J. Koppenjan (eds) (1997), *Managing Complex Networks. Strategies for the Public Sector*, London: Sage.

Kilinç, M. (2006), 'Institutional environment and place attachment as determinants of elders' life satisfaction', a thesis submitted to The Graduate School of Social Sciences of Middle East Technical University.

Klein, L.R. (2003), 'Creating virtual product experiences: the role of tele-presence', *Journal of Interactive Marketing*, **17** (1), 41–55.

Knox, S. and D. Bickerton (2003), 'The six conventions of corporate branding', *European Journal of Marketing*, **37** (7/8), 998–1016.

Kolb, B. (2006), *Tourism Marketing for Cities and Towns: Using Branding and Events to Attract Tourists*, Amsterdam: Elsevier.

Kong, L. (2000), 'Culture, economy, policy: trends and developments', *Geoforum*, **31** (4), 385–90.

Konken, M. (2004), *Stadtmarketing: Kommunikation mit Zukunft*, Messkirch: Gmeiner-Verlag.

Kotler, P. (1997), *Marketing management: Analysis, planning, implementation and control* (9th edition), Upper Saddle River, NJ: Pearson Prentice Hall.

Kotler, P., C. Asplund, I. Rein and D. Haider (1999), *Marketing Places Europe: Attracting Investments, Industries and Visitors to European Cities, Communities, Regions and Nations*, Harlow: Financial Times Prentice Hall.

Kotler, P. and D. Gertner (2002), 'Country as brand, product and beyond: a place marketing and brand management perspective', in N. Morgan, A. Pritchard and R. Pride (eds), *Destination Branding: Creating the Unique Destination Proposition*, Amsterdam: Elsevier, 40–56.

Kotler, P., D. Haider and I. Rein (1993), *Marketing Places: Attracting Investment, Industry, and Tourism to Cities, States and Nations*, New York: The Free Press.

Kotler, P. and K.L. Keller (2006), *Marketing Management* (12th edition), Upper Saddle River, NJ: Pearson Prentice Hall.

Krantz, M. and L. Schaetzl (1997), 'Marketing the city', in C.N. Jensen-Butler, A. Shachar and J. Van Weesep (eds), *European Cities in Competition*, Aldershot: Avebury, 468–93.

Krätke, S. (2002), *Medienstadt. Urbane Cluster und globale Zentren der Kulturproduktion*, Opladen: Leske & Budrich.

Krätke, S. (2003), 'Global media cities in a worldwide urban network', *European Planning Studies*, **11** (6): 605–28.

Krätke, S. (2004a), 'Economic restructuring and the making of a financial crisis: Berlin's socio-economic development path 1989 to 2004', *DISP*, **156**, 58–63.

Krätke, S. (2004b), 'City of talents? Berlin's regional economy, socio-spatial fabric and "worst practice" urban governance', *International Journal of Urban and Regional Research*, **28** (3), 511–29.

Krätke, S. and R. Borst (2000), *Berlin. Metropole zwischen Boom und Krise*, Opladen: Leske & Budrich.

Kress, G. and Leeuwen, T. van (1996), *Reading images: Grammar of visual design*, London: Routledge.

Kvale, S. (1996), *InterViews. An Introduction to Qualitative Research Interviewing*, London: Sage.

La Gory, M., R. Ward and S. Sherman (1985), 'The ecology of aging: neighborhood satisfaction in an older population', *Sociological Quarterly*, **26**, 405–18.

Landry, C. (2000), *Creative City: A Toolkit for Urban Innovators*, London: Earthscan Publications.

Landry, C. (2006), *The Art of City Making*, London: Earthscan Publications.

Lange, B. (2007), *Die Räume der Kreativszenen – Culturepreneurs und ihre Orte in Berlin*, Bielefeld: Transcript-Verlag.

Langeard, E., J. Bateson, C. Lovelock and P. Eiglier (1981), 'Marketing of services: new insights from consumers and managers', Report No. 81–104, Cambridge, MA: Marketing Sciences Institute.

Lash, S. and J. Urry (1994), *Economies of Signs and Space*, London: Sage Publications.

Lavin, I. (2005), 'Discorso in occasione della consegna del Premio Galilei', available at: http://www.humnet.unipi.it/galileo/fondazione/Home/home.htm (last accessed August 2009).

Lazzeretti, L. (2003), 'City of art as High Culture local system and cultural districtualization processes', *International Journal of Urban and Regional Research*, **27** (3), 635–48.

Lee, D.J. and M.J. Sirgy (2004), 'Quality-of-life (QOL) marketing: proposed antecedents and consequences', *Journal of Macromarketing*, **24** (1), 44–58.

Lee, D.J., M.J. Sirgy, V. Larsen and N.D. Wright (2002), 'Developing a subjective measure of consumer well-being', *Journal of Macromarketing*, **22** (2), 158–69.

Leelakulthanit, O., R. Day and R. Walters (1991), 'Investigating the relationship between marketing and overall satisfaction with life in a developing country', *Journal of Macromarketing*, **11**, 3–23.

Lehrer, U. (2002), 'Image production and globalization: city building processes at Potsdamer Platz', unpublished PhD dissertation, Department of Urban Planning, Los Angeles: University of California.

Leisen, B. (2001), 'Image segmentation: the case of a tourism destination', *Journal of Services Marketing*, **5** (1), 49–66.

Leitch, S. and N. Richardson (2003), 'Corporate branding in the new economy', *European Journal of Marketing*, **37** (7/8), 1066–79.

Liddle, J. and J. Diamond (2007), 'Reflections on regeneration management skills research', *Public Money and Management*, **27** (3), 189–92.

Loukissas, P., A. Deffner, A. Adamou, E. Koutseris and T. Metaxas (2002), 'Globalisation, sustainable development and the social context: the case of the National Marine Park of Alonnisos – Northern Sporades Islands in Greece', in A.G. Kungolos, A.B. Liakopoulos and G.P. Korfiatis (eds), *Protection and Restoration of the Environment VI, Proceedings of an International Conference, vol. III*, Skiathos, 1385–92.

Lovelock, C. and J. Wirtz (2007), *Services Marketing* (6th edition), Upper Saddle River, NJ: Pearson Prentice Hall.

Low, G. and R. Fullerton (1994), 'Brands, brand management and the brand manager system: a critical-historical evaluation', *Journal of Marketing Research*, **31** (May), 173–90.

Low, S.M. and I. Altman (1992), 'Place attachment: a conceptual inquiry', in I. Altman and S.M. Low (eds), *Human Behavior and Environment*, New York: Plenum, 1–12.

Mahizhnan, A. (1999), 'Smart cities: the Singapore case', *Cities*, **16** (1), 13–18.

Manale, M. (2003), 'La modernité faite mythe', *Les Temps Modernes*, **625**, 196–215.

Manzanti, B. and J. Ploger (2003), 'Community planning – from politicised places to lived spaces', *Journal of Housing and the Built Environment*, **19** (4), 309–29.

Marenco, P. (2003), *Progetto Arnovalley*, Pisa: Scuola Superiore Sant'Anna and Università di Pisa.

Maslow, A.H. (1943) 'A theory of human motivation', *Psychological Review*, **50**, 370–96.

McCann, E.J. (2004), 'Best places: interurban competititiveness', *Urban Studies*, **41** (10), 1909–29.

McCarthy, J. (1960), *Basic Marketing*, Homewood, IL: Irwin.

McCarthy, J. (1998), 'Reconstruction, regeneration and re-imaging: the case of Rotterdam', *Cities*, **15** (5), 337–44.

McLuhan, C. (1987), *Letters of Marshall McLuhan*, Oxford: Oxford University Press.

Meadow, H.L. (1983), 'The relationship between consumer satisfaction and life satisfaction for the elderly', PhD dissertation, Virginia Polytechnic Institute and State University, Blacksburg, VA.

Meler, M. and D. Ruzic (1999), 'Marketing identity of the tourist product of the Republic of Croatia', *Tourism Management*, **20** (5), 635–43.

Melewar, T.C. (2003), 'Determinants of the corporate identity construct: a review of the literature', *Journal of Marketing Communications*, **9**, 195–220.

Melewar T.C., K. Bassett and C. Simoes (2006), 'The role of communication and visual identity in modern organisation', *Corporate Communications: An International Journal*, **11** (2), 138–47.

Melewar, T.C. and E. Jenkins (2002), 'Defining the corporate identity construct', *Corporate Reputation Review*, **5** (1), 76–90.

Melewar, T.C. and J. Saunders (2000), 'Global corporate visual identity systems: using an extended marketing mix', *European Journal of Marketing*, **34**, 538–50.

Metadesign (n/d), South Tyrol, Berlin: MetaDesgin AG.

Metaxas, T. (2003), 'The image of the city as a "good": The creation of a city's promotional package through a strategic framework analysis of City Marketing procedure', in Beriatos, E. et al. (eds), *Sustainable Planning and Development*, Wessex Institute of Technology and Department of Planning and Regional Development, University of Thessaly, 427–38.

Metcalf, H., T. Modood and S. Virdee (1996), *Asian Self-Employment: The Interaction of Culture and Economics in England*, London: Policy Studies Institute.

Miles, M.B. and M.A. Huberman (2003), *Qualitative Data Analysis*, London: Sage.

Millington, S., C. Young and J. Lever (1997), 'A bibliography of city marketing', *Journal of Regional and Local Studies*, **17**, 16–42.

Misiura, S. (2006), *Heritage Marketing*, Oxford: Butterworth-Heinemann/ Elsevier.

Mommaas, H. (2002), 'City branding: the necessity of socio-cultural goals', in T. Hauben, M. Vermeulen and V. Patteeuw (eds), *City Branding: Image Building and Building Images*, Rotterdam: NAI Uitgevers, 34–44.

Moran, W.R. (1973), 'Why new products fail', *Journal of Advertising Research*, **13** (1), 5–13.

Morgan, N. and A. Pritchard (eds) (2001), *Advertising in Tourism and Leisure*, Oxford: Butterworth-Heinemann.

Morgan, N. and A. Pritchard (2002), 'Meeting the destination branding challenge', in N. Morgan, A. Pritchard and R. Pride (eds), *Destination Branding: Creating the Unique Destination Proposition*, Oxford: Butterworth-Heinemann, 59–78.

Morgan, N., A. Pritchard and R. Piggott (2002), 'New Zealand, 100% pure: the creation of a powerful niche destination brand', *Journal of Brand Management*, **9** (4/5), 335–54.

Morgan N., A. Pritchard and R. Pride (eds) (2002/2004), *Destination Branding: Creating the Unique Destination Proposition*, Oxford: Butterworth-Heinemann.

Morrison, A.M. (1989/2001), *Hospitality and Travel Marketing*, Florence, Kentucky: Delmar Learning.

Murphy, B., P. Maguiness, C. Pescott, S. Wislang, J. Ma and R. Wang (2005), 'Stakeholder perceptions presage holistic stakeholder relationship marketing performance', *European Journal of Marketing*, **39** (9/10), 1049–59.

Murphy P., M.P. Pritchard and B. Smith (2000), 'The destination product and its impact on traveller perceptions', *Tourism Management*, **21** (1), 43–52.

Murray, C. (2001), *Making Sense of Place: New Approaches to Place Marketing*, Stroud/ Leicester: Comedia/ International Cultural Planning and Policy Unit.

Neill, W.J.V. (2004), *Urban Planning and Cultural Identity*, London: Routledge.

Nordjyllands Amt (2003), 'Nordjysk Erhvervsredegørelse 2003 – Fra afvikling til udvikling', Aalborg: Nordjyllands Amt.

Novelli, M. (2003), 'Wine tourism events: Apulia, Italy', in I. Yeoman, M. Robertson, J. Ali-Knight and S. Drummond (eds), *Festival and Events Management: An International Arts and Culture Perspective*, Oxford: Butterworth Heinemann, 805–22.

Nuttavuthisit, K. (2007), 'Branding Thailand: correcting the negative image of sex tourism', *Place Branding and Public Diplomacy*, **3** (1), 21–30.

Nwankwo, S. and A. Lindridge (1998), 'Marketing to ethnic minorities in Britain', *Journal of Marketing Practice: Applied Marketing Science*, **4** (7), 200–16.

Nykiel, R.A. and E. Jascolt (1998/2008), *Marketing Your City, U.S.A: A Guide to Developing a Strategic Tourism Marketing Plan*, Binghamton, NY: Haworth.

ODPM (2004), 'The future of local government: developing a 10 year vision', Office of the Deputy Prime Minister, HMSO.

Olins, W. (1989), *Corporate Identity: Making Business Strategy Visible Through Design*, London: Thames & Hudson.

Olins, W. (2004), 'Branding the nation: the historical context', in N. Morgan, A. Pritchard and R. Pride (eds), *Destination Branding: Creating the Unique Destination Proposition*, Oxford: Butterworth-Heinemann.

O'Loughlin, C. and G. Coenders (2002), 'Application of the European Customer Satisfaction Index to postal services: structural equation models versus partial least squares', Working Papers of the Department of Economics, University of Girona.

Olsen, L.L. and M.D. Johnson (2003), 'Service equity, satisfaction, and loyalty: from transaction-specific to cumulative evaluations', *Journal of Service Research*, **5**, 184–95.

Ooi, C.S. (2004), 'Poetics and politics of destinational branding: Denmark', *Scandinavian Journal of Hospitality and Tourism*, **4** (2), 107–28.

Oppermann, M. (1996), 'Convention destination images: analysis of association meeting planner's perceptions', *Tourism Management*, **17** (3), 175–82.

O'Shaughnessy, J. (1995), *Competitive Marketing: A Strategic Approach* (3rd edition), London: Routledge.

O'Shaughnessy, J. and N.J. O'Shaughnessy (2000), 'Treating the nation as a brand: some neglected issues', *Journal of Macromarketing*, **20** (1), 56–64.

Ouseley, H. (2001), 'Community pride not prejudice: making diversity work in Bradford', report to Bradford Vision, July 2001.

Oxford English Dictionary (1936), Oxford: Pergamon.

Özer, M. (2004), 'A study on the life satisfaction of elderly individuals living in family environment and nursing homes', *Turkish Journal Of Geriatrics*, **7** (1), 33–6.

Paddison, R. (1993), 'City marketing, image reconstruction and urban regeneration', *Urban Studies*, **30** (2), 339–50.

Papadopoulos, N. and L. Heslop (2002), 'Country equity and country branding: problems and prospects', *Journal of Brand Management*, **9** (4/5), 294–315.

Park, C.W., B. Jaworski and D. McInnis (1986), 'Strategic brand concept management', *Journal of Marketing*, **50** (October), 135–45.

Patton, M.Q. (2002), *Qualitative Evaluation and Research Methods* (3rd edition), Newby Park, CA: Sage.

Pavot, W. and E. Diener (1993), 'Review of the satisfaction with life scale', *Psychological Assessment*, **5** (2), 164–72.

Pearce, C.L. and M.D. Ensley (2003), 'A reciprocal and longitudinal investigation of the innovation process: the central role of shared vision in product and process innovation teams (PPITs)', *Journal of Organization Behavior*, **24**, 1–20.

Pearce, P.L. (1982), 'Perceived changes in holiday destinations', *Annals of Tourism Research*, **9** (2), 145–64.

Peirce, C.S. (1965), *The Collected Papers of Charles Sanders Peirce*, Cambridge, MA: Harvard University Press.

Peirce, C.S. (1978), *Collected Papers of Charles Sanders Peirce, Vol. 1 & 2* (4th edition), Cambridge: The Belknap Press of Harvard University Press.

Pelsmacker, P. de, M. Geuens and J. van den Bergh (2004), *Marketing Communications: A European Perspective* (2nd edition), Harlow: Prentice Hall Financial Times.

Penaloza, L. and M.C. Gilly (1999), 'Marketer acculturation: the changer and the changed', *Journal of Marketing*, **63**, 84–104.

Philo, C. and G. Kearns (1993), 'Culture, history, capital: a critical introduction to the selling of places', in G. Kearns and C. Philo (eds), *Selling Places. The City as Culture Capital, Past and Present*, Oxford: Pergmanon Press, 1–32.

Piercy, N. and D. Cravens (1995), 'The network paradigm and the marketing organisation: developing a new management agenda', *European Journal of Marketing*, **29** (3), 7–34.

Pink, S. (2001), *Doing Visual Ethnography*, Newby Park, CA: Sage.

Pires, G. and J. Stanton (2000), 'Marketing services to ethnic consumers in culturally diverse markets: Issues and implications', *The Journal of Services Marketing*, **14** (7), 143–58.

Plan del Turismo Español 2008–2012, available at: www.turismo2020.es.

Porter, M.E. (1980), *Competitive Strategy: Techniques for Analysing Industries and Competitors*, New York: Free Press.

Porter, M.E. (1995), 'The competitive advantage of the inner city', *Harvard Business Review*, May/June, 55–71.

Pratchett, L. (2002), 'Local democracy and local government at the end of Labour's first term', *Parliamentary Affairs*, **55**, 331–46.

Pratchett, L., C. Durose, V. Lowndes, G. Smith, G. Stoker and C. Wales (2009), 'Empowering communities to influence local decision making: evidence based lessons for policy making and practitioners', Department for Communities and Local Government, HMSO.

Pratt, A.C. (1997), 'The cultural industries production system: a case study of employment change in Britain 1984–91', *Environment and Planning A*, **29** (11), 1953–74.

Price, R. and R.J. Brodie (2001), 'Transforming a public service organization from inside out to outside in: the case of Auckland, New Zealand', *Journal of Service Research*, **4** (1) 50–59.

Pride, R. (2002), 'Brand Wales: national revival', in N. Morgan, A. Pritchard and R. Pride (eds), *Destination Branding: Creating the Unique Destination Proposition*, Oxford: Butterworth-Heineman.

Pride, R. (2004), 'A challenger brand: Wales, golf as it should be', in: N. Morgan, A. Pritchard and R. Pride (eds), *Destination Branding: Creating the Unique Destination Proposition*, Oxford: Butterworth-Heinemann.

Pride, R. (2008), 'The Welsh brand – connecting image with reality', Wales and the World Institute of Welsh Affairs Seminar, Cardiff, October.

Pritchard, A. and N. Morgan (1996), 'Selling the Celtic Arc to the USA: a comparative analysis of the destination brochure images used in the marketing of Ireland, Scotland and Wales', *Journal of Vacation Marketing*, **2** (4), 346–65.

Pritchard, A. and N. Morgan (1998), 'Mood marketing – the new destination marketing strategy. A case study of Wales the brand', *Journal of Vacation Marketing*, **4** (3), 215–29.

Pritchard, A. and N. Morgan (2001), 'Culture, identity and representation. Marketing Cymru or Wales?', *Tourism Management*, **22** (2) 167–79.

Pritchard, A. and N. Morgan (2003), 'Mythic geographies of representation and identity: contemporary postcards of Wales', *Journal of Tourism and Cultural Change*, **1** (2), 111–30.

Rabe, H. and W. Süss (1995), 'Stadtmarketing zwischen Innovation und Krisendeutung. Eine Berliner Fallstudie', apt-papers 1/95, Berlin: Freie Universität Berlin, Arbeitsstelle Politik und Technik.

Rada, U. (2008a), 'Wir sind Rütli, wir sind Berlin' die Tageszeitung, 12 March, (online), available at: http://www.taz.de/regional/berlin/aktuell/artikel/1/wir-sind-ruetli-wir-sind-berlin/?src=SE&cHash=bc56f235d2 (last accessed 15 January 2009).

Rada, U. (2008b), 'Wir-Gefühl gegen soziale Spaltung' die Tageszeitung, 12 March, (online), available at: http://www.taz.de/regional/berlin/aktuell/artikel/1/wir-gefuehl-gegen-soziale-spaltung/?src=SE&cHash=a 660bbfb8f (last accessed 15 January 2009).

Rainisto, S. (2003), 'Success factors of place marketing: a study of place marketing practices in Northern Europe and the United States', PhD thesis, Helsinki University of Technology, Institute of Strategy and International Business.

Region Nordjylland Vækstforum (2007), *Vækst og balance. Erhvervsudviklingsstrategi for Nordjylland 2007–10*, Aalborg, Region Nordjylland Vækstforum.

Rein, I. and B. Shields (2007), 'Place branding sports: strategies for differentiating emerging, transitional, negatively viewed and newly industrialised nations', *Place Branding and Public Diplomacy*, **3** (1), 73–85.

Riel, C.B.M. van (1995), *Principles of Corporate Communication*, London: Prentice Hall.

Ries, A. and J. Trout (1981), *Positioning: The Battle for your Mind*, Maidenhead: McGraw-Hill.

Ritchie, J.R. (1984), 'Assessing the impact of hallmark events: conceptual and research issues', *Journal of Travel Research*, **23**, 2–11.

Rizzi, P. and A. Scaccheri (2006), *Promuovere il territorio: guida al marketing territoriale e strategie di sviluppo locale*, Milan: Franco Angeli.

Rogerson, R.J. (1999), 'Quality of life and city competitiveness', *Urban Studies*, **36** (5/6), 969–85.

Rowles, G.D. (1990), 'Place attachment among the small town elderly', *Journal of Rural Community Psychology*, **11**, 103–20.

Royales, E. (2008), 'Welsh paradiplomacy: future directions and priorities', Wales and the World Institute of Welsh Affairs Seminar, Cardiff, October.

Rubinstein, L. and P.A. Parmelee (1992), 'Attachment to place and the representation of the life course by the elderly', in I. Altman and S.M. Low (eds), *Human Behavior and Environment*, New York: Plenum, 139–63.

Sacco, P.L., G. Ferilli and S. Pedrini (2008), 'System-wide cultural districts: an introduction from the Italian viewpoint', paper presented at the ERSA 2008 Conference, Liverpool, UK.

Sadler, D. (1993), 'Place marketing, competitive places and the construction of hegemony in Britain in the 1980s', in G. Kearns and C. Philo (eds), *Selling Places: the City as Cultural Capital Past and Present*, Oxford: Pergamon Press, 175–92.

Saussure, F. De (1974), *Course in General Linguistics*, New York: Fontana/Collins.

Schmitt, B. (1999), *Experiential marketing*, New York: The Free Press.

Schultz, M. and L. de Chernatony (2002), 'Introduction: the challenges of corporate branding', *Corporate Reputation Review*, **5** (2/3), 105–12.

Schütz, E. and K. Siebenhaar (1996), *Berlin wirbt! Metropolenwerbung zwischen Verkehrsreklame und Stadtmarketing, 1920–1995*, Berlin: Institute für Kommunikationsgeschichte und angewandte Kulturwissenschaften der Freien Universität Berlin, FAB Verlag.

Seisdedos, G. and P. Vaggione, (2004), 'The city branding processes: the case of Madrid', available at: http://www.isocarp.net/Data/case_studies/658.pdf.

Selby, M. (2004), *Understanding Urban Tourism*, London: Macmillan.

Selby, M. and N.J. Morgan (1996), 'Reconstructing place image: a case study of its role in destination market research', *Tourism Management*, **17** (4), 287–94.

Senatskanzlei Berlin (2007), Berlin Stadt des Wandels, (online), available at: http://www.berlin.de/stadtdeswandels/ (last accessed 15 January 2009).

Senatsverwaltung für Wirtschaft, Arbeit und Frauen (2005),

'Kulturwirtschaftsbericht', Berlin: Senatsverwaltung für Wirtschaft, Arbeit und Frauen.

Shields, R. (1991), *Places on the Margin: Alternative Geographies of Modernity*, London: Routledge.

Shimp, T.A. (2007), *Integrated Marketing Communications in Advertising and Promotion* (7th edition), Mason, OH: Thomson South Western.

Short, J.R. (1999), 'Urban imagineers: boosterism and the representation of cities', in A.E.G. Jonas and D. Wilson (eds), *The Urban Growth Machine: Critical Perspectives Two Decades Later*, New York: State University of New York Press, 37–54.

Short, J.R. and Y.H. Kim (1998), 'Urban crises/urban representations: selling the city in difficult times', in T. Hall and P. Hubbard (eds), *The Entrepreneurial City: Geographies of Politics, Regimes and Representations*, Chichester: John Wiley, 55–75.

Short, J.R. and Y.H. Kim (1999), *Globalisation and the City*, Harlow: Longman.

Shostack, G.L. (1977), 'Breaking free from product marketing', *Journal of Marketing*, **41** (April), 73–80.

Shostack, G.L. (1984), 'Designing services that deliver', *Harvard Business Review*, **62** (January–February), 133–9.

Shumaker, S.A. and R.B. Taylor (1983), 'Toward a clarification of people-place relationships: a model of attachment to place', in N. Feimer and E.S. Geller (eds), *Environmental Psychology: Directions and Perspectives*, New York: Praeger, 219–51.

Simoes, C. and S. Dibb (2001), 'Rethinking the brand concept: new brand orientation', *Corporate Communications: An International Journal*, **6** (4), 217–24.

Simon, C. (2005), 'Commodification of regional identities: the "selling" of Waterland', in G.J. Ashworth and B. Graham (eds), *Senses of Place: Senses of Time*, London: Ashgate.

Simpson, F. and M. Chapman (1999), 'Comparison of urban governance and planning policy: East looking West', *Cities*, **16** (5), 353–64.

Sirgy, M.J. and C. Su (2000), 'Destination image, self-congruity, and travel behaviour: towards an integrative model', *Journal of Travel Research*, **38** (May), 340–52.

Skinner, H. (2008), 'The emergence and development of place marketing's confused identity', *Journal of Marketing Management*, **24** (9/10), 915–28.

Sleipen, W. (1988), *Marketing van de Historische Omgeving*, Breda: Netherlands Research Institute for Tourism.

Smyth, H. (1994), *Marketing the City: The Role of Flagship Developments in Urban Regeneration*, London: E. & F. N. Spon.

Soanes, C. (2002), *Paperback Oxford English Dictionary*, Oxford: Oxford University Press.

Sotarranto, M. (2005), 'Shared leadership and dynamic capabilities in regional development', in M. Sagan and A. Halker (eds), *Regionalism Contested: Institutions, Society and Governance*, Cornwall: Ashgate.

STADTart, K. Kunzmann and Culture Concepts (2007), *Kreativeräume in der Stadt – Integration von Kunst, Kultur und Co. in die Berliner Stadtentwicklung*, Berlin: Senatsverwaltung für Stadtentwicklung.

Standard & Poor's (2006), *World's Top 10 Economic Centers*, Maidenhead: MacGraw-Hill.

Strom, E. (2001), *Building the new Berlin: the Politics of Urban Development in Germany's Capital City*, Landham, MD: Lexington Books.

Süchting, W. and P. Weiss (2001), 'A new plan for Berlin's inner city: Planwerk Innenstadt', in W.J.V. Neill and H.U. Schwedler (eds), *Urban Planning and Cultural Inclusion: Lessons from Belfast and Berlin*, Basingtoke: Palgrave, 57–68.

Svendsen, A. (1997), 'Building relationships with microcommunities', *Marketing News*, **13** (12).

Tasci, A. and M. Kozak (2006), 'Destination brands vs. destination images: do we know what we mean?', *Journal of Vacation Marketing*, **12**, 299–317.

Taylor, P.J. (2004), 'Leading world cities: empirical evaluations of urban nodes in multiple networks', *Urban Studies*, **42** (9), 1593–603.

Teknologisk Institut (2000), 'Nordjyllands IKT-kompetencer – Hovedrapport'. Høje Tåstrup: Teknologisk Institut.

The Communication Group plc (2006), 'The Power of Destinations. Why it matters to be different', London, available at: http://www.thecom municationgroup.co.uk (last accessed June 2009).

The Independent (2008), 'Reborn to be wild: Berlin's 24-hour party people', *The Independent*, 10 January, (online), available at: http:// www.independent.co.uk/news/europe/reborn-to-be-wild-berlins-24hour-party-people-769246.html (last accessed 15 January 2009).

Theodori, G.L. (2004), 'Exploring the association between length of residence and community attachment: a research note', *Southern Rural Sociology*, **20** (1), 107–22.

Therkelsen, A. and H. Halkier (2004), 'Umbrella place branding. A study of friendly exoticism and exotic friendliness in coordinated national tourism and business promotion', Spirit Discussion Papers (26).

Therkelsen, A. and H. Halkier (2008), 'Contemplating place branding umbrellas. The case of coordinated national tourism and business promotion', *Scandinavian Journal of Hospitality and Tourism*, **8** (2), 159–75.

Thomas, R.S. (1992), *Cymru or Wales?*, Llandysul, Dyfed: Gomer Press.

Till, K.E. (2003), 'Construction sites and showcases: tourism, maps, and spatial practices of the New Berlin', in S. Hanna and V. Del Casino (eds), *Mapping Tourism Spaces*, Minneapolis: University of Minnesota Press, 51–78.

Till, K.E. (2005), *The New Berlin: Memory, Politics, Place*, Minneapolis: University of Minnesota Press.

Tilley, C. (1999), 'Built-in branding: how to engineer a leadership brand', *Journal of Marketing Management*, **15** (1/3), 181–91.

Tinagli, I. and R. Florida (2005), *L'Italia nell'era creativa*, Milan: Creativity Group Europe.

Travino, L.K., and G.R. Weaver (2003), *Managing Ethics in Business Organizations: Social scientific properties*, Stanford, CA: Stanford University Press.

Tresserras, J.J. (2008), 'Identitat(s), marca i destinacions turístiques. Límits i riscos dels models turístics', DCIDOB 93, Turisme i sostenibilitat cultural, available at: www.cidob.org (last accessed January 2008).

Trueman, M. (2001), 'Bradford in the Premier League? A multidisciplinary approach to branding and re-positioning a city', Working Paper 01/04, Bradford University, School of Management, Bradford.

Trueman, M., D. Cook and N. Cornelius (2008), 'Creative dimensions for branding and regneration: overcoming negative perceptions of a city', *Place Branding and Public Diplomacy*, **4** (1), 29–44.

Trueman, M. and N. Cornelius (2006), 'Hanging baskets or basket cases? Managing the complexity of city brands and regeneration', Working Paper 06/13, Bradford University School of Management, Bradford.

Trueman, M., M. Klemm and A. Giroud (2004), 'Can a city communicate? Bradford as a corporate brand', *Corporate Communications: An International Journal*, **9** (4), 317–30.

Tunbridge, J.E. and G.J. Ashworth (1996), *Dissonant Heritage: The Past as a Resource in Conflict*, Chichester: Wiley.

Twigger-Ross, C.L. and D. Uzzell (1996), 'Place and identity processes', *Journal of Environmental Psychology*, **16** (3), 205–20.

UNESCO (1998), *World Culture Report 1998: Culture, creativity and markets*, Paris: UNESCO.

Urban, F. (2002), 'Small town, big website? Cities and their representation on the internet', *Cities*, **19** (1), 49–59.

Urde, M. (1999), 'Brand orientation: a mindset for building brands into strategic resources', *Journal of Marketing Management*, **15** (1/3), 117–33.

Urde, M. (2003), 'Core value-based corporate brand building', *European Journal of Marketing*, **37** (7/8), 1017–40.

Urry, J. (1990), *The Tourist Gaze*, London: Sage Publications.

Virgo, B. and L. de Chernatony (2006), 'Delphic brand visioning to align stakeholder buy-in to the city of Birmingham brand', *Journal of Brand Management*, **13** (6), 379–92.

VisitAalborg (2005), 'Vild med værten. Håndbog for succesfulde kongresarrangører' (3. udgave), Aalborg: VisitAalborg.

VisitAalborg (2006), 'Vi har sat et nyt ansigt på turismen i Den nye Aalborg Kommune', Aalborg: VisitAalborg.

www.visitbritain.com

www.visitwales.com

Wahl, H.W. and G.D. Weisman (2003), 'Environmental gerontology at the beginning of the new millenium: reflections on its historical empirical and theoretical development', *The Gerontologist*, **43** (5), 616–27.

Wales Tourist Board (WTB) (1994), *Tourism 2000: A Strategy for Wales*, Cardiff: Wales Tourist Board.

Ward, J. (2004), 'Berlin, the virtual global city', *Journal of Visual Culture*, **3** (2), 239–56.

Ward, K.G. (2000), 'From Rentiers to Rantiers: "Active Entrepreneurs", "Structural Speculators" and the politics of marketing the city', *Urban Studies*, **37** (7), 1093–1107.

Ward, S.V. (1998), *Selling Places: The Marketing and Promotion of Towns and Cities 1850–2000*, London: E. & F.N. Spon/Routledge.

Ward, S.V. and J.R. Gold (1994), 'Introduction', in J.R. Gold and S.V. Ward (eds), *Place Promotion: The Use of Publicity and Marketing to Sell Towns and Regions*, Chichester: John Wiley, 1–17.

Warnaby, G. and D. Bennison (2006), 'Reciprocal urban place marketing and co-branding? Retail applications', *Place Branding and Public Diplomacy*, **2** (3), 297–310.

Warnaby, G., D. Bennison and J.B. Davies (2005), 'Marketing town centers: retailing and town centre management', *Local Economy*, **20** (2), 183–204.

Warnaby, G., D. Bennison, B.J. Davies and H. Hughes (2002), 'Marketing UK towns and cities as shopping destinations', *Journal of Marketing Management*, **18** (9/10), 877–904.

Warnaby, G., D. Bennison, B.J. Davies and H. Hughes (2004), 'People and partnerships: marketing urban retailing', *International Journal of Retail & Distribution Management*, **32** (11), 545–56.

Warnaby, G. and B. Davies (1997), 'Commentary: cities as service factories? Using the Servuction System for marketing cities as shopping destinations', *International Journal of Retail & Distribution Management*, **25** (6), 204–10.

Webster, C. (1992), 'The effects of Hispanic subcultural identification on information search behaviour', *Journal of Advertising Research*, **32** (5), 54–62.

Webster, C. (1994), 'Effects of ethnic identification on marital roles in the purchase decision process', *Journal of Consumer Research*, **21**, 319–31.

Welch-Guerra, M. (1999), *Haupstadt Einig Vaterland: Planung und Politik zwischen Bonn und Berlin*, Berlin: Verlag Bauwesen.

White, G., S. Dickinson, N. Miles, L. Richardson, H. Russell and H. Taylor (2006), 'Exemplars of local governance', Department for Communities and Local Government, HMSO.

Wilkie, W. (1986), *Consumer Behaviour*, New York: John Wiley.

Williams, A., P. Kitchen, J. Randall and N. Muhajarine (2008), 'Changes in quality of life perceptions in Saskatoon, Saskatchewan: comparing survey results from 2001 and 2004', *Social Indicators Research*, **85** (1), 5–22.

Wise, M.Z. (1998), *Capital Dilemma*, New York: Princeton Architectural Press.

Woodside, A. and Lyonski, S. (1989), 'Towards a general model of traveler destination choice', *Journal of Travel Research*, **Spring**, 8–14.

Woodward, R.B. (2005), 'For young artists, all roads now lead to a happening Berlin', *New York Times*, 13 March, (online), available at: http://travel.nytimes.com/2005/03/13/travel/13berlin.html (last accessed 30 April 2008).

Young, C. and J. Lever (1997), 'Place promotion, economic location and consumption of the city image', *Tijdschrift voor Economische en Sociale Geografie*, **88**, 332–41.

Zakia, R.D. and M. Nadin (1987), 'Semiotics, advertising and marketing', *Journal of Consumer Marketing*, **4** (2), 5–12.

Zeithaml V., M. Bitner and D. Gremler (2006), *Services Marketing* (4th edition), Maidenhead: McGraw-Hill.

Zerres, M. and I. Zerres (eds) (2000), *Kooperatives Stadtmarketing: Konzepte, Strategien und Instrumente zur Erhöhung der Attraktivität einer Stadt*, Stuttgart: Kohlhammer.

Zineldin, M. (2004), 'Co-opetition: the organisation of the future', *Marketing Intelligence and Planning*, **22** (27), 780–89.

Zukin, S. (1988), *Loft Living: Culture and Capital in Urban Change*, London: Radius.

Zukin, S. (1995), *The Cultures of Cities*, Oxford: Blackwell.

Index